AMST

CITY GUIDE

SHOPS, RESTAURANTS, COFFEE SHOPS & NIGHTLIFE

The Most Positively Reviewed and Recommended by Locals and Travelers

EGP
Editorial

AMSTERDAM

CITY GUIDE

SHOPS, RESTAURANTS, COFFEE SHOPS & NIGHTLIFE

AMSTERDAM CITY GUIDE 2022
Shops, Restaurants, Coffee Shops, Attractions & Nightlife

© Duncan J. Emerson
© E.G.P. Editorial

Printed in USA.

ISBN-13: 9798747725065

INDEX

AMSTERDAM CITY GUIDE

Shops, Restaurants, Attractions & Nightlife

*This directory is dedicated to Amsterdam Business Owners and Managers
who provide the experience that the locals and tourists enjoy.
Thanks you very much for all that you do and thank for being the "People Choice".*

*Thanks to everyone that posts their reviews online and
the amazing reviews sites that make our life easier.*

*The places listed in this book are the most positively reviewed
and recommended by locals and travelers from around the world.*

*You will find in this book 2,200 places to visit organized in five groups
to make your life easier when you decide to go out.*

*500 Shops, 500 Restaurants, 500 Attractions,
500 Nightlife Spots and 200 Cannabis Coffee Shops.*

*Thank you for your time and enjoy the directory that is
designed with locals and tourist in mind!*

TOP 500 SHOPS

Recommended by Locals & Trevelers
(From #1 to #500)

#1
De Melkweg
Category: Art Gallery
Average price: Modest
Area: Centrum
Address: Lijnbaansgracht 234 1017 PH
Amsterdam The Netherlands
Phone: +31 20 5318181

#2
Scandinavian Embassy
Category: Coffee & Tea,
Scandinavian, Fashion
Average price: Modest
Area: Zuid, De Pijp
Address: Sarphatipark 34 1072 PB
Amsterdam The Netherlands
Phone: +31 619 518199

#3
Apple Store
Category: Electronics, Computers
Average price: Expensive
Area: Centrum
Address: Hirschgebouw 1017 PS
Amsterdam The Netherlands
Phone: +31 20 5302200

#4
Concerto
Category: Vinyl Records, Music & DVDs
Average price: Modest
Area: Centrum
Address: Utrechtsestraat 52-60 1017 VP
Amsterdam The Netherlands
Phone: +31 20 6235228

#5
P.G.C.
Category: Tobacco Shops
Average price: Expensive
Area: Centrum
Address: Rokin 92-I 1012 KZ
Amsterdam The Netherlands
Phone: +31 20 6237494

#6
Hema
Category: Department Stores
Average price: Inexpensive
Area: Centrum
Address: Kalvertoren Kalverstraat 212
1012 WP Amsterdam The Netherlands
Phone: +31 20 4228988

#7
Duikelman
Category: Shopping
Average price: Exclusive
Area: Zuid, De Pijp
Address: Ferdinand Bolstraat 68-68A
1072 LM Amsterdam The Netherlands
Phone: +31 20 6712230

#8
De Bijenkorf
Category: Department Stores
Average price: Expensive
Area: Centrum, De Wallen
Address: Dam 1 1012 JS Amsterdam
The Netherlands
Phone: +31 20 6255832

#9
Foam Fotografiemuseum
Category: Museum, Art Gallery
Average price: Modest
Area: Centrum
Address: Keizersgracht 609 1017 DS
Amsterdam The Netherlands
Phone: +31 20 5516500

#10
I Love Vintage
Category: Vintage& Consignment,
Women's Clothing
Average price: Modest
Area: Centrum
Address: Prinsengracht 201 1015 DT
Amsterdam The Netherlands
Phone: +31 20 3301950

#11
Lyppens
Category: Jewelry
Average price: Modest
Area: Centrum, De Wallen
Address: Langebrugsteeg 8 1012 GB
Amsterdam The Netherlands
Phone: +31 20 6270901

#12
Marks & Spencer
Category: Men's Clothing, Women's
Clothing, Children's Clothing
Average price: Modest
Area: Centrum
Address: Kalverstraat 226 1012 XJ
Amsterdam The Netherlands
Phone: +31 20 3300080

#13
De Kinderboekwinkel
Category: Bookstores
Average price: Modest
Area: Centrum, Jordaan
Address: Rozengracht 34 1016 NC
Amsterdam The Netherlands
Phone: +31 20 6224761

#14
Deksels! keukenspullen
Category: Kitchen & Bath, Hobby Shops
Average price: Expensive
Area: Centrum, Haarlemmerbuurt
Address: Haarlemmerdijk 129 1013 KE
Amsterdam The Netherlands
Phone: +31 20 5289613

#15
Hutspot
Category: Art Gallery, Cafe
Average price: Expensive
Area: Zuid, De Pijp
Address: Van Woustraat 4 1073 LL
Amsterdam The Netherlands
Phone: +31 613 651566

#16
Kitsch Kitchen
Category: Flowers & Gifts
Average price: Modest
Area: Centrum, Jordaan
Address: Rozengracht 8-12 1016 NB
Amsterdam The Netherlands
Phone: +31 20 6228261

#17
The American Book Center
Category: Books, Mags, Music & Video
Average price: Modest
Area: Centrum
Address: Spui 12 1012 XA Amsterdam
The Netherlands
Phone: +31 20 6255537

#18
Flying Tiger
Category: Gift Shops, Home Decor
Average price: Inexpensive
Area: Centrum
Address: Rembrandtplein 2 1017 CV
Amsterdam The Netherlands
Phone: +31 20 4212959

#19
Diva Amsterdam
Category: Jewelry
Average price: Modest
Area: Centrum
Address: Heiligeweg 20 1012 XR
Amsterdam The Netherlands
Phone: +31 20 6278517

#20
River Island
Category: Fashion
Average price: Modest
Area: Centrum
Address: Kalverstraat 22-26 1012 PD
Amsterdam The Netherlands
Phone: +31 20 3302640

#21
Tiffany & Co
Category: Jewelry, Bridal
Average price: Expensive
Area: Zuid, Museumkwartier
Address: Pieter Cornelisz Hooftstraat 86
1071 CB Amsterdam The Netherlands
Phone: +31 20 6756875

#22
By Popular Demand
Category: Gift Shops
Average price: Modest
Area: Centrum
Address: Raadhuisstraat 2 1012 TJ
Amsterdam The Netherlands
Phone: +31 20 6245231

#23
Mendo
Category: Bookstores
Average price: Expensive
Area: Centrum, Negen Straatjes
Address: Berenstraat 11 1016 GG
Amsterdam The Netherlands
Phone: +31 20 6121216

#24
Cloud9
Category: Shopping
Average price: Expensive
Area: Centrum, Haarlemmerbuurt
Address: Haarlemmerdijk 119-B 1013
KE Amsterdam The Netherlands
Phone: +31 20 4288004

#25
MAC Cosmetics
Category: Makeup Artists, Cosmetics &Beauty
Average price: Expensive
Area: Centrum
Address: Heiligeweg 5 1012 XN Amsterdam The Netherlands
Phone: +31 20 3300748

#26
Friday Next
Category: Furniture Stores, Jewelry, Women's Clothing
Average price: Expensive
Area: West, Helmersbuurt
Address: Overtoom 31 1054 HB Amsterdam The Netherlands
Phone: +31 20 6123292

#27
Skins Cosmetics
Category: Cosmetics &Beauty, Skin Care
Average price: Exclusive
Area: Centrum, Negen Straatjes
Address: Runstraat 11 1016 GJ Amsterdam The Netherlands
Phone: +31 20 5286922

#28
The English Hatter
Category: Accessories, Men's Clothing, Outlet Stores
Average price: Expensive
Area: Centrum
Address: Heiligeweg 40 1012 XS Amsterdam The Netherlands
Phone: +31 20 5285700

#29
La Casa del Habano
Category: Tobacco Shops
Average price: Modest
Area: Zuid, Museumkwartier
Address: The Conservatorium Hotel 1071 AN Amsterdam The Netherlands
Phone: +31 20 7530781

#30
Atelier Molenpad
Category: Art Gallery, Local Flavor
Average price: Modest
Area: Centrum
Address: Molenpad 17d 1016 GL Amsterdam The Netherlands
Phone: +31 610 915544

#31
Droog Amsterdam
Category: Home Decor, Furniture Stores, Concept Shops
Average price: Modest
Area: Centrum
Address: Staalstraat 7B 1011 JJ Amsterdam The Netherlands
Phone: +31 20 5235059

#33
Backstage Make-Up en Grime
Category: Cosmetics &Beauty
Average price: Expensive
Area: Centrum, Jordaan
Address: Rozengracht 101-103 1016 LV Amsterdam The Netherlands
Phone: +31 20 6221267

#32
Jacob Hooy Amsterdam
Category: Drugstores
Average price: Modest
Area: Centrum, De Wallen
Address: Kloveniersburgwal 10 1012 CT Amsterdam The Netherlands
Phone: +31 20 6243041

#34
Blond-Amsterdam
Category: Shopping
Average price: Expensive
Area: Zuid, De Pijp
Address: Gerard Doustraat 69 1071 VL Amsterdam The Netherlands
Phone: +31 20 4284929

#35
Athenaeum Boekhandel
Category: Bookstores
Average price: Modest
Area: Centrum
Address: Spui 14-16 1012 XA Amsterdam The Netherlands
Phone: +31 20 5141460

#36
Condomerie Het Gulden Vlies
Category: Adult
Average price: Inexpensive
Area: Centrum, De Wallen
Address: Warmoesstraat 141 1012 JB Amsterdam The Netherlands
Phone: +31 20 6274174

#37
Episode
Category: Thrift Stores, Vintage&
Consignment
Average price: Modest
Area: Centrum, Negen Straatjes
Address: Berenstraat 1 1016 GG
Amsterdam The Netherlands
Phone: +31 20 6264679

#38
Hema
Category: Department Stores
Average price: Modest
Area: Zuid, De Pijp
Address: Ferdinand Bolstraat 93-93 A
1072 LD Amsterdam The Netherlands
Phone: +31 20 6763222

#39
Hoogstins Boekhandel
Category: Office Equipment, Bookstores
Average price: Modest
Area: West, Oud West
Address: Kinkerstraat 117 1053 DL
Amsterdam The Netherlands
Phone: +31 20 6854600

#40
Record Palace
Category: Vinyl Records, Thrift Stores
Average price: Expensive
Area: Centrum
Address: Weteringschans 33d 1017 RV
Amsterdam The Netherlands
Phone: +31 20 6223904

#41
De Kinderfeestwinkel
Category: Shopping
Average price: Modest
Area: Zuid, De Pijp
Address: Gerard Doustraat 65 1072 LV
Amsterdam The Netherlands
Phone: +31 20 6722215

#42
De Emaillekeizer
Category: Home Decor
Average price: Modest
Area: Zuid, De Pijp
Address: Eerste Sweelinckstraat 15
1073 CL Amsterdam The Netherlands
Phone: +31 20 6641847

#43
Suit Supply
Category: Fashion
Average price: Modest
Area: Zuid, Museumkwartier
Address: Willemsparkweg 37-41 1071
GR Amsterdam The Netherlands
Phone: +31 20 4713362

#44
Intratuin
Category: Nurseries & Gardening
Average price: Modest
Area: Oost, Watergraafsmeer
Address: Nobelweg 10 1097 AR
Amsterdam The Netherlands
Phone: +31 20 4622922

#45
De Stadsfiets
Category: Bikes
Average price: Inexpensive
Area: Zuid, De Pijp
Address: Ceintuurbaan 354 1072 GP
Amsterdam The Netherlands
Phone: +31 20 6766006

#46
Studio Bazar
Category: Kitchen & Bath
Average price: Expensive
Area: Centrum
Address: Keizersgracht 709 1017 DW
Amsterdam The Netherlands
Phone: +31 20 6222858

#47
De boekenmarkt op Het Spui
Category: Bookstores
Average price: Inexpensive
Area: Centrum
Address: Spui Amsterdam, Noord-
Holland The Netherlands
Phone: +31 299 401021

#48
Hema
Category: Department Stores
Average price: Modest
Area: Oost, Oosterparkbuurt
Address: Linnaeusstraat 245 1093 ER
Amsterdam The Netherlands
Phone: +31 20 6949292

#49
Streetclothes
Category: Shoe Stores, Women's
Clothing, Accessories
Average price: Expensive
Area: Zuid, De Pijp
Address: Albert Cuypstraat 128 1072 EA
Amsterdam The Netherlands
Phone: +31 20 4702488

#50
Vodafone Winkel
Category: Electronics
Average price: Modest
Area: Centrum
Address: Kalverstraat 173 1012 XB
Amsterdam The Netherlands
Phone: +31 20 4124329

#51
De Stofzuigerkoning
Category: Electronics
Average price: Expensive
Area: West, Bos en Lommer
Address: Jan van Galenstraat 163 1056
BR Amsterdam The Netherlands
Phone: +31 20 6182181

#52
Gunters en Meuser
Category: Hardware Stores
Average price: Modest
Area: Centrum, Jordaan
Address: Egelantiersgracht 2-BG 1015
RL Amsterdam The Netherlands
Phone: +31 20 6221666

#53
Lambiek
Category: Comic Books
Average price: Modest
Area: Centrum
Address: Kerkstraat 132 1017 GP
Amsterdam The Netherlands
Phone: +31 20 6267543

#54
Chanel
Category: Fashion
Average price: Exclusive
Area: Zuid, Museumkwartier
Address: P.C. Hooftstraat 66/68 1071
CA Amsterdam The Netherlands
Phone: +31 20 3053777

#55
American Apparel
Category: Women's Clothing, Men's
Clothing, Accessories
Average price: Expensive
Area: Centrum
Address: Utrechtsestraat 85 1015 VK
Amsterdam The Netherlands
Phone: +31 20 6246635

#56
Maranon Hammocks Amsterdam
Category: Home Decor
Average price: Modest
Area: Centrum
Address: Singel 488-490 1017 AW
Amsterdam The Netherlands
Phone: +31 20 6225938

#57
Jan de Grote Kleinvakman
Category: Hobby Shops
Average price: Exclusive
Area: Zuid, De Pijp
Address: Albert Cuypstraat 203 1073 BE
Amsterdam The Netherlands
Phone: +31 20 6738247

#58
Zipper
Category: Vintage& Consignment
Average price: Modest
Area: Centrum, Negen Straatjes
Address: Huidenstraat 7 1016 ER
Amsterdam The Netherlands
Phone: +31 20 6237302

#59
Independent Outlet
Category: Sports Wear, Vinyl Records
Average price: Modest
Area: Centrum
Address: Vijzelstraat 77 1017 HG
Amsterdam The Netherlands
Phone: +31 20 4212096

#60
Vanilia
Category: Women's Clothing
Average price: Expensive
Area: Zuid, Museumkwartier
Address: Van Baerlestraat 30 1071 AX
Amsterdam The Netherlands
Phone: +31 20 6795449

#61
Karen Millen
Category: Women's Clothing
Average price: Expensive
Area: Centrum
Address: Leidsestraat 13 1017 NS
Amsterdam The Netherlands
Phone: +31 20 6223818

#62
The Otherist
Category: Antiques, Jewelry,
Concept Shops
Average price: Modest
Area: Centrum
Address: Leliegracht 6 1015 DE
Amsterdam The Netherlands
Phone: +31 20 3200420

#63
Arnold Booden Unique
Eyefashion
Category: Eyewear & Opticians
Average price: Expensive
Area: Zuid, Museumkwartier
Address: Van Baerlestraat 95 1071 AT
Amsterdam The Netherlands
Phone: +31 20 6628378

#64
Inglot Cosmetics
Category: Cosmetics &Beauty
Average price: Expensive
Area: Zuid, Museumkwartier
Address: Van Baerlestraat 8 1071 AW
Amsterdam The Netherlands
Phone: +31 20 6700919

#65
Rituals Store
Category: Cosmetics &Beauty
Average price: Expensive
Area: Centrum
Address: Kalverstraat 73 1012 NZ
Amsterdam The Netherlands
Phone: +31 20 3449222

#66
The Frozen Fountain
Category: Interior Design, Furniture
Stores, Home Decor
Average price: Inexpensive
Area: Centrum
Address: Prinsengracht 645 1016 HV
Amsterdam The Netherlands
Phone: +31 20 6229375

#67
Itemz
Category: Flowers & Gifts,
Discount Store
Average price: Modest
Area: Oost, Oosterparkbuurt
Address: Wibautstraat 45 1091 GH
Amsterdam The Netherlands
Phone: +31 20 4683690

#68
G.W.
Category: Hardware Stores
Average price: Expensive
Area: Zuid, De Pijp
Address: Gerard Doustraat 62-3 1072
VV Amsterdam The Netherlands
Phone: +31 20 6712016

#69
De Winkel Van Nijntje
Category: Toy Stores
Average price: Exclusive
Area: Zuid, Rivierenbuurt
Address: Scheldestraat 61 1078 GH
Amsterdam The Netherlands
Phone: +31 20 6648054

#70
Tenue de Nimes
Category: Fashion
Average price: Expensive
Area: Centrum, Jordaan
Address: Elandsgracht 60 1016 TX
Amsterdam The Netherlands
Phone: +31 20 3204012

#71
The Mad Bakers
Category: Specialty Food, Hobby Shops
Average price: Modest
Area: Centrum, Haarlemmerbuurt
Address: Haarlemmerdijk 97 1013 KD
Amsterdam The Netherlands
Phone: +31 20 8100386

#72
Soap Company
Category: Day Spas,
Cosmetics &Beauty
Average price: Expensive
Area: Zuid, Museumkwartier
Address: Van Baerlestraat 122 1071 BD
Amsterdam The Netherlands
Phone: +31 20 6737599

#73
Raak Amsterdam
Category: Home Decor,
Women's Clothing
Average price: Expensive
Area: Zuid, De Pijp
Address: 1e van der Helststraat 46 1072
NV Amsterdam The Netherlands
Phone: +31 20 6704206

#74
Dam Square Souvenirs
Category: Shopping
Average price: Expensive
Area: Centrum, De Wallen
Address: Dam 19 1012 JS Amsterdam
The Netherlands
Phone: +31 20 4287167

#75
The Gamekeeper
Category: Toy Stores
Average price: Modest
Area: Centrum, Negen Straatjes
Address: Hartenstraat 14 1016 CB
Amsterdam The Netherlands
Phone: +31 20 6381579

#76
Laura Dols
Category: Thrift Stores,
Vintage& Consignment
Average price: Modest
Area: Centrum, Negen Straatjes
Address: Wolvenstraat 6 en 7 1016 EM
Amsterdam The Netherlands
Phone: +31 20 6249066

#77
Denham
Category: Men's Clothing,
Women's Clothing
Average price: Expensive
Area: Centrum, Negen Straatjes
Address: Prinsengracht 495 1016 HR
Amsterdam The Netherlands
Phone: +31 20 3315039

#78
Louis Wittenburg
Category: Hobby Shops
Average price: Expensive
Area: Centrum
Address: Raadhuisstraat 16 1016 DE
Amsterdam The Netherlands
Phone: +31 20 6246886

#79
Tutti Frutti
Category: Vintage& Consignment
Average price: Modest
Area: West, Oud West, Kinkerbuurt
Address: De Clercqstraat 112 1052 NN
Amsterdam The Netherlands
Phone: +31 20 6160508

#80
Magna Plaza
Category: Shopping Centers
Average price: Modest
Area: Centrum
Address: Nieuwezijds Voorburgwal 182-
1 1012 SJ Amsterdam The Netherlands
Phone: +31 20 6269199

#81
BIHP
Category: Art Gallery, French
Average price: Expensive
Area: Centrum, Negen Straatjes
Address: Keizersgracht 335 1016 EG
Amsterdam The Netherlands
Phone: +31 20 4282609

#82
Haastje Repje Amsterdam
Category: Women's Clothing
Average price: Expensive
Area: Zuid, De Pijp
Address: Ferdinand Bolstraat 96-VII
1072 LN Amsterdam The Netherlands
Phone: +31 20 6791403

#83
Soraya's Shoesz
Category: Shoe Stores
Average price: Expensive
Area: West, Oud West, Helmersbuurt
Address: 1e Constatijn Huygenstraat 69
1054 BT Amsterdam The Netherlands
Phone: +31 20 6189887

#84
A.
Category: Shopping
Average price: Expensive
Area: Centrum
Address: Nieuwe Hoogstraat 31-33
1011 HD Amsterdam The Netherlands
Phone: +31 20 6267205

#85
Tony Cohen
Category: Women's Clothing,
Accessories
Average price: Expensive
Area: Centrum, Negen Straatjes
Address: Huidenstraat 28 1016 ET
Amsterdam The Netherlands
Phone: +31 20 3203211

#86
2Theloo
Category: Shopping
Average price: Modest
Area: Centrum
Address: Kalverstraat 126 1012 PK
Amsterdam The Netherlands
Phone: +31 20 4202833

#87
Bril Amsterdam
Category: Eyewear & Opticians,
Optometrists
Average price: Expensive
Area: Zuid, Museumkwartier
Address: Cornelis Schuytstraat 23 1071
JD Amsterdam The Netherlands
Phone: +31 20 6767050

#88
Nieuws The Peoples Giftstore
Category: Cards & Stationery,
Gift Shops
Average price: Expensive
Area: Centrum
Address: Prinsengracht 297 1016 GX
Amsterdam The Netherlands
Phone: +31 20 6279540

#89
De Beestenwinkel
Category: Gift Shops, Toy Stores
Average price: Expensive
Area: Centrum
Address: Staalstraat 26 1011 JM
Amsterdam The Netherlands
Phone: +31 20 6231805

#90
Papillon
Category: Sports Wear,
Women's Clothing
Average price: Expensive
Area: Centrum
Address: Rokin 104 1012 KZ
Amsterdam The Netherlands
Phone: +31 20 6230648

#91
Fashion Helmet
Category: Accessories
Average price: Expensive
Area: Zuid, De Pijp
Address: Albert Cuypstraat 27h 1072
CK Amsterdam The Netherlands
Phone: +31 20 6750597

#92
Foto Mignon
Category: Photography Store
Average price: Modest
Area: Zuid, De Pijp
Address: Van Woustraat 56 1073 LN
Amsterdam The Netherlands
Phone: +31 20 6620145

#93
Superfood Centre
Category: Food, Shopping
Average price: Modest
Area: Centrum, Jordaan
Address: Eerste Rozendwarsstraat 10
1016 PC Amsterdam The Netherlands
Phone: +31 20 4897676

#94
Thinking of Holland
Category: Department Stores
Average price: Modest
Area: Oost
Address: Piet Heinkade 23 1019 BR
Amsterdam The Netherlands
Phone: +31 20 4191229

#95
Art Unlimited
Category: Cards & Stationery
Average price: Modest
Area: Centrum
Address: Leidsestraat 57 1012 NV
Amsterdam The Netherlands
Phone: +31 317 25074868

#96
Himalaya New Age Shop
Category: Books, Mags, Music & Video,
Breakfast & Brunch
Average price: Modest
Area: Centrum, De Wallen
Address: Warmoesstraat 56 1012 JG
Amsterdam The Netherlands
Phone: +31 20 6260899

#97
Tangram
Category: Shopping
Average price: Modest
Area: Centrum
Address: Herenstraat 9 1015 BX
Amsterdam The Netherlands
Phone: +31 20 6244286

#98
P.W.
Category: Office Equipment
Average price: Expensive
Area: Centrum, De Wallen
Address: Langebrugsteeg 13 1012 GB
Amsterdam The Netherlands
Phone: +31 20 6231649

#99
Laundry Industry
Category: Women's Clothing
Average price: Expensive
Area: Centrum
Address: Spuistraat 137 1012 SV
Amsterdam The Netherlands
Phone: +31 20 6253960

#100
Bever
Category: Outdoor Gear
Average price: Expensive
Area: West
Address: Stadhouderskade 4 1054 ES
Amsterdam The Netherlands
Phone: +31 20 6894639

#101
Second Life Music
Category: Thrift Stores, Vinyl Records,
Music & DVDs
Average price: Inexpensive
Area: Centrum, Jordaan
Address: Prinsengracht 366 1016 JA
Amsterdam The Netherlands
Phone: +31 20 6205200

#102
Boekhandel van Rossum
Category: Bookstores
Average price: Modest
Area: Zuid, Apollobuurt
Address: Beethovenstraat 32-4 1077 JH
Amsterdam The Netherlands
Phone: +31 20 4707077

#103
&Klevering
Category: Home Decor
Average price: Expensive
Area: Centrum, Haarlemmerbuurt
Address: Haarlemmerstraat 8 1013 ER
Amsterdam The Netherlands
Phone: +31 20 4222708

#104
B.J.
Category: Beer, Wine & Spirits,
Wineries, Wholesale Stores
Average price: Expensive
Area: Zuid, Apollobuurt
Address: Beethovenstraat 27 1077 HM
Amsterdam The Netherlands
Phone: +31 20 6626208

#105
Acne studio
Category: Women's Clothing,
Men's Clothing
Average price: Expensive
Area: Centrum
Address: Oude Spiegelstraat 8 1016 KJ
Amsterdam The Netherlands
Phone: +31 20 4226845

#106
Moooi
Category: Interior Design,
Home Decor, Art Gallery
Average price: Expensive
Area: Centrum, Jordaan
Address: Westerstraat 187 1015 MA
Amsterdam The Netherlands
Phone: +31 20 5287760

#107
Lush
Category: Cosmetics &Beauty
Average price: Expensive
Area: Centrum
Address: Leidsestraat 14 1017 PA
Amsterdam The Netherlands
Phone: +31 20 4234315

#108
Stout
Category: Adult, Lingerie
Average price: Expensive
Area: Centrum, Negen Straatjes
Address: Berenstraat 9-BG 1016 GG
Amsterdam The Netherlands
Phone: +31 20 6201676

#109
De Knopenwinkel
Category: Shopping
Average price: Expensive
Area: Centrum
Address: Herengracht 389 1016 BC
Amsterdam The Netherlands
Phone: +31 20 6269472

#110
De Kinderboekwinkel
Category: Bookstores
Average price: Modest
Area: Centrum
Address: Nieuwezijds Voorburgwal 344
1012 RX Amsterdam The Netherlands
Phone: +31 20 6227741

#111
Biec
Category: Accessories
Average price: Modest
Area: Centrum
Address: Staalstraat 28 1011 JM
Amsterdam The Netherlands
Phone: +31 20 7894006

#112
Maison de Bonneterie
Category: Fashion
Average price: Expensive
Area: Centrum
Address: Rokin 150 1012 LE
Amsterdam The Netherlands
Phone: +31 20 4898165

#113
Perry Sport
Category: Sports Wear
Average price: Modest
Area: Centrum
Address: Kalverstraat 99 1012 PA
Amsterdam The Netherlands
Phone: +31 20 6247131

#114
De Vredespijp
Category: Coffee & Tea, Art Gallery
Average price: Modest
Area: Zuid, De Pijp
Address: Eerste van der Helststraat 11a
1073 AA Amsterdam The Netherlands
Phone: +31 20 6764855

#115
Mobilia Woonstudio
Category: Interior Design, Shopping
Average price: Exclusive
Area: Centrum
Address: Utrechtsestraat 62 1017 VR
Amsterdam The Netherlands
Phone: +31 20 6229075

#116
Harten Amsterdam
Category: Accessories,
Women's Clothing
Average price: Modest
Area: Centrum
Address: Utrechtsestraat 25 1017 VH
Amsterdam The Netherlands
Phone: +31 20 3200035

#117
Fred de la Bretoniere Amsterdam
Category: Shoe Stores
Average price: Expensive
Area: Centrum
Address: Utrechtsestraat 77 1017 VJ
Amsterdam The Netherlands
Phone: +31 20 6269627

#118
Episode
Category: Vintage& Consignment
Average price: Modest
Area: Centrum
Address: Waterlooplein 1 1011 NV
Amsterdam The Netherlands
Phone: +31 20 3203000

#119
Studio Bazar
Category: Kitchen & Bath, Home Decor
Average price: Expensive
Area: Centrum
Address: Reguliersdwarsstraat 60-62
1017 BM Amsterdam The Netherlands
Phone: +31 20 6220830

#120
Saton Optiek Amsterdam
Category: Eyewear & Opticians,
Optometrists
Average price: Expensive
Area: Zuid, De Pijp
Address: 1e van der Helststraat 3a 1073
AA Amsterdam The Netherlands
Phone: +31 20 5788500

#121
Urban Outfitters
Category: Women's Clothing,
Men's Clothing, Concept Shops
Average price: Expensive
Area: Centrum
Address: Kalverstraat 31-33 1012 NX
Amsterdam The Netherlands
Phone: +31 20 6226729

#122
Aurora
Category: Electronics
Average price: Modest
Area: Centrum
Address: Vijzelstraat 27-35 1017 HD
Amsterdam The Netherlands
Phone: +31 20 6234062

#123
1953 Retro & Chic
Category: Vintage& Consignment
Average price: Expensive
Area: Centrum
Address: Staalstraat 2 1011 JL
Amsterdam The Netherlands
Phone: +31 642 808455

#124
Sprmrkt
Category: Fashion
Average price: Exclusive
Area: Centrum, Jordaan
Address: Rozengracht 191 1016 LZ
Amsterdam The Netherlands
Phone: +31 20 3305601

#125
Douglas
Category: Cosmetics &Beauty,
Skin Care
Average price: Expensive
Area: Centrum
Address: Kalverstraat 71 1012 NZ
Amsterdam The Netherlands
Phone: +31 20 6276663

#126
Patta
Category: Shoe Stores
Average price: Expensive
Area: Centrum, De Wallen
Address: Zeedijk 67 1012 AS
Amsterdam The Netherlands
Phone: +31 20 3318571

#127
Hema
Category: Department Stores
Average price: Modest
Area: Centrum
Address: Nieuwendijk 174-176 1012 MT
Amsterdam The Netherlands
Phone: +31 20 6234176

#128
iCentre
Category: Computers
Average price: Expensive
Area: Centrum
Address: Prins Hendrikkade 26 1012 TM
Amsterdam The Netherlands
Phone: +31 900 5202020

#129
Goochem Speelgoed
Category: Toy Stores
Average price: Expensive
Area: West, Oud West, Helmersbuurt
Address: 1e C Huygensstr 80 1054 BW
Amsterdam The Netherlands
Phone: +31 20 6124704

#130
Gerda's Bloemen en Planten
Category: Florists
Average price: Exclusive
Area: Centrum, Negen Straatjes
Address: Runstraat 16 1016 GK
Amsterdam The Netherlands
Phone: +31 20 6242912

#131
De Bruidssuite
Category: Bridal
Average price: Expensive
Area: Zuid, Apollobuurt
Address: Stadionweg 186 1077 TC
Amsterdam The Netherlands
Phone: +31 20 6710449

#132
Lucie's Amsterdam
Category: Jewelry
Average price: Modest
Area: Centrum
Address: St Luciensteeg 22 1012 PM
Amsterdam The Netherlands
Phone: +31 20 4284213

#133
Knutsel Frutsel
Category: Toy Stores
Average price: Modest
Area: Zuid, Hoofddorppleinbuurt
Address: Hoofddorpweg 21 1059 CT
Amsterdam The Netherlands
Phone: +31 20 6153994

#134
Gassan Dam Square
Category: Jewelry
Average price: Exclusive
Area: Centrum
Address: Rokin 1-5 1012 KK Amsterdam
The Netherlands
Phone: +31 20 6245787

#135
Pina
Category: Fashion
Average price: Expensive
Area: Centrum, Negen Straatjes
Address: Keizersgracht 233 1016 EA
Amsterdam The Netherlands
Phone: +31 20 3208225

#136
Zuiderziel
Category: Gift Shops
Average price: Modest
Area: Zuid, Museumkwartier
Address: Roelof Hartstraat 18 1071 VH
Amsterdam The Netherlands
Phone: +31 20 7370191

#137
Salon De Lingerie
Category: Lingerie
Average price: Expensive
Area: Centrum
Address: Utrechtsestraat 38 1017 VP
Amsterdam The Netherlands
Phone: +31 20 6239857

#138
Dede's Underworld
Category: Lingerie
Average price: Expensive
Area: Zuid, Apollobuurt
Address: Beethovenstraat 40-A 1077 JJ
Amsterdam The Netherlands
Phone: +31 20 6705653

#139
Carhartt Store
Category: Women's Clothing,
Men's Clothing
Average price: Modest
Area: Centrum, Negen Straatjes
Address: Hartenstraat 18 1016 CB
Amsterdam The Netherlands
Phone: +31 20 3305666

#140
Tinkerbell
Category: Toy Stores
Average price: Expensive
Area: Centrum
Address: Spiegelgracht 10-BG 1017 JR
Amsterdam The Netherlands
Phone: +31 20 6258830

#141
Wolford Flagship Store
Category: Lingerie
Average price: Exclusive
Area: Zuid, Museumkwartier
Address: P Cornelisz Hooftstr 83-1 1071
BP Amsterdam The Netherlands
Phone: +31 20 4701737

#142
Eenvoud
Category: Jewelry
Average price: Expensive
Area: Centrum, Jordaan
Address: Prinsengracht 310-HS 1016
HW Amsterdam The Netherlands
Phone: +31 20 6226374

#143
SeventyFive
Category: Shoe Stores
Average price: Modest
Area: Centrum, Haarlemmerbuurt
Address: Haarlemmerdijk 55-C 1013 KB
Amsterdam The Netherlands
Phone: +31 20 3306328

#144
Montblanc Boutique
Category: Leather Goods
Average price: Expensive
Area: Zuid, Museumkwartier
Address: Pieter Cornelisz Hooftstraat 57
1071 BN Amsterdam The Netherlands
Phone: +31 20 4700220

#145
De Sperwer
Category: Local Flavor,
Bookstores, Hobby Shops
Average price: Modest
Area: Zuid, De Pijp
Address: Gerard doustraat 226 1073 XC
Amsterdam The Netherlands
Phone: +31 20 6736896

#146
Nivo Schweitzer
Category: Photography Store
Average price: Expensive
Area: Centrum, Haarlemmerbuurt
Address: Haarlemmerdijk 114 1013 JH
Amsterdam The Netherlands
Phone: +31 20 6233159

#147
Broekmans en Van Poppel
Category: Books, Mags, Music & Video
Average price: Modest
Area: Zuid, Museumkwartier
Address: Van Baerlestraat 92 1071 BB
Amsterdam The Netherlands
Phone: +31 20 6796575

#148
La Savonnerie
Category: Cosmetics &Beauty
Average price: Modest
Area: Centrum, Jordaan
Address: Prinsengracht 294 1016 HJ
Amsterdam The Netherlands
Phone: +31 20 4281139

#149
Cine-Qua-Non Filmposters
Category: Shopping
Average price: Modest
Area: Centrum
Address: Staalstraat 14 1011 JL
Amsterdam The Netherlands
Phone: +31 20 6255588

#150
Mood over West
Category: Shopping
Average price: Modest
Area: West, Helmersbuurt
Address: Overtoom 60-62 1054 HL
Amsterdam The Netherlands
Phone: +31 20 7539993

#151
Menno Kroon
Category: Flowers & Gifts
Average price: Expensive
Area: Zuid, Museumkwartier
Address: Cornelis Schuytstraat 11 1071
JC Amsterdam The Netherlands
Phone: +31 20 6791950

#152
Hema
Category: Department Stores
Average price: Modest
Area: Zuid, Apollobuurt
Address: Stadionweg 43 1077 RX
Amsterdam The Netherlands
Phone: +31 20 6625145

#153
Van Beek
Category: Art Supplies,
Cards & Stationery
Average price: Modest
Area: Centrum
Address: Weteringschans 201-205 1017
XG Amsterdam The Netherlands
Phone: +31 20 6239647

#154
Fashion Flairs Parisienne
Category: Accessories
Average price: Expensive
Area: Centrum, Negen Straatjes
Address: Berenstraat 4 1016 GH
Amsterdam The Netherlands
Phone: +31 20 4280834

#155
The Shirt Shop
Category: Men's Clothing
Average price: Modest
Area: Centrum
Address: Reguliersdwarsstraat 64 1017
BM Amsterdam The Netherlands
Phone: +31 20 4232088

#156
Concerto Audio
Category: Electronics
Average price: Exclusive
Area: Centrum
Address: Utrechtsestraat 40 1017 VP
Amsterdam The Netherlands
Phone: +31 20 6222856

#157
H & M
Category: Women's Clothing, Accessories, Children's Clothing
Average price: Modest
Area: Centrum
Address: Kalverstraat 114-118 1012 PK Amsterdam The Netherlands
Phone: +31 20 5567799

#158
Linnaeus Boekhandel
Category: Bookstores
Average price: Modest
Area: Oost, Watergraafsmeer
Address: Middenweg 29-II BG 1098 AB Amsterdam The Netherlands
Phone: +31 20 4687192

#159
Beadies
Category: Hobby Shops
Average price: Expensive
Area: Centrum, Negen Straatjes
Address: Huidenstraat 6 1016 ES Amsterdam The Netherlands
Phone: +31 20 4285161

#160
Teuntje
Category: Toy Stores
Average price: Expensive
Area: Centrum, Haarlemmerbuurt
Address: Haarlemmerdijk 132 1013 JJ Amsterdam The Netherlands
Phone: +31 20 6253432

#161
Beadazzled
Category: Jewelry, Hobby Shops
Average price: Modest
Area: Zuid, De Pijp
Address: Sarphatipark 6-HS 1072 PA Amsterdam The Netherlands
Phone: +31 20 6734587

#162
Vlieger
Category: Office Equipment, Cards & Stationery, Hobby Shops
Average price: Modest
Area: Centrum
Address: Amstel 34 1017 AB Amsterdam The Netherlands
Phone: +31 20 6235834

#163
P.C.
Category: Shopping, Arts & Entertainment, Restaurant, Local Flavor
Average price: Expensive
Area: Zuid, Museumkwartier
Address: Pieter Cornelisz Hooftstraat 1071 BR Amsterdam The Netherlands
Phone: +31 20 6702606

#164
Lock Stock & Barrel
Category: Fashion
Average price: Expensive
Area: Centrum, Negen Straatjes
Address: Hartenstraat 26 1016 CC Amsterdam The Netherlands
Phone: +31 20 4213348

#165
SKY
Category: Fashion
Average price: Expensive
Area: Centrum, Negen Straatjes
Address: Herengracht 228-BG 1016 BT Amsterdam The Netherlands
Phone: +31 20 3200081

#166
Petit Bateau
Category: Children's Clothing
Average price: Exclusive
Area: Zuid, Museumkwartier
Address: Van Baerlestraat 19 1071 AN Amsterdam The Netherlands
Phone: +31 20 6709873

#167
Leuk
Category: Women's Clothing
Average price: Expensive
Area: Centrum
Address: Utrechtsestraat 35 1017 VH Amsterdam The Netherlands
Phone: +31 20 6387768

#168
De Tuinen
Category: Cosmetics &Beauty
Average price: Expensive
Area: Centrum
Address: Kalverstraat 11 1012 NX Amsterdam The Netherlands
Phone: +31 20 3202914

#169
Vrolijk Boekhandel
Category: Bookstores
Average price: Modest
Area: Centrum
Address: Paleisstraat 135 1012 ZL
Amsterdam The Netherlands
Phone: +31 20 6235142

#170
Chique de Friemel
Category: Vintage& Consignment
Average price: Modest
Area: Centrum, Haarlemmerbuurt
Address: Haarlemmerdijk 172 1013 JK
Amsterdam The Netherlands
Phone: +31 20 6273533

#171
Het Grote Avontuur
Category: Home Decor, Home Services
Average price: Modest
Area: Centrum, Haarlemmerbuurt
Address: Haarlemmerstraat 25 1013 EJ
Amsterdam The Netherlands
Phone: +31 20 6268597

#172
360Volt
Category: Thrift Stores, Home Services
Average price: Modest
Area: Centrum, Negen Straatjes
Address: Prinsengracht 397 1016 HL
Amsterdam The Netherlands
Phone: +31 20 8100101

#173
Vanmoof
Category: Bikes
Average price: Modest
Area: Oost, Oosterparkbuurt
Address: Mauritskade 55 1092 AD
Amsterdam The Netherlands
Phone: +31 20 3307401

#174
Jan
Category: Home Decor, Accessories
Average price: Expensive
Area: Centrum
Address: Utrechtsestraat 74 1017 VR
Amsterdam The Netherlands
Phone: +31 20 6264301

#175
The Darling
Category: Women's Clothing
Average price: Modest
Area: Centrum, Negen Straatjes
Address: Runstraat 4 1016 GK
Amsterdam The Netherlands
Phone: +31 20 4223142

#176
Chimera
Category: Toy Stores
Average price: Modest
Area: Centrum, De Wallen
Address: Damstraat 32 1012 JM
Amsterdam The Netherlands
Phone: +31 20 6246199

#177
Reisboekhandel Pied à Terre
Category: Bookstores
Average price: Modest
Area: West, Oud West
Address: Overtoom 135-137 1054 HG
Amsterdam The Netherlands
Phone: +31 20 6274455

#178
Xenos
Category: Discount Store
Average price: Inexpensive
Area: Centrum
Address: Kalverstraat 228 1012 XJ
Amsterdam The Netherlands
Phone: +31 20 4229163

#179
Daniele Dentici
Category: Shoe Stores
Average price: Expensive
Area: Zuid, De Pijp
Address: van Woustraat 76 1073 LP
Amsterdam The Netherlands
Phone: +31 20 6732686

#180
Pylones
Category: Flowers & Gifts
Average price: Modest
Area: Centrum
Address: Leidsestraat 65 1017 NX
Amsterdam The Netherlands
Phone: +31 20 3301847

#181
Sjerpetine
Category: Accessories,
Women's Clothing
Average price: Modest
Area: Zuid, De Pijp
Address: 1e van der Helststraat 33 1073
AC Amsterdam The Netherlands
Phone: +31 20 6641362

#182
Waterstone's
Category: Bookstores
Average price: Modest
Area: Centrum
Address: Kalverstraat 152 1012 XE
Amsterdam The Netherlands
Phone: +31 20 6383821

#183
Xenos
Category: Discount Store
Average price: Inexpensive
Area: West, Oud West
Address: Bilderdijkstraat 49-53 1053 KK
Amsterdam The Netherlands
Phone: +31 20 4121430

#184
De Klaproos
Category: Women's Clothing
Average price: Expensive
Area: Oost, Watergraafsmeer
Address: Middenweg 41 1098 AC
Amsterdam The Netherlands
Phone: +31 20 4630204

#185
Fashion Corner
Category: Men's Clothing
Average price: Modest
Area: Centrum
Address: Nieuwendijk 131 1012 MD
Amsterdam The Netherlands
Phone: +31 20 6248385

#186
Foto Fransen
Category: Photography Store
Average price: Expensive
Area: Oost, Oosterparkbuurt
Address: Beukenweg 31 1092 AZ
Amsterdam The Netherlands
Phone: +31 20 6650471

#187
&Klevering
Category: Flowers & Gifts
Average price: Expensive
Area: Centrum
Address: Staalstraat 11 1011 JK
Amsterdam The Netherlands
Phone: +31 20 4213029

#188
Wah Kiu
Category: Shopping
Average price: Modest
Area: Centrum, De Wallen
Address: Geldersekade 104 1012 BM
Amsterdam The Netherlands
Phone: +31 20 6264010

#189
Villeroy & Boch Tableware
Category: Flowers & Gifts
Average price: Expensive
Area: Zuid, Museumkwartier
Address: Van Baerlestraat 70 1071 BA
Amsterdam The Netherlands
Phone: +31 20 6640210

#190
Amsterdamse Matrassen Centrale
Category: Mattresses
Average price: Modest
Area: Zuid, De Pijp
Address: Albert Cuypstraat 116 D 1072
CZ Amsterdam The Netherlands
Phone: +31 20 6751268

#191
Radio Rotor
Category: Electronics
Average price: Modest
Area: West, Oud West, Da Costabuurt
Address: Kinkerstraat 55 1053 DE
Amsterdam The Netherlands
Phone: +31 20 6125759

#192
Joe Merino
Category: Men's Clothing
Average price: Expensive
Area: Centrum
Address: Kerkstraat 169 1017 GH
Amsterdam The Netherlands
Phone: +31 20 3415777

#193
Penelope Craft
Category: Art Supplies, Knitting
Supplies, Hobby Shops
Average price: Modest
Area: Centrum
Address: Kerkstraat 117 1017 GE
Amsterdam The Netherlands
Phone: +31 614 277733

#194
Primera Middenweg
Category: Shopping
Average price: Modest
Area: Oost, Watergraafsmeer
Address: Middenweg 49-BG 1098 AC
Amsterdam The Netherlands
Phone: +31 20 6927586

#195
Mulberry Shops
Category: Leather Goods
Average price: Exclusive
Area: Zuid, Museumkwartier
Address: Pieter Cornelisz Hooftstraat 46
1071 BZ Amsterdam The Netherlands
Phone: +31 20 6738086

#196
Minerva Boekhandel
Category: Books, Mags, Music & Video
Average price: Modest
Area: Zuid, Willemspark
Address: Koninginneweg 229 1075 CS
Amsterdam The Netherlands
Phone: +31 20 6620877

#197
Lucky Star Videotheek
Category: Videos & Video Game Rental
Average price: Inexpensive
Area: Zuid
Address: Amstelveenseweg 81 1075
VW Amsterdam The Netherlands
Phone: +31 20 6735529

#198
't Hoekje
Category: Florists
Average price: Modest
Area: Oost, Watergraafsmeer
Address: Cornelis Drebbelstraat 12
1097 AL Amsterdam The Netherlands
Phone: +31 20 6650377

#199
Papabubble II
Category: Candy Stores, Arts & Crafts
Average price: Modest
Area: Centrum
Address: Staalstraat 16 1011 JL
Amsterdam The Netherlands
Phone: +31 20 6262662

#200
Boterham
Category: Concept Shops
Average price: Modest
Area: Oost, Oosterparkbuurt
Address: Andreas Bonnstraat 2 1091 AX
Amsterdam The Netherlands
Phone: +31 20 3541465

#201
Occhiali
Category: Eyewear & Opticians
Average price: Expensive
Area: Centrum
Address: Koningsplein 15 1017 BB
Amsterdam The Netherlands
Phone: +31 20 4210520

#202
Woontante
Category: Furniture Stores, Home Decor
Average price: Modest
Area: Zuid, De Pijp
Address: Van Woustraat 163-165 1074
AK Amsterdam The Netherlands
Phone: +31 20 6766926

#203
Charlie + Mary
Category: Women's Clothing, Men's
Clothing, Accessories
Average price: Modest
Area: Zuid, Rivierenbuurt
Address: Gerard Doustraat 84 1072 VW
Amsterdam The Netherlands
Phone: +31 20 6628281

#204
Zwartjes Van 1883
Category: Shoe Stores
Average price: Expensive
Area: Centrum
Address: Utrechtsestraat 123 1017 VL
Amsterdam The Netherlands
Phone: +31 20 6233701

#205
Rams Interieur
Category: Home Decor
Average price: Expensive
Area: Centrum
Address: Utrechtsestraat 120 1017 VT
Amsterdam The Netherlands
Phone: +31 20 4204585

#206
De Badjassenwinkel
Category: Accessories
Average price: Exclusive
Area: Centrum
Address: Vijzelgracht 41 1017 HP
Amsterdam The Netherlands
Phone: +31 20 3201617

#207
**Gebroeders Winter
Kantoorvakhandel**
Category: Office Equipment
Average price: Modest
Area: Zuid, Apollobuurt
Address: Beethovenstraat 5 1077 HK
Amsterdam The Netherlands
Phone: +31 20 6714162

#208
Leonore Sieraden
Category: Jewelry
Average price: Exclusive
Area: Centrum
Address: Utrechtsestraat 53 1017 VJ
Amsterdam The Netherlands
Phone: +31 20 6245655

#209
Klamboe Collection
Category: Home Decor
Average price: Modest
Area: Centrum, Jordaan
Address: Rozengracht 141 1016 LW
Amsterdam The Netherlands
Phone: +31 20 6229492

#210
Relaxed Clothing
Category: Accessories, Men's Clothing,
Women's Clothing
Average price: Expensive
Area: Centrum, Negen Straatjes
Address: Huidenstraat 19 1016 ER
Amsterdam The Netherlands
Phone: +31 20 3202001

#211
De Hoed Van Tijn
Category: Accessories
Average price: Exclusive
Area: Centrum
Address: Nieuwe Hoogstraat 15 1011
HC Amsterdam The Netherlands
Phone: +31 20 6232759

#212
Hunkemöller
Category: Lingerie, Cosmetics &Beauty
Average price: Modest
Area: Centrum
Address: Kalverstraat 203 1012 XC
Amsterdam The Netherlands
Phone: +31 20 6265036

#213
Tenue de Nîmes
Category: Women's Clothing,
Men's Clothing
Average price: Expensive
Area: Centrum, Haarlemmerbuurt
Address: Haarlemmerstraat 92-94 1013
EV Amsterdam The Netherlands
Phone: +31 20 3312778

#214
Wonen 2000
Category: Furniture Stores
Average price: Exclusive
Area: Centrum, Jordaan
Address: Rozengracht 215-217 1016 LZ
Amsterdam The Netherlands
Phone: +31 20 5218712

#215
Yogisha
Category: Sports Wear
Average price: Expensive
Area: Zuid, De Pijp
Address: Ceintuurbaan 378 1073 EM
Amsterdam The Netherlands
Phone: +31 20 6640743

#216
Bouman Mode
Category: Women's Clothing
Average price: Expensive
Area: Zuid, De Pijp
Address: Albert Cuypstraat 189-191
1073 BD Amsterdam The Netherlands
Phone: +31 20 6623986

#217
**Gebroeders Winter
Kantoorvakhandel**
Category: Office Equipment
Average price: Modest
Area: Centrum, Jordaan
Address: Rozengracht 62 1016 NE
Amsterdam The Netherlands
Phone: +31 20 6234715

#218
**Gebroeders Winter
Kantoorvakhandel**
Category: Office Equipment
Average price: Modest
Area: Centrum, Jordaan
Address: Rozengracht 62 1016 NE
Amsterdam The Netherlands
Phone: +31 20 6234715

#219
Paul Warmer
Category: Shoe Stores
Average price: Expensive
Area: Centrum
Address: Leidsestraat 41 1017 NV
Amsterdam The Netherlands
Phone: +31 20 4278011

#220
Buhjah
Category: Jewelry
Average price: Expensive
Area: Zuid, Museumkwartier
Address: Hobbemastraat 13 1071 XZ
Amsterdam The Netherlands
Phone: +31 20 6700673

#221
Centre Neuf
Category: Women's Clothing
Average price: Expensive
Area: Centrum
Address: Utrechtsestraat 139-BG 1017
VM Amsterdam The Netherlands
Phone: +31 20 5285040

#222
OOK
Category: Flowers & Gifts
Average price: Modest
Area: Centrum, Haarlemmerbuurt
Address: Haarlemmerdijk 147 1013 KH
Amsterdam The Netherlands
Phone: +31 20 4273287

#223
Bizar Fashion
Category: Women's Clothing
Average price: Exclusive
Area: Centrum
Address: Leidsestraat 47 1017 NV
Amsterdam The Netherlands
Phone: +31 20 3206908

#224
Wolford
Category: Lingerie, Women's Clothing
Average price: Expensive
Area: Zuid, Apollobuurt
Address: Beethovenstraat 67 1077 HN
Amsterdam The Netherlands
Phone: +31 20 6763364

#225
Soulcycle
Category: Bikes
Average price: Expensive
Area: Centrum
Address: Weteringschans 221 1017 XH
Amsterdam The Netherlands
Phone: +31 20 6895522

#226
Dam Feestwinkel
Category: Hobby Shops
Average price: Modest
Area: Oost, Watergraafsmeer
Address: Middenweg 40-42 1097 BP
Amsterdam The Netherlands
Phone: +31 20 6938886

#227
Paul Noyen Amsterdam
Category: Shoe Stores
Average price: Expensive
Area: Zuid, Museumkwartier
Address: Van Baerlestraat 64-HS 1071
BA Amsterdam The Netherlands
Phone: +31 20 6769791

#228
Nijhof & Lee
Category: Bookstores
Average price: Expensive
Area: Centrum
Address: Staalstraat 13-A 1011 JK
Amsterdam The Netherlands
Phone: +31 20 6203980

#229
Joe's Vliegerwinkel
Category: Hobby Shops
Average price: Modest
Area: Centrum
Address: Nieuwe Hoogstraat 19 1011
HD Amsterdam The Netherlands
Phone: +31 20 6250139

#230
Van Ravenstein
Category: Women's Clothing
Average price: Exclusive
Area: Centrum, Negen Straatjes
Address: Keizersgracht 359 1016 EJ
Amsterdam The Netherlands
Phone: +31 20 6390067

#231
Bis
Category: Thrift Stores
Average price: Modest
Area: Centrum
Address: Sint Antoniesbreestraat 25-A
1011 HB Amsterdam The Netherlands
Phone: +31 20 6203467

#232
Fred de la Bretoniere
Category: Shoe Stores
Average price: Expensive
Area: Centrum
Address: Sint Luciënsteeg 20 1012 PM
Amsterdam The Netherlands
Phone: +31 20 6234152

#233
Santa Jet
Category: Shopping
Average price: Modest
Area: Centrum
Address: Prinsenstraat 7 1015 DA
Amsterdam The Netherlands
Phone: +31 20 6200794

#234
Front Runner
Category: Sporting Goods
Average price: Expensive
Area: Centrum
Address: Nieuwendijk 134 1012 MS
Amsterdam The Netherlands
Phone: +31 20 4280202

#235
Hay Store Amsterdam
Category: Furniture Stores, Home Decor
Average price: Expensive
Area: Centrum
Address: Spuistraat 281abc 1012 VR
Amsterdam The Netherlands
Phone: +31 20 3708851

#236
Six & Sons
Category: Antiques,
Vintage& Consignment
Average price: Expensive
Area: Centrum, Haarlemmerbuurt
Address: Haarlemmerdijk 31 1013 EJ
Amsterdam The Netherlands
Phone: +31 20 2330092

#237
Christie's
Category: Art Gallery
Average price: Exclusive
Area: Zuid, Museumkwartier
Address: Cornelis Schuytstraat 57 1071
JG Amsterdam The Netherlands
Phone: +31 20 5755255

#238
Au Bonheur Des Dames
Category: Shopping
Average price: Expensive
Area: Zuid, Apollobuurt
Address: Beethovenstraat 92 1077 JN
Amsterdam The Netherlands
Phone: +31 20 6794938

#239
LifeStyle Amsterdam
Category: Home Decor
Average price: Expensive
Area: Zuid, Museumkwartier
Address: P.C. Hooftstraat 116 1071 CD
Amsterdam The Netherlands
Phone: +31 20 4709913

#240
KANT
Category: Lingerie
Average price: Expensive
Area: Oost, Watergraafsmeer
Address: Middenweg 50 1097 BR
Amsterdam The Netherlands
Phone: +31 20 6630020

#241
KANT
Category: Lingerie
Average price: Expensive
Area: Oost, Watergraafsmeer
Address: Middenweg 50 1097 BR
Amsterdam The Netherlands
Phone: +31 20 6630020

#242
Schmidt Optiek
Category: Eyewear & Opticians
Average price: Expensive
Area: Centrum
Address: Rokin 72 1012 KW
Amsterdam The Netherlands
Phone: +31 20 6231981

#243
Henk Comics & Manga Store
Category: Books, Mags, Music & Video
Average price: Expensive
Area: Centrum, De Wallen
Address: Zeedijk 136 1012 BC
Amsterdam The Netherlands
Phone: +31 20 4213688

#244
Betsy Palmer
Category: Shoe Stores
Average price: Expensive
Area: Centrum, De Wallen
Address: Rokin 15 1012 KK
Amsterdam The Netherlands
Phone: +31 20 4221040

#245
Ellebelle
Category: Women's Clothing
Average price: Expensive
Area: Zuid, Museumkwartier
Address: Cornelis Schuytstraat 30 1071
JJ Amsterdam The Netherlands
Phone: +31 20 4707040

#246
290 Square Meters
Category: Shoe Stores,
Men's Clothing, Women's Clothing
Average price: Exclusive
Area: Centrum
Address: Houtkopersdwarsstraat 3 1011
NK Amsterdam The Netherlands
Phone: +31 20 4192525

#247
Mooi
Category: Thrift Stores,
Vintage& Consignment
Average price: Modest
Area: Zuid, Rivierenbuurt
Address: Scheldestraat 58 1078 GM
Amsterdam The Netherlands
Phone: +31 20 3795768

#248
Frantzen Wintersport
Category: Sports Wear
Average price: Expensive
Area: Zuid, Rivierenbuurt
Address: Churchilllaan 83 1078 DJ
Amsterdam The Netherlands
Phone: +31 20 6625988

#249
Uitgeverij en Boekhandel Jimmink
Category: Bookstores
Average price: Modest
Area: Zuid, Rivierenbuurt
Address: Rooseveltlaan 62 1078 NL
Amsterdam The Netherlands
Phone: +31 20 6791244

#250
't Stomerijtje
Category: Cards & Stationery
Average price: Modest
Area: Centrum, Haarlemmerbuurt
Address: Haarlemmerdijk 56 1013 JE
Amsterdam The Netherlands
Phone: +31 20 6269860

#251
Action
Category: Shopping
Average price: Inexpensive
Area: Zuid
Address: Europaboulevard 17 1079 PC
Amsterdam The Netherlands
Phone: +31 228 565656

#252
Royal Delft
Category: Home & Garden
Average price: Exclusive
Area: Centrum, De Wallen
Address: Munttoren 1012 WR
Amsterdam The Netherlands
Phone: +31 20 6232271

#253
Dept Store
Category: Fashion
Average price: Expensive
Area: Centrum
Address: Heiligeweg 49-51 1012 XP
Amsterdam The Netherlands
Phone: +31 20 5287907

#254
Linhard
Category: Fashion
Average price: Expensive
Area: Zuid, Museumkwartier
Address: Van Baerlestraat 50 1071 AZ
Amsterdam The Netherlands
Phone: +31 20 6790755

#255
Wanuskewin
Category: Bookstores
Average price: Modest
Area: Zuid, De Pijp
Address: Ferdinand Bolstraat 28 1072
LK Amsterdam The Netherlands
Phone: +31 20 6794649

#256
Lush
Category: Cosmetics &Beauty
Average price: Expensive
Area: Centrum
Address: Kalverstraat 98 1012 PJ
Amsterdam The Netherlands
Phone: +31 20 3306376

#257
BeboB Design
Category: Furniture Stores
Average price: Expensive
Area: Centrum
Address: Prinsengracht 764 1017 LE
Amsterdam The Netherlands
Phone: +31 20 6245763

#258
Ramona
Category: Shoe Stores
Average price: Expensive
Area: Centrum, Haarlemmerbuurt
Address: Haarlemmerdijk 124 1013 JJ
Amsterdam The Netherlands
Phone: +31 20 6251870

#259
Blau
Category: Women's Clothing
Average price: Expensive
Area: Centrum, Haarlemmerbuurt
Address: Haarlemmerdijk 174 1013 JK
Amsterdam The Netherlands
Phone: +31 20 6256990

#260
Wulf Wonen
Category: Home Decor
Average price: Expensive
Area: Centrum, Jordaan
Address: Rozengracht 74-76-78 1016
NE Amsterdam The Netherlands
Phone: +31 20 6265011

#261
1401 Footwear
Category: Shoe Stores, Outdoor Gear
Average price: Expensive
Area: West, Oud West, Helmersbuurt
Address: J.P. Heijestraat 153 1054 MG
Amsterdam The Netherlands
Phone: +31 20 6161734

#262
Rituals
Category: Cosmetics &Beauty
Average price: Modest
Area: Centrum
Address: Leidsestraat 62 1017 PC
Amsterdam The Netherlands
Phone: +31 20 6252311

#263
Hampe & Berkel Muziek
Category: Musical Instruments
Average price: Expensive
Area: Centrum
Address: Spui 11 1012 WX
Amsterdam The Netherlands
Phone: +31 20 6242323

#264
**Spare Time Street
Beach & Snowwear**
Category: Fashion
Average price: Expensive
Area: Zuid, Rivierenbuurt
Address: Rijnstraat 205-BG 1079 HE
Amsterdam The Netherlands
Phone: +31 20 6460807

#265
Wini Vintage
Category: Vintage& Consignment,
Women's Clothing, Men's Clothing
Average price: Modest
Area: Centrum, Haarlemmerbuurt
Address: Haarlemmerstraat 29 1013 EJ
Amsterdam The Netherlands
Phone: +31 20 4279393

#266
De Pittenkoning
Category: Local Flavor, Hobby Shops
Average price: Expensive
Area: Zuid, De Pijp
Address: 1e van der Helststraat 35 1073
AC Amsterdam The Netherlands
Phone: +31 20 6716308

#267
Profiles Hair & Body Spa
Category: Cosmetics &Beauty, Hair
Salons, Day Spas
Average price: Expensive
Area: Centrum
Address: Spuistraat 330 1012 VX
Amsterdam The Netherlands
Phone: +31 20 6276337

#268
Fame Music Store
Category: Music & DVDs
Average price: Expensive
Area: Centrum
Address: Kalverstraat 2-4 1012 PC
Amsterdam The Netherlands
Phone: +31 20 6236546

#269
Hema
Category: Department Stores
Average price: Inexpensive
Area: Centrum
Address: Reguliersbreestraat 20 1017
CN Amsterdam The Netherlands
Phone: +31 20 4273782

#270
Boekhandel Mulder
Category: Bookstores
Average price: Modest
Area: Zuid, Museumkwartier
Address: Cornelis Schuytstraat 14 1071
JH Amsterdam The Netherlands
Phone: +31 20 6625680

#271
Fraai Fashion
Category: Women's Clothing
Average price: Expensive
Area: Zuid, Apollobuurt
Address: Stadionweg 49 1077 RX
Amsterdam The Netherlands
Phone: +31 20 4703936

#272
Beverly Beethoven
Category: Women's Clothing,
Accessories
Average price: Expensive
Area: Zuid, Apollobuurt
Address: Beethovenstraat 75 1077 HP
Amsterdam The Netherlands
Phone: +31 20 6709669

#273
l'Occitane en Provence
Category: Cosmetics &Beauty
Average price: Expensive
Area: Centrum
Address: Heiligeweg 24 1012 XR
Amsterdam The Netherlands
Phone: +31 20 5285146

#274
Het is Liefde
Category: Bridal, Flowers & Gifts
Average price: Expensive
Area: Zuid, De Pijp
Address: Eerste van der Helststraat 13-
15 1073 AB Amsterdam The Netherlands
Phone: +31 20 6717818

#275
Vezjun
Category: Women's Clothing
Average price: Modest
Area: Centrum, Jordaan
Address: Rozengracht 110,
1016 NH Amsterdam, The Netherlands
Phone: +31 20 6745788

#276
Pinc Sale
Category: Women's Clothing
Average price: Modest
Area: Zuid, WTC, Buitenveldert
Address: Gustav Mahlerlaan 316
Amsterdam, Noord-Holland The
Netherlands
Phone: +31 652 300165

#277
NAN Amsterdam
Category: Fashion
Average price: Exclusive
Area: Zuid, Apollobuurt
Address: Beethovenstraat 15 1077 HL
Amsterdam The Netherlands
Phone: +31 20 4004370

#278
AKO
Category: Bookstores,
Newspapers & Magazines
Average price: Modest
Area: Zuid, Apollobuurt
Address: Beethovenstraat 42 1077 JJ
Amsterdam The Netherlands
Phone: +31 881 338022

#279
Het Martyrium
Category: Books, Mags, Music & Video
Average price: Modest
Area: Zuid
Address: Van Baerlestraat 170-172
1071 BH Amsterdam The Netherlands
Phone: +31 20 6732092

#280
Restored
Category: Concept Shops
Average price: Expensive
Area: Centrum, Haarlemmerbuurt
Address: Haarlemmerdijk 39 1013 KA
Amsterdam The Netherlands
Phone: +31 20 3376473

#281
Zenza
Category: Home Decor
Average price: Expensive
Area: Centrum
Address: Utrechtsestraat 101 1017 VK
Amsterdam The Netherlands
Phone: +31 20 4230070

#282
Welikefashion.com
Category: Women's Clothing,
Accessories
Average price: Modest
Area: Zuid, Museumkwartier
Address: Van Baerlestraat 108 1071 BC
Amsterdam The Netherlands
Phone: +31 20 6649922

#283
Red Carpet Queen store
Category: Makeup Artists, Skin Care,
Cosmetics &Beauty, Eyelash Service
Average price: Expensive
Area: Centrum, Haarlemmerbuurt
Address: Haarlemmerstraat 140 1013
EZ Amsterdam The Netherlands
Phone: +31 20 6140140

#284
Nes Optiek
Category: Optometrists,
Eyewear & Opticians
Average price: Exclusive
Area: Centrum, De Wallen
Address: Grimburgwal 3 1012 GA
Amsterdam The Netherlands
Phone: +31 20 4123911

#285
Amsterdam Watch Company
Category: Jewelry, Watches
Average price: Expensive
Area: Centrum, Negen Straatjes
Address: Reestraat 3 1016 DM
Amsterdam The Netherlands
Phone: +31 20 3892789

#286
Axi Schoen
Category: Shoe Stores
Average price: Inexpensive
Area: Zuid, De Pijp
Address: Eerste Sweelinckstraat 1-3
1073 CK Amsterdam The Netherlands
Phone: +31 20 6739922

#287
Wollepop
Category: Toy Stores, Fashion,
Baby Gear & Furniture
Average price: Inexpensive
Area: West, Helmersbuurt
Address: Bosboom Toussaintstraat 49-II
1054 AN Amsterdam The Netherlands
Phone: +31 20 6854176

#288
Vero Moda
Category: Women's Clothing
Average price: Modest
Area: Centrum
Address: Nieuwendijk 116-118 1012 MS
Amsterdam The Netherlands
Phone: +31 20 6221606

#289
Hebbes in Speelgoed
Category: Toy Stores
Average price: Expensive
Area: Centrum, Haarlemmerbuurt
Address: Haarlemmerdijk 18 1013 JC
Amsterdam The Netherlands
Phone: +31 20 6255115

#290
Avviso
Category: Women's Clothing,
Hair Salons
Average price: Modest
Area: Zuid, De Pijp
Address: Van Woustraat 52 1073 LM
Amsterdam The Netherlands
Phone: +31 20 3791560

#291
Printerette
Category: Cards & Stationery,
Printing Services
Average price: Modest
Area: Centrum
Address: Vijzelstraat 76 1017 HL
Amsterdam The Netherlands
Phone: +31 20 6254604

#292
Pol's Potten
Category: Home Decor
Average price: Expensive
Area: Oost, Java Eiland
Address: Knsm-Laan 39 1019 LA
Amsterdam The Netherlands
Phone: +31 20 4193541

#293
Costa Rijwielhandel
Category: Bikes
Average price: Modest
Area: Oost, Dapperbuurt
Address: Oosterspoorplein 1 1093 JW
Amsterdam The Netherlands
Phone: +31 20 6923439

#294
Color Me Mine
Category: Venues & Events, Arts &
Crafts, Hobby Shops
Average price: Expensive
Area: Zuid, Museumkwartier
Address: Roelof Hartstraat 22 1071 VJ
Amsterdam The Netherlands
Phone: +31 20 6752987

#295
Klevering Zuid
Category: Home Decor
Average price: Expensive
Area: Zuid, Museumkwartier
Address: Jacob Obrechtstraat 19-A
1071 KD Amsterdam The Netherlands
Phone: +31 20 6703623

#296
H&M
Category: Accessories,
Men's Clothing, Women's Clothing
Average price: Modest
Area: Centrum
Address: Leidseplein 1-3 1017 PR
Amsterdam The Netherlands
Phone: +31 900 1988

#297
Run2Day
Category: Sporting Goods
Average price: Exclusive
Area: Zuid, West
Address: Overtoom 345-351 1054 JM
Amsterdam The Netherlands
Phone: +31 20 6167272

#298
Postkantoor
Category: Personal Shopping,
Post Offices
Average price: Modest
Area: Centrum
Address: Singel 250 1016 AB
Amsterdam The Netherlands
Phone: +31 20 3300555

#299
Blokker
Category: Home Decor
Average price: Modest
Area: Centrum
Address: Kalverstraat 41 1012 NZ
Amsterdam The Netherlands
Phone: +31 20 6234454

#300
Gassan Diamonds
Category: Jewelry
Average price: Exclusive
Area: Centrum
Address: Nieuwe Uilenburgerstraat
173-175 1011 LN Amsterdam
The Netherlands
Phone: +31 20 6225333

#301
Betsy Palmer
Category: Shoe Stores
Average price: Expensive
Area: Zuid, De Pijp
Address: Van Woustraat 46 1073 LM
Amsterdam The Netherlands
Phone: +31 20 4709795

#302
Zara
Category: Fashion
Average price: Expensive
Area: Centrum
Address: Kalverstraat 66-72 1012 PG
Amsterdam The Netherlands
Phone: +31 20 5304050

#303
Raak Amsterdam
Category: Fashion
Average price: Expensive
Area: Centrum
Address: Leidsestraat 79 1017 NX
Amsterdam The Netherlands
Phone: +31 20 4211324

#304
America Today
Category: Men's Clothing, Women's
Clothing
Average price: Modest
Area: Plantagebuurt, Centrum
Address: Sarphatistraat 48 1018 GN
Amsterdam The Netherlands
Phone: +31 20 6389847

#305
Cats & Things
Category: Pet Stores, Home Decor,
Pet Training
Average price: Modest
Area: Centrum, Jordaan
Address: Hazenstraat 26 1016 SP
Amsterdam The Netherlands
Phone: +31 20 4283028

#306
G Star Women
Category: Women's Clothing
Average price: Modest
Area: Centrum
Address: Leidsestraat 111017 NS
Amsterdam, The Netherlands
Phone: +31 20 4285432

#307
Streetlife
Category: Women's Clothing
Average price: Modest
Area: Zuid, De Pijp
Address: Ferdinand Bolstraat 45 1072
LB Amsterdam The Netherlands
Phone: +31 20 4702488

#308
De Klederij
Category: Thrift Stores
Average price: Modest
Area: Zuid, De Pijp
Address: Van Woustraat 116 1073 LS
Amsterdam The Netherlands
Phone: +31 20 4709522

#309
Runnersworld
Category: Sporting Goods
Average price: Modest
Area: Centrum
Address: Vijzelgracht 7 1017 HM
Amsterdam The Netherlands
Phone: +31 20 4208700

#310
BOO Shoes
Category: Shoe Stores
Average price: Expensive
Area: Zuid, Rivierenbuurt
Address: Scheldestraat 42 1078 GL
Amsterdam The Netherlands
Phone: +31 20 6723993

#311
Waar
Category: Shopping
Average price: Expensive
Area: Centrum
Address: Heiligeweg 45 1012 XP
Amsterdam The Netherlands
Phone: +31 20 3307727

#312
Zara Home
Category: Home Decor
Average price: Modest
Area: Zuid, Museumkwartier
Address: Van Baerlestraat 25 1071 AN
Amsterdam The Netherlands
Phone: +31 20 4713403

#313
Raw materials
Category: Furniture Stores
Average price: Expensive
Area: Centrum, Jordaan
Address: Rozengracht 229 - 233 1016
NA Amsterdam The Netherlands
Phone: +31 20 4213893

#314
Cartier
Category: Jewelry
Average price: Exclusive
Area: Zuid, Museumkwartier
Address: P.C. Hooftstraat 132-134 1071
BR Amsterdam The Netherlands
Phone: +31 20 6703434

#315
Plantenmarkt van Tol
Category: Flowers & Gifts,
Nurseries & Gardening
Average price: Modest
Area: Zuid, De Pijp
Address: Albert Cuypstraat 203 1073 BE
Amsterdam The Netherlands
Phone: +31 20 6626440

#316
Lansuplant
Category: Florists
Average price: Modest
Area: Zuid, Hoofddorppleinbuurt
Address: Hoofddorpweg 32 1058 PC
Amsterdam The Netherlands
Phone: +31 20 6170689

#317
**De Ru Verf en
Behangspeciaalzaak**
Category: Home Decor,
Hardware Stores
Average price: Exclusive
Area: Zuid, De Pijp
Address: Van Woustraat 143-145 1074
AJ Amsterdam The Netherlands
Phone: +31 20 6626821

#318
Adidas
Category: Sports Wear
Average price: Expensive
Area: Centrum
Address: Leidsestraat 7 1017 NS
Amsterdam The Netherlands
Phone: +31 20 4287634

#319
Parfumerie Marjo
Category: Cosmetics &Beauty,
Drugstores
Average price: Modest
Area: Centrum, De Wallen
Address: Damstraat 27-29 1012 JL
Amsterdam The Netherlands
Phone: +31 20 6255785

#320
Cynthia
Category: Shoe Stores
Average price: Modest
Area: Centrum
Address: Leidsestraat 86 1017 PE
Amsterdam The Netherlands
Phone: +31 20 6265519

#321
Exota
Category: Fashion
Average price: Modest
Area: Centrum, Negen Straatjes
Address: Hartenstraat 10 1016 CB
Amsterdam The Netherlands
Phone: +31 20 6209102

#322
Fred de la Bretoniere
Category: Leather Goods, Shoe Stores
Average price: Expensive
Area: Zuid, Museumkwartier
Address: Van Baerlestraat 34-II 1071
AX Amsterdam The Netherlands
Phone: +31 20 4709320

#323
Daniele Dentici
Category: Shoe Stores
Average price: Expensive
Area: Centrum, Jordaan
Address: Elandsgracht 10-A 1016 TV
Amsterdam The Netherlands
Phone: +31 20 4236995

#324
Hans Winkel Brillen
Category: Eyewear & Opticians
Average price: Expensive
Area: Centrum
Address: Rokin 130 1012 LD
Amsterdam The Netherlands
Phone: +31 20 6238175

#325
Danie Bles Styling
Category: Personal Shopping
Average price: Exclusive
Area: Slotervaart
Address: Koningin Wilhelminaplein 13
1062 HH Amsterdam The Netherlands
Phone: +31 20 4083220

#326
Property Of...
Category: Accessories
Average price: Expensive
Area: Centrum
Address: Herenstraat 2 1015 CA
Amsterdam The Netherlands
Phone: +31 20 6225909

#327
Schaap & Citroen
Category: Jewelry
Average price: Exclusive
Area: Zuid, Museumkwartier
Address: P.C. Hooftstraat 40 1071 BZ
Amsterdam The Netherlands
Phone: +31 20 6714714

#328
Kiehl's
Category: Cosmetics &Beauty
Average price: Expensive
Area: Zuid, Museumkwartier
Address: Hobbemastraat 4 1071 ZA
Amsterdam The Netherlands
Phone: +31 20 6750891

#329
Juggle Store
Category: Hobby Shops
Average price: Modest
Area: Centrum
Address: Staalstraat 3 1011 JJ
Amsterdam The Netherlands
Phone: +31 20 4202080

#330
Lemon
Category: Women's Clothing,
Men's Clothing, Accessories
Average price: Modest
Area: Centrum
Address: Nieuwendijk 115 1012 MD
Amsterdam The Netherlands
Phone: +31 20 6223155

#331
Universe on a T-Shirt
Category: Women's Clothing,
Men's Clothing, Concept Shops
Average price: Modest
Area: Centrum, Jordaan
Address: Nieuwe Leliestraat 6 1015 SP
Amsterdam The Netherlands
Phone: +31 20 7370081

#332
De Kweker
Category: Food Delivery Services,
Wholesale Stores, Organic Stores
Average price: Modest
Area: West, Bos en Lommer
Address: Jan van Galenstraat 4 1051
KM Amsterdam The Netherlands
Phone: +31 20 6063606

#333
AU Bout DU Monde
Category: Bookstores
Average price: Modest
Area: Centrum
Address: Singel 313 1012 WJ
Amsterdam The Netherlands
Phone: +31 20 6251397

#334
Pauw
Category: Women's Clothing
Average price: Exclusive
Area: Zuid, Museumkwartier
Address: Van Baerlestraat 72 1071 BA
Amsterdam The Netherlands
Phone: +31 20 6717322

#335
NOA NOA
Category: Women's Clothing
Average price: Exclusive
Area: Centrum
Address: Kalverstraat 163 1012 XB
Amsterdam The Netherlands
Phone: +31 20 4209879

#336
Douglas
Category: Cosmetics &Beauty,
Skin Care
Average price: Expensive
Area: Zuid, Museumkwartier
Address: P.C. Hooftstraat 107-109 1071
BR Amsterdam The Netherlands
Phone: +31 20 6795822

#337
Vishandel Tel
Category: Grocery, Shopping
Average price: Inexpensive
Area: Centrum
Address: Kloveniersburgwal 11 1011 JT
Amsterdam The Netherlands
Phone: +31 20 6255776

#338
Drake's of Los Angeles
Category: Adult
Average price: Expensive
Area: Centrum
Address: Damrak 61 1012 LM
Amsterdam The Netherlands
Phone: +31 20 6279544

#339
Knuffels
Category: Toy Stores
Average price: Modest
Area: Centrum
Address: Sint Antoniesbreestraat 39-51
1011 HB Amsterdam The Netherlands
Phone: +31 20 6230632

#340
Van Beek Art Supplies
Category: Art Supplies
Average price: Expensive
Area: Zuid, De Pijp
Address: Stadhouderskade 63 - 65 1072
AD Amsterdam The Netherlands
Phone: +31 20 6621670

#341
Artis Winkel
Category: Shopping
Average price: Expensive
Area: Plantagebuurt, Centrum
Address: Artis 1018 CZ Amsterdam
The Netherlands
Phone: +31 20 5233400

#342
Skatezone
Category: Sporting Goods
Average price: Modest
Area: Zuid, De Pijp
Address: Ceintuurbaan 59 1072 EV
Amsterdam The Netherlands
Phone: +31 20 6622822

#343
Het Werkmanspaleis
Category: Fashion
Average price: Expensive
Area: Centrum
Address: Nieuwendijk 47/49 1012 MB
Amsterdam The Netherlands
Phone: +31 20 6242700

#344
Second Female
Category: Women's Clothing,
Accessories
Average price: Expensive
Area: Centrum, Negen Straatjes
Address: Prinsengracht 417-419
Amsterdam, Noord-Holland The
Netherlands
Phone: +31 20 4204151

#345
1 Euro Winkel
Category: Discount Store
Average price: Modest
Area: Oost, Dapperbuurt
Address: Dapperstraat 283,
1093 BS Amsterdam, The Netherlands
Phone: +31 20 4789151

#346
World Press Photo
Category: Festival, Art Gallery
Average price: Modest
Area: Centrum, De Wallen
Address: Oudekerksplein 23 1012 GX
Amsterdam The Netherlands
Phone: +31 20 6766096

#347
De Mof
Category: Men's Clothing,
Women's Clothing
Average price: Modest
Area: Centrum, Haarlemmerbuurt
Address: Haarlemmerdijk 109 1013 KD
Amsterdam The Netherlands
Phone: +31 20 6231798

#348
Moondrop
Category: Fashion
Average price: Modest
Area: Centrum
Address: nieuwendijk 41-43 1012 ma
Amsterdam The Netherlands
Phone: +31 20 4289448

#349
Daniele Alessandrini
Category: Men's Clothing,
Women's Clothing
Average price: Expensive
Area: Centrum, Negen Straatjes
Address: Hartenstraat 20-A 1016 CC
Amsterdam The Netherlands
Phone: +31 20 6381744

#350
Jack en Jones Nieuwendijk
Category: Men's Clothing
Average price: Modest
Area: Centrum
Address: Nieuwendijk 170 1012 MT
Amsterdam The Netherlands
Phone: +31 20 4890504

#351
Vlerk
Category: Women's Clothing
Average price: Exclusive
Area: Zuid, Museumkwartier
Address: Willemsparkweg 159 1071 GZ
Amsterdam The Netherlands
Phone: +31 20 6766320

#352
Het Speelgoedhemeltje
Category: Toy Stores
Average price: Modest
Area: Zuid, Hoofddorppleinbuurt
Address: Jacob Marisstraat 2 1058 HZ
Amsterdam The Netherlands
Phone: +31 20 6696853

#353
Hella Pais Interieurs
Category: Home Decor
Average price: Modest
Area: Zuid, Stadionbuurt
Address: Laan der Hesperiden 170 1076
DX Amsterdam The Netherlands
Phone: +31 20 6271341

#354
Cream
Category: Women's Clothing
Average price: Modest
Area: Centrum
Address: Leidsestraat 56 1017 PC
Amsterdam The Netherlands
Phone: +31 20 4203094

#355
MC Bloom
Category: Florists
Average price: Expensive
Area: Zuid, Apollobuurt
Address: Beethovenstraat 13 1077 HL
Amsterdam The Netherlands
Phone: +31 20 6629780

#356
Sukha Amsterdam
Category: Shopping
Average price: Expensive
Area: Centrum, Haarlemmerbuurt
Address: Haarlemmerstraat 110 1013
EW Amsterdam The Netherlands
Phone: +31 20 3304001

#357
Florale Haircare
Category: Cosmetics &Beauty
Average price: Modest
Area: Zuid, Rivierenbuurt
Address: Maasstraat 133 1078 HH
Amsterdam The Netherlands
Phone: +31 20 6755550

#358
Megazino
Category: Fashion, Outlet Stores
Average price: Modest
Area: Centrum, Jordaan
Address: Rozengracht 207-213
1016 LZ Amsterdam The Netherlands
Phone: +31 20 3301031

#359
Hoeden M/V
Category: Accessories
Average price: Expensive
Area: Centrum
Address: Herengracht 422-B 1017 BZ
Amsterdam The Netherlands
Phone: +31 20 6263038

#360
Demmenie
Category: Outdoor Gear
Average price: Expensive
Area: Centrum, Jordaan
Address: Marnixstraat 2 1015 XH
Amsterdam The Netherlands
Phone: +31 20 6243652

#361
Chez Merav
Category: Accessories,
Women's Clothing
Average price: Expensive
Area: Zuid, Rivierenbuurt
Address: Maasstraat 109 1078 HH
Amsterdam The Netherlands
Phone: +31 20 6711195

#362
Palazzina
Category: Lingerie
Average price: Exclusive
Area: Centrum
Address: Paleisstraat 17 1012 RB
Amsterdam The Netherlands
Phone: +31 20 6234865

#363
Fabulous Woman
Category: Women's Clothing
Average price: Expensive
Area: Oost, Watergraafsmeer
Address: Middenweg 31 1098 AB
Amsterdam The Netherlands
Phone: +31 20 6630889

#364
Bever Women's Outdoor World
Category: Outdoor Gear, Sports Wear
Average price: Expensive
Area: West
Address: Overtoom 51-53 1054 HB
Amsterdam The Netherlands
Phone: +31 20 4122879

#365
De Fietsentuin
Category: Bike Repair/Maintenance,
Self Storage, Bikes
Average price: Modest
Area: Zuid, Hoofddorppleinbuurt
Address: Weissenbruchstraat 23 1058
KL Amsterdam The Netherlands
Phone: +31 20 6158142

#366
Dille & Kamille
Category: Kitchen & Bath
Average price: Modest
Area: Centrum
Address: Nieuwendijk 16-18 1012 MK
Amsterdam The Netherlands
Phone: +31 20 3303797

#367
Cherry Sue
Category: Women's Clothing
Average price: Expensive
Area: Centrum, Jordaan
Address: Eerste Leliedwarsstraat 6
1015 TA Amsterdam The Netherlands
Phone: +31 20 6233766

#368
Het Cleijne Verschil
Category: Flowers & Gifts
Average price: Expensive
Area: Centrum
Address: Nieuwe Hoogstraat 14
1011 HE Amsterdam The Netherlands
Phone: +31 20 4275424

#369
Het Cleijne Verschil
Category: Flowers & Gifts
Average price: Expensive
Area: Centrum
Address: Nieuwe Hoogstraat 14
1011 HE Amsterdam The Netherlands
Phone: +31 20 4275424

#370
The Natural Special Vitaminshop
Category: Drugstores
Average price: Modest
Area: Zuid, De Pijp
Address: Ceintuurbaan 39-41
1072 ET Amsterdam The Netherlands
Phone: +31 20 6737891

#371
Ace & Dik Juweliers
Category: Jewelry
Average price: Expensive
Area: Zuid, Museumkwartier
Address: Van Baerlestraat 46 1071 AZ
Amsterdam The Netherlands
Phone: +31 20 5711560

#372
Slaapkamer Amsterdam
Category: Home Decor, Mattresses
Average price: Modest
Area: Zuid, De Pijp
Address: Ceintuurbaan 81-BG
1072 EW Amsterdam The Netherlands
Phone: +31 20 6712938

#373
MeCHICas
Category: Jewelry, Accessories
Average price: Expensive
Area: Centrum
Address: Gasthuismolensteeg 11 1016
AM Amsterdam The Netherlands
Phone: +31 20 4203092

#374
Bloemenstal 't Lievertje
Category: Florists
Average price: Modest
Area: Centrum
Address: Spui 7, t/o Kalverstraat 152
1012 XE Amsterdam The Netherlands
Phone: +31 20 6279062

#375
**Geraldine's English
Country Style**
Category: Home Decor
Average price: Expensive
Area: Zuid, De Pijp
Address: Stadhouderskade 116 1073
AZ Amsterdam The Netherlands
Phone: +31 20 6763947

#376
Ennu
Category: Men's Clothing,
Women's Clothing
Average price: Exclusive
Area: Zuid, Museumkwartier
Address: Cornelis Schuytstraat 15 1071
JC Amsterdam The Netherlands
Phone: +31 20 6735265

#377
Parfumerie Coco
Category: Drugstores
Average price: Modest
Area: Oost, Watergraafsmeer
Address: Middenweg 46-III 1097 BR
Amsterdam The Netherlands
Phone: +31 20 6651925

#378
De Lakenhal
Category: Tobacco Shops,
Newspapers & Magazines
Average price: Modest
Area: Centrum
Address: Staalstraat 16 1011 JL
Amsterdam The Netherlands
Phone: +31 20 6243120

#379
Ici Paris XL
Category: Cosmetics &Beauty
Average price: Expensive
Area: Zuid, Apollobuurt
Address: Beethovenstraat 34 1077 JH
Amsterdam The Netherlands
Phone: +31 318 579111

#380
Aboriginal Art & Instruments
Category: Musical Instruments
Average price: Expensive
Area: Centrum
Address: Paleisstraat 137 1012 ZL
Amsterdam The Netherlands
Phone: +31 20 4231333

#381
Imagine
Category: Toy Stores, Baby Gear &
Furniture, Children's Clothing
Average price: Modest
Area: Zuid, Willemspark
Address: Amstelveenseweg 131 1075
VX Amsterdam The Netherlands
Phone: +31 20 6708899

#382
Cees Tak
Category: Shoe Stores
Average price: Expensive
Area: West, Oud West, Da Costabuurt
Address: Bilderdijkstraat 69 1053 KM
Amsterdam The Netherlands
Phone: +31 20 6129465

#383
oTTo Bikes
Category: Appliances & Repair, Bikes
Average price: Inexpensive
Area: West, Oud West
Address: Overtoom 402 1054 JS
Amsterdam The Netherlands
Phone: +31 20 7860609

#384
Xenos
Category: Discount Store
Average price: Inexpensive
Area: Centrum
Address: Nieuwendijk 202 1012 MX
Amsterdam The Netherlands
Phone: +31 20 4274153

#385
Bloemsierkunst Isabel
Category: Flowers & Gifts
Average price: Modest
Area: Zuid, Rivierenbuurt
Address: Scheldestraat 104 1078 GP
Amsterdam The Netherlands
Phone: +31 20 6769054

#386
't Klompenhuisje
Category: Shoe Stores,
Children's Clothing
Average price: Expensive
Area: Centrum
Address: Nieuwe Hoogstraat 9-A 1011
HC Amsterdam The Netherlands
Phone: +31 20 6228100

#387
Brom
Category: Hardware Stores
Average price: Modest
Area: Zuid, Museumkwartier
Address: Cornelis Schuytstraat 41-43
1071 JE Amsterdam The Netherlands
Phone: +31 20 6621878

#388
Bed Habits
Category: Home & Garden, Interior
Design
Average price: Expensive
Area: Centrum
Address: Reguliersdwarsstraat 57-A
1017 BK Amsterdam The Netherlands
Phone: +31 20 3203024

#389
Tom 's Skateshop
Category: Sports Wear, Outdoor Gear
Average price: Expensive
Area: Centrum, De Wallen
Address: Oude Hoogstraat 35 1012 CD
Amsterdam The Netherlands
Phone: +31 20 6254922

#390
Seventyfive
Category: Shoe Stores
Average price: Modest
Area: Centrum
Address: Nieuwe Hoogstraat 24-II 1011
HG Amsterdam The Netherlands
Phone: +31 20 6264611

#391
Compromis Store
Category: Fashion
Average price: Expensive
Area: Zuid, Apollobuurt
Address: Beethovenstraat 61 1077 HN
Amsterdam The Netherlands
Phone: +31 20 6648015

#392
Groeno Rijwielen Amsterdam
Category: Wholesale Stores
Average price: Modest
Area: West, Frederik Hendrikbuurt
Address: 2de Hugo de Grootstraat 18
1052 LC Amsterdam The Netherlands
Phone: +31 20 6844270

#393
Sissy-Boy Homeland
Magna Plaza
Category: Fashion
Average price: Modest
Area: Centrum
Address: Nieuwezijds Voorburgwal 182
1012 SJ Amsterdam The Netherlands
Phone: +31 20 3892589

#394
Nicnic Fashion En Design
Category: Women's Clothing,
Antiques, Thrift Stores
Average price: Modest
Area: Centrum
Address: Gasthuismolensteeg 5 1016
am Amsterdam The Netherlands
Phone: +31 20 6228523

#395
Objet
Category: Fashion, Home Decor
Average price: Modest
Area: West, Oud West
Address: Jan Pieter Heijestraat 98 1053
GT Amsterdam The Netherlands
Phone: +31 20 4122227

#396
McCarthy's
Category: Beer, Wine & Spirits,
Tobacco Shops
Average price: Expensive
Area: Centrum, De Wallen
Address: Oudezijds Kolk 71 1012 AL
Amsterdam The Netherlands
Phone: +31 20 6393525

#397
Swatch Store
Category: Watches
Average price: Modest
Area: Centrum
Address: Singel 457-B16 1012 WP
Amsterdam The Netherlands
Phone: +31 20 4228878

#398
Hoopman
Category: Hobby Shops
Average price: Expensive
Area: Centrum, Jordaan
Address: Marnixstraat 47 1015 VA
Amsterdam The Netherlands
Phone: +31 20 6246045

#399
Hans Appenzeller
Category: Jewelry
Average price: Expensive
Area: Centrum, De Wallen
Address: Grimburgwal 1 1012 GA
Amsterdam The Netherlands
Phone: +31 20 6268218

#400
Warmer Schoenen
Category: Shoe Stores
Average price: Expensive
Area: West, Oud West, Da Costabuurt
Address: Bilderdijkstraat 134-5 1053 LA
Amsterdam The Netherlands
Phone: +31 20 6169627

#401
Charly Amsterdam
Category: Women's Clothing
Average price: Expensive
Area: Zuid, Museumkwartier
Address: Cornelis Schuytstraat 45-BG
1071 JG Amsterdam The Netherlands
Phone: +31 20 6720404

#402
Intercodam
Category: Flooring, Kitchen & Bath
Average price: Expensive
Area: Plantagebuurt, Centrum
Address: Amstel 135 1018 EN
Amsterdam The Netherlands
Phone: +31 20 6225115

#403
Firma Moes
Category: Home & Garden
Average price: Modest
Area: Zuid, De Pijp
Address: Eerste van der Helstsraat 67
1073 AD Amsterdam The Netherlands
Phone: +31 20 6626347

#404
Closed Woman
Category: Women's Clothing
Average price: Expensive
Area: Centrum, Negen Straatjes
Address: Wolvenstraat 17 1016 EM
Amsterdam The Netherlands
Phone: +31 20 3307303

#405
Spikes & More
Category: Fashion
Average price: Modest
Area: Centrum
Address: Prinsenstraat 23-C 1015 DB
Amsterdam The Netherlands
Phone: +31 20 7705679

#406
American Apparel
Category: Fashion
Average price: Modest
Area: Centrum, Jordaan
Address: Westerstraat 59-61 1015 LV
Amsterdam The Netherlands
Phone: +31 20 3302391

#407
Rivièra Maison
Category: Home Decor
Average price: Expensive
Area: Zuid, Museumkwartier
Address: Van Baerlestraat 2-4 1071 AW
Amsterdam The Netherlands
Phone: +31 20 4711699

#408
WE Women
Category: Women's Clothing,
Accessories
Average price: Modest
Area: Zuid, Apollobuurt
Address: Beethovenstraat 48 1077 JK
Amsterdam The Netherlands
Phone: +31 20 6793808

#409
WE Women
Category: Women's Clothing,
Accessories
Average price: Modest
Area: Zuid, Apollobuurt
Address: Beethovenstraat 48 1077 JK
Amsterdam The Netherlands
Phone: +31 20 6793808

#410
Emotions Fashion
Category: Fashion
Average price: Expensive
Area: West, Oud West, Kinkerbuurt
Address: Kinkerstraat 240 1053 EN
Amsterdam The Netherlands
Phone: +31 20 6121559

#411
The End
Category: Thrift Stores
Average price: Modest
Area: Centrum
Address: Nieuwe Hoogstraat 27 1011
HD Amsterdam The Netherlands
Phone: +31 20 6253162

#412
Reflex New Art Gallery
Category: Art Gallery
Average price: Exclusive
Area: Centrum
Address: Weteringschans 83 1017 RZ
Amsterdam The Netherlands
Phone: +31 20 4235423

#413
Lee Amsterdam
Category: Men's Clothing,
Women's Clothing
Average price: Modest
Area: Centrum, Negen Straatjes
Address: Wolvenstraat 8 1016 EP
Amsterdam The Netherlands
Phone: +31 20 6206704

#414
Nottinghill
Category: Accessories
Average price: Expensive
Area: Centrum, Haarlemmerbuurt
Address: Haarlemmerstraat 85 1013 EL
Amsterdam The Netherlands
Phone: +31 20 3313714

#415
Sunglass Hut
Category: Eyewear & Opticians
Average price: Expensive
Area: Centrum
Address: Leidsestraat 78 1017 PD
Amsterdam The Netherlands
Phone: +31 20 6258991

#416
Young Designers United
Category: Fashion
Average price: Expensive
Area: Centrum
Address: Keizersgracht 447 1017 DK
Amsterdam The Netherlands
Phone: +31 20 6269191

#417
A Space Oddity
Category: Hobby Shops
Average price: Expensive
Area: Centrum, Jordaan
Address: Prinsengracht 204-3 1016 HD
Amsterdam The Netherlands
Phone: +31 20 4274036

#418
Buise
Category: Women's Clothing
Average price: Expensive
Area: Zuid, Museumkwartier
Address: Cornelis Schuytstraat 12 1071
JH Amsterdam The Netherlands
Phone: +31 20 6704904

#419
Azzurro
Category: Women's Clothing
Average price: Exclusive
Area: Zuid, Museumkwartier
Address: P Cornelisz Hooftstr 142a
1071 CE Amsterdam The Netherlands
Phone: +31 20 6716804

#420
Elka's Casual Fashion
Category: Fashion
Average price: Modest
Area: West, Oud West
Address: Kinkerstraat 85-IV 1053 DH
Amsterdam The Netherlands
Phone: +31 20 6126910

#421
COPA Football Store
Category: Sports Wear, Men's Clothing
Average price: Modest
Area: Centrum
Address: Prins Hendrikkade 20-B 1012
TL Amsterdam The Netherlands
Phone: +31 20 6201660

#422
French Connection
Category: Women's Clothing
Average price: Modest
Area: Zuid, Museumkwartier
Address: Cornelis Schuytstraat 36 1071
JK Amsterdam The Netherlands
Phone: +31 20 6700668

#423
Homely
Category: Home Decor
Average price: Expensive
Area: Zuid
Address: Zeilstraat 10 1075 SG
Amsterdam The Netherlands
Phone: +31 20 6791781

#424
Rijwielhandel Ciclo
Category: Appliances & Repair,
Bikes, Thrift Stores
Average price: Inexpensive
Area: Zuid, Museumkwartier
Address: Ruysdaelstraat 35 1071 XA
Amsterdam The Netherlands
Phone: +31 20 6764511

#425
I DO I DO
Category: Bridal
Average price: Exclusive
Area: Zuid, Apollobuurt
Address: Beethovenstraat 105 1077 HX
Amsterdam The Netherlands
Phone: +31 20 4705474

#426
Manwood Mode Schoenen
Category: Shoe Stores
Average price: Expensive
Area: Oost, Watergraafsmeer
Address: Middenweg 17 1098 AA
Amsterdam The Netherlands
Phone: +31 20 4682615

#427
Stenelux
Category: Hobby Shops
Average price: Modest
Area: Zuid, De Pijp
Address: 1e Jacob van Campenstr 2-HS
1072 BE Amsterdam The Netherlands
Phone: +31 20 6621490

#428
La Boite
Category: Children's Clothing
Average price: Expensive
Area: Zuid
Address: Zeilstraat 29-33 1075 SB
Amsterdam The Netherlands
Phone: +31 20 6790362

#429
Interbasics Meubels
Category: Furniture Stores
Average price: Modest
Area: Zuid, De Pijp
Address: 1e van der Helststraat 41 1073
AC Amsterdam The Netherlands
Phone: +31 20 6622371

#430
**Undressed by Marlies Dekkers,
Berenstraat**
Category: Lingerie
Average price: Expensive
Area: Centrum, Negen Straatjes
Address: Berenstraat 18 1016 GH
Amsterdam The Netherlands
Phone: +31 20 4211900

#431
DOTShop Furniture &Gifts
Category: Home Decor
Average price: Expensive
Area: West, Oud West
Address: Jan Pieter Heijestraat 108
1053 GT Amsterdam The Netherlands
Phone: +31 20 6129016

#432
Quiksilver
Category: Shopping
Average price: Modest
Area: Centrum
Address: Kalverstraat 212-22 1012 PD
Amsterdam The Netherlands
Phone: +31 20 6260610

#433
Christine Le Duc
Category: Adult
Average price: Expensive
Area: Centrum, De Wallen
Address: Oude Doelenstraat 10 1012
ED Amsterdam The Netherlands
Phone: +31 20 6226753

#434
Rumors Vintage & Design
Category: Women's Clothing,
Vintage& Consignment, Thrift Stores
Average price: Modest
Area: Centrum, Haarlemmerbuurt
Address: Haarlemmerstraat 99 1013 EL
Amsterdam The Netherlands
Phone: +31 20 7529874

#435
Cosmic Cowboys
Category: Accessories, Shoe Stores
Average price: Exclusive
Area: Zuid, Museumkwartier
Address: Pieter Cornelisz. Hooftstraat
50 1071 CA Amsterdam The Netherlands
Phone: +31 20 6738238

#436
Parfumerie Marjo
Category: Cosmetics &Beauty
Average price: Inexpensive
Area: Centrum, De Wallen
Address: Zeedijk 68-70 1012 BA
Amsterdam The Netherlands
Phone: +31 20 6241742

#437
Breekbaar
Category: Home Decor
Average price: Inexpensive
Area: Centrum
Address: Weteringschans 209 1017 XG
Amsterdam The Netherlands
Phone: +31 20 6261260

#438
Designsales
Category: Furniture Stores
Average price: Expensive
Area: West, Bos en Lommer
Address: Haarlemmerweg 331A 1051
LH Amsterdam The Netherlands
Phone: +31 20 6863863

#439
Hartman Cigars & More
Category: Tobacco Shops
Average price: Modest
Area: Zuid, Apollobuurt
Address: Beethovenstraat 88 1077 JN
Amsterdam The Netherlands
Phone: +31 20 6705770

#440
Mono
Category: Accessories
Average price: Modest
Area: Centrum, Haarlemmerbuurt
Address: Haarlemmerstraat 16 1013 ER
Amsterdam The Netherlands
Phone: +31 20 4215378

#441
Run-Inn
Category: Sports Wear
Average price: Expensive
Area: Oost, Oosterparkbuurt
Address: Linnaeuskade 5 1098 BC
Amsterdam The Netherlands
Phone: +31 20 4635771

#442
't Groene Paradijs
Category: Florists
Average price: Expensive
Area: West, Staatsliedenbuurt
Address: van Hallstraat 99 - 103 1051
HA Amsterdam The Netherlands
Phone: +31 20 6845054

#443
Zondag
Category: Women's Clothing
Average price: Expensive
Area: Zuid, Museumkwartier
Address: Willemsparkweg 181 1071 GZ
Amsterdam The Netherlands
Phone: +31 20 6756826

#444
Fair Trade Shop
Category: Shopping
Average price: Modest
Area: Centrum
Address: Heiligeweg 45 1012 XP
Amsterdam The Netherlands
Phone: +31 20 6252245

#445
Maskshopvenice
Category: Arts & Crafts
Average price: Expensive
Area: Centrum, De Wallen
Address: Warmoesstraat 18a 1012 JD
Amsterdam The Netherlands
Phone: +31 20 3203389

#446
COS
Category: Women's Clothing,
Men's Clothing, Children's Clothing
Average price: Expensive
Area: Centrum
Address: Leidsestraat 20-22 1017 PA
Amsterdam The Netherlands
Phone: +31 20 6389843

#447
Mycom Computers
Category: Computers
Average price: Modest
Area: Zuid, De Pijp
Address: Ceintuurbaan 113-3 1072 EZ
Amsterdam The Netherlands
Phone: +31 20 4709595

#448
Saturn
Category: Electronics
Average price: Modest
Area: Centrum
Address: Oosterdokskade 67 1011 DL
Amsterdam The Netherlands
Phone: +31 20 5213600

#449
De Tuinen
Category: Drugstores
Average price: Expensive
Area: Centrum
Address: Leidsestraat 54-BG 1017 PC
Amsterdam The Netherlands
Phone: +31 20 4202063

#450
Carl Denig
Category: Outdoor Gear
Average price: Expensive
Area: Centrum
Address: Weteringschans 113-115 1017
SB Amsterdam The Netherlands
Phone: +31 20 6262436

#451
Out Of The Closet
Category: Thrift Stores
Average price: Inexpensive
Area: Centrum
Address: Jodenbreestraat 158 1011 NS
Amsterdam The Netherlands
Phone: +31 20 6206261

#452
De Ruilhoek
Category: Vintage& Consignment
Average price: Modest
Area: Zuid, Rivierenbuurt
Address: Maasstraat 174 1079 BL
Amsterdam The Netherlands
Phone: +31 20 4421422

#453
't Runnertje
Category: Antiques
Average price: Expensive
Area: Centrum, Negen Straatjes
Address: Prinsengracht 531 1016 HR
Amsterdam The Netherlands
Phone: +31 20 6243735

#454
Keukenspullen
Category: Kitchen & Bath
Average price: Expensive
Area: Zuid, De Pijp
Address: Van Woustraat 151 1074 AJ
Amsterdam The Netherlands
Phone: +31 20 6620643

#455
Bij Ons Vintage
Category: Thrift Stores
Average price: Modest
Area: Centrum
Address: Nieuwezijds Voorburgwal 150
1012 SJ Amsterdam The Netherlands
Phone: +31 611 871278

#456
Etos
Category: Drugstores
Average price: Modest
Area: Centrum, Haarlemmerbuurt
Address: Haarlemmerdijk 81- 85 1013
KC Amsterdam The Netherlands
Phone: +31 20 5289238

#457
Metz & Co
Category: Department Stores
Average price: Exclusive
Area: Centrum
Address: Leidsestraat 34-36 1017 PB
Amsterdam The Netherlands
Phone: +31 20 5207020

#458
The Old Man
Category: Sports Wear
Average price: Expensive
Area: Centrum, De Wallen
Address: Damstraat 14-16 1012 JM
Amsterdam The Netherlands
Phone: +31 20 6270043

#459
Christine le Duc
Category: Adult
Average price: Exclusive
Area: Centrum
Address: Spui 6 1012 WZ Amsterdam
The Netherlands
Phone: +31 20 6248265

#460
Perry Sport
Category: Sports Wear
Average price: Modest
Area: West, Helmersbuurt
Address: Overtoom 2-8 1054 HH
Amsterdam The Netherlands
Phone: +31 20 6189111

#461
Second Best
Category: Vintage& Consignment
Average price: Expensive
Area: Centrum, Negen Straatjes
Address: Wolvenstraat 18 1016 EP
Amsterdam The Netherlands
Phone: +31 20 4220274

#462
**Tweedehands Kleding
Over en Weer**
Category: Thrift Stores
Average price: Modest
Area: Zuid, Rivierenbuurt
Address: Rijnstraat 234-BG 1079 HV
Amsterdam The Netherlands
Phone: +31 20 6444632

#463
Oger Fashion
Category: Men's Clothing
Average price: Exclusive
Area: Zuid, Museumkwartier
Address: P.C. Hooftstraat 75-81 1071
BP Amsterdam The Netherlands
Phone: +31 20 6768695

#464
Coster Diamonds
Category: Jewelry, Museum
Average price: Expensive
Area: Zuid, Museumkwartier
Address: Paulus Potterstraat 2-8 1071
CZ Amsterdam The Netherlands
Phone: +31 20 3055555

#465
Mycom Computers
Category: Computers
Average price: Modest
Area: Zuid, De Pijp
Address: Ceintuurbaan 113-3 1072 EZ
Amsterdam The Netherlands
Phone: +31 20 4709595

#466
Zacht
Category: Children's Clothing, Baby
Gear & Furniture, Toy Stores
Average price: Modest
Area: Oost, Watergraafsmeer
Address: Middenweg 53-B 1098 AD
Amsterdam The Netherlands
Phone: +31 20 4631200

#467
Witbaard
Category: Shopping
Average price: Inexpensive
Area: Zuid, De Pijp
Address: Ferdinand Bolstraat 22-HS
1072 LJ Amsterdam The Netherlands
Phone: +31 20 6626144

#468
PartyHouse
Category: Hobby Shops
Average price: Modest
Area: Centrum, Jordaan
Address: Rozengracht 92 1016 NG
Amsterdam The Netherlands
Phone: +31 20 6247851

#469
Filippa K
Category: Fashion
Average price: Expensive
Area: Zuid, Museumkwartier
Address: P Cornelisz Hooftstr 129 1071
BS Amsterdam The Netherlands
Phone: +31 20 6732343

#470
Zilch
Category: Women's Clothing
Average price: Modest
Area: Centrum, Haarlemmerbuurt
Address: Haarlemmerstraat 1 1013 EH
Amsterdam The Netherlands
Phone: +31 20 4206268

#471
Rood
Category: Shopping
Average price: Modest
Area: Centrum, De Wallen
Address: Warmoesstraat 137-A 1012 JB
Amsterdam The Netherlands
Phone: +31 20 4210350

#472
Internova
Category: Furniture Stores
Average price: Modest
Area: Zuid, De Pijp
Address: Ferdinand Bolstraat 162-164
1072 LT Amsterdam The Netherlands
Phone: +31 20 4707192

#473
Pieces Kalverstraat
Category: Accessories,
Women's Clothing
Average price: Modest
Area: Centrum
Address: Kalverstraat 198 1012 XH
Amsterdam The Netherlands
Phone: +31 20 4286389

#474
Coppenhagen Kralen / Beads
Category: Hobby Shops,
Venues & Events
Average price: Modest
Area: Centrum, Jordaan
Address: Rozengracht 54 1016 ND
Amsterdam The Netherlands
Phone: +31 20 6243681

#475
Etos
Category: Drugstores
Average price: Modest
Area: Zuid, Apollobuurt
Address: Beethovenstraat 37 -39 1077
HM Amsterdam The Netherlands
Phone: +31 20 6757561

#476
Blokker
Category: Home Decor
Average price: Modest
Area: Oost, Indische Buurt
Address: Javastraat 24 1094 HH
Amsterdam The Netherlands
Phone: +31 20 4636754

#477
SubRosa
Category: Home Decor
Average price: Expensive
Area: Centrum, Jordaan
Address: Rozengracht 49-E 1016 LR
Amsterdam The Netherlands
Phone: +31 20 6200286

#478
Zarzana
Category: Shoe Stores
Average price: Modest
Area: West, Oud West
Address: Bilderdijkstraat 177 1053 KG
Amsterdam The Netherlands
Phone: +31 20 6164616

#479
Shu Shu Schoenwinkel
Category: Accessories, Shoe Stores,
Leather Goods
Average price: Modest
Area: Zuid
Address: Zeilstraat 17H 1075 RZ
Amsterdam The Netherlands
Phone: +31 20 6738083

#480
Subliminal
Category: Fashion
Average price: Expensive
Area: Centrum
Address: Nieuwendijk 134-A 1012 MS
Amsterdam The Netherlands
Phone: +31 20 4282606

#481
Imps & Elfs
Category: Children's Clothing
Average price: Expensive
Area: Zuid, Hoofddorppleinbuurt
Address: Sloterkade 41-44 1058 HE
Amsterdam The Netherlands
Phone: +31 20 3460180

#482
Seventyfive
Category: Shoe Stores
Average price: Modest
Area: Zuid, De Pijp
Address: Van Woustraat 14-3 1073 LL
Amsterdam The Netherlands
Phone: +31 20 3795335

#483
Suitable Amsterdam
Category: Men's Clothing
Average price: Expensive
Area: Centrum
Address: Singel 466 1017 AW
Amsterdam The Netherlands
Phone: +31 20 4234000

#484
Paris Blanco
Category: Women's Clothing
Average price: Inexpensive
Area: Centrum, Haarlemmerbuurt
Address: Haarlemmerdijk 117 1013 KE
Amsterdam The Netherlands
Phone: +31 20 4273640

#485
sZen
Category: Women's Clothing
Average price: Modest
Area: Zuid, De Pijp
Address: Cornelis Troostplein 5bg 1072
JJ Amsterdam The Netherlands
Phone: +31 20 6702780

#486
Luba for girls
Category: Women's Clothing
Average price: Expensive
Area: West, Oud West, Kinkerbuurt
Address: Kinkerstraat 160 1053 EH
Amsterdam The Netherlands
Phone: +31 20 4897430

#487
Kort Shoes
Category: Shoe Stores
Average price: Modest
Area: Zuid, Museumkwartier
Address: Van Baerlestraat 54 1071 BA
Amsterdam The Netherlands
Phone: +31 20 6799245

#488
HIP Wonen
Category: Home Decor
Average price: Expensive
Area: West, Oud West
Address: Overtoom 412 1054 JT
Amsterdam The Netherlands
Phone: +31 20 6161300

#489
Van Beek Art Supplies
Category: Office Equipment,
Hobby Shops
Average price: Modest
Area: Centrum
Address: Weteringschans 201 1017 XG
Amsterdam The Netherlands
Phone: +31 20 6239647

#490
Louise Bloemsierkunst
Category: Florists
Average price: Modest
Area: Zuid, De Pijp
Address: Van Woustraat 187 1074 AM
Amsterdam The Netherlands
Phone: +31 20 4004113

#491
Kunstmarkt Spui
Category: Art Gallery
Average price: Modest
Area: Centrum
Address: Spui 1012 XK
Amsterdam The Netherlands
Phone: +31 35 5416078

#492
Siebel Juweliers
Category: Jewelry
Average price: Modest
Area: Centrum
Address: Kalverstraat 121 1012 PA
Amsterdam The Netherlands
Phone: +31 20 6238590

#493
Robel Schoenen
Category: Shoe Stores
Average price: Modest
Area: West, Oud West, Kinkerbuurt
Address: Kinkerstraat 316-318 1053 GD
Amsterdam The Netherlands
Phone: +31 20 6184440

#494
Sacha Shoes
Category: Shoe Stores
Average price: Modest
Area: Centrum
Address: Kalverstraat 20 1012 PD
Amsterdam The Netherlands
Phone: +31 20 6238165

#495
Bitter
Category: Shoe Stores
Average price: Expensive
Area: Centrum
Address: Leidsestraat 20 1017 PA
Amsterdam The Netherlands
Phone: +31 20 4235412

#496
Cafe Moda Shoes
Category: Shoe Stores
Average price: Inexpensive
Area: Centrum
Address: Kalverstraat 54 1012 PE
Amsterdam The Netherlands
Phone: +31 20 6255228

#497
Kosiuko
Category: Women's Clothing
Average price: Modest
Area: Centrum
Address: Kalvertoren 1012 WP
Amsterdam The Netherlands
Phone: +31 20 6185800

#498
Ladyland
Category: Thrift Stores
Average price: Inexpensive
Area: Zuid, De Pijp
Address: van Woustraat 99 1074 AG
Amsterdam The Netherlands
Phone: +31 643 134624

#499
Praxis
Category: Hardware Stores
Average price: Expensive
Area: Oost
Address: Molukkenstraat 190 1098 TW
Amsterdam The Netherlands
Phone: +31 20 6634116

#500
Manwood Mode Schoenen
Category: Shoe Stores
Average price: Expensive
Area: Zuid, Museumkwartier
Address: Willemsparkweg 173 1071 GZ
Amsterdam The Netherlands
Phone: +31 20 6736013

TOP 500 RESTAURANTS

Recommended by Locals & Trevelers
(From #1 to #500)

#1
Gartine
Category: Breakfast & Brunch
Average price: €8-20
Area: Centrum
Address: Taksteeg 7 1012 PB
Amsterdam The Netherlands
Phone: +31 20 3204132

#2
Vlaams Friteshuis Vleminckx
Category: Do-It-Yourself Food, Street
Vendors, Food Stands
Average price: Under €7
Area: Centrum
Address: Voetboogstraat 33 1012 XK
Amsterdam The Netherlands
Phone: +31 654 787000

#3
Restaurant Blauw
Category: Indonesian
Average price: €21-40
Area: Zuid
Address: Amstelveenseweg 158-160
1075 XN Amsterdam The Netherlands
Phone: +31 20 6755000

#4
De Kas
Category: Do-It-Yourself Food
Average price: Above €41
Area: Oost, Watergraafsmeer
Address: Kamerlingh Onneslaan 3 1097
DE Amsterdam The Netherlands
Phone: +31 20 4624562

#5
Winkel
Category: Soup, Seafood, Vegetarian
Average price: €8-20
Area: Centrum, Jordaan
Address: Noordermarkt 43 1015 NA
Amsterdam The Netherlands
Phone: +31 20 6230223

#6
Tales & Spirits
Category: Cocktail Bar, European
Average price: €21-40
Area: Centrum
Address: Lijnbaanssteeg 5-7 1012 TE
Amsterdam The Netherlands
Phone: +31 655 356467

#7
Scandinavian Embassy
Category: Coffee & Tea,
Scandinavian, Fashion
Average price: €8-20
Area: Zuid, De Pijp
Address: Sarphatipark 34 1072 PB
Amsterdam The Netherlands
Phone: +31 619 518199

#8
Café De Klos
Category: GastroPub, Steakhouses
Average price: €8-20
Area: Centrum
Address: Kerkstraat 41-II 1017 GB
Amsterdam The Netherlands
Phone: +31 20 6253730

#9
Cafe Brecht
Category: Bar, Cafe
Average price: €8-20
Area: Centrum
Address: Weteringschans 157 1017 SE
Amsterdam The Netherlands
Phone: +31 20 6272211

#10
Omelegg
Category: Breakfast & Brunch
Average price: €8-20
Area: Zuid, De Pijp
Address: Ferdinand Bolstraat 143 1072
LH Amsterdam The Netherlands
Phone: +31 20 3701134

#11
Mystique
Category: Bar, Diners
Average price: €21-40
Area: Centrum
Address: Utrechtsestraat 30a 1017 VN
Amsterdam The Netherlands
Phone: +31 20 3302994

#12
Moeders
Category: Salad, Soup
Average price: €8-20
Area: Centrum, Jordaan, West
Address: Rozengracht 251 1016 SX
Amsterdam The Netherlands
Phone: +31 20 6267957

#13
Brouwerij 't IJ
Category: Breweries, Cafe
Average price: Under €7
Area: Centrum
Address: Funenkade 7 1018 AL
Amsterdam The Netherlands
Phone: +31 20 6228325

#14
Café Bern
Category: Fondue, GastroPub
Average price: €8-20
Area: Centrum
Address: Nieuwmarkt 9 1011 JP
Amsterdam The Netherlands
Phone: +31 20 6220034

#15
Castell
Category: Steakhouses
Average price: €21-40
Area: Centrum
Address: Lijnbaansgracht 253 1017 RK
Amsterdam The Netherlands
Phone: +31 20 6228606

#16
Vis Aan De Schelde
Category: Seafood
Average price: €21-40
Area: Zuid, Rivierenbuurt
Address: Scheldeplein 4 1078 GR
Amsterdam The Netherlands
Phone: +31 20 6751583

#17
Pancakes! Amsterdam
Category: Creperies
Average price: €8-20
Area: Centrum, Negen Straatjes
Address: Berenstraat 38 1016 GH
Amsterdam The Netherlands
Phone: +31 20 5289797

#18
Pannenkoekenhuis Upstairs
Category: Creperies
Average price: €8-20
Area: Centrum, De Wallen
Address: Grimburgwal 2 1012 GA
Amsterdam The Netherlands
Phone: +31 20 6265603

#19
Burger-Bar
Category: Fast Food
Average price: €8-20
Area: Centrum
Address: Kolksteeg 2 1012 PT
Amsterdam The Netherlands
Phone: +31 20 6249049

#20
Balthazar's Keuken
Category: Mediterranean
Average price: €21-40
Area: Centrum, Jordaan
Address: Elandsgracht 108 1016 VA
Amsterdam The Netherlands
Phone: +31 20 4202114

#21
Bakers & Roasters
Category: Breakfast & Brunch, Cafe
Average price: €8-20
Area: Zuid, De Pijp
Address: Eerste Jacob van
Campenstraat 54 1072 BH Amsterdam
The Netherlands
Phone: +31 614 699645

#22
Café Loetje
Category: Steakhouses
Average price: €8-20
Area: Zuid, Museumkwartier
Address: Johannes Vermeerstraat 52-III
1071 DT Amsterdam The Netherlands
Phone: +31 20 6628173

#23
The Pancake Bakery
Category: Creperies
Average price: €8-20
Area: Centrum
Address: Prinsengracht 191 1015 DS
Amsterdam The Netherlands
Phone: +31 20 6251333

#24
**Belgisch Bierproeflokaal
De Zotte**
Category: Pub, Belgian
Average price: €8-20
Area: Centrum, Jordaan
Address: Raamstraat 29 1016 XL
Amsterdam The Netherlands
Phone: +31 20 6268694

#25
Yamazato
Category: Sushi Bar, Japanese
Average price: Above €41
Area: Zuid, De Pijp
Address: Yamazato Restaurant 1072 LH
Amsterdam The Netherlands
Phone: +31 20 6787450

#26
Bird
Category: Thai
Average price: €8-20
Area: Centrum, De Wallen
Address: Zeedijk 72 1012 BA
Amsterdam The Netherlands
Phone: +31 20 6201442

#27
Restaurant Koh-I-Noor
Category: Indian
Average price: €8-20
Area: Centrum
Address: Westermarkt 29 1016 DJ
Amsterdam The Netherlands
Phone: +31 20 6233133

#28
Warung Spang Makandra
Category: Diners, Indonesian,
Ethnic Food
Average price: €8-20
Area: Zuid, De Pijp
Address: Gerard Doustraat 39 1072 VK
Amsterdam The Netherlands
Phone: +31 20 6705081

#29
Seasons Restaurant
Category: Salad, Soup, European
Average price: €8-20
Area: Centrum
Address: Herenstraat 16 1015 CA
Amsterdam The Netherlands
Phone: +31 20 3303800

#30
Sugar & Spice Bakery
Category: Bakeries, Coffee & Tea,
Breakfast & Brunch
Average price: €8-20
Area: Centrum, De Wallen
Address: Zeedijk 75 1012 AS
Amsterdam The Netherlands
Phone: +31 686 045183

#31
La Boutique Del Caffe Torrefazione
Category: Coffee & Tea, Cafe
Average price: Under €7
Area: Zuid, De Pijp
Address: Eerste Jacob Van
Campenstraat 38 Amsterdam, Noord-
Holland The Netherlands
Phone: +31 20 3640500

#33
Manneken Pis
Category: Fast Food
Average price: Under €7
Area: Centrum
Address: Damrak 41 1012 LK
Amsterdam The Netherlands
Phone: +31 20 6384568

#32
Kantjil & de Tijger
Category: Indonesian
Average price: €8-20
Area: Centrum
Address: Spuistraat 291-293 1012 VS
Amsterdam The Netherlands
Phone: +31 20 6200994

#34
The Pantry
Category: Creperies
Average price: €8-20
Area: Centrum
Address: Leidsekruisstraat 21-III 1017
RE Amsterdam The Netherlands
Phone: +31 20 6200922

#35
De Pizzabakkers
Category: Pizza
Average price: €8-20
Area: Centrum, Haarlemmerbuurt
Address: Haarlemmerdijk 128-BG 1013
JJ Amsterdam The Netherlands
Phone: +31 20 4274144

#36
Valerius
Category: Breakfast & Brunch,
Sandwiches
Average price: €8-20
Area: Zuid, Museumkwartier
Address: Banstraat 14 1071 DP
Amsterdam The Netherlands
Phone: +31 20 4713976

#37
Coffee Bru
Category: Restaurant, Coffee & Tea
Average price: Under €7
Area: Oost, Oosterparkbuurt
Address: Beukenplein 14 1091 KG
Amsterdam The Netherlands
Phone: +31 20 7519956

#38
Latei
Category: Restaurant, Coffee & Tea
Average price: €8-20
Area: Centrum, De Wallen
Address: Zeedijk 143 1012 AW
Amsterdam The Netherlands
Phone: +31 20 6257485

#39
Thaise Snackbar Bird
Category: Thai
Average price: €8-20
Area: Centrum, De Wallen
Address: Zeedijk 77-I 1012 AS
Amsterdam The Netherlands
Phone: +31 20 4206289

#40
The Butcher
Category: Burgers
Average price: €8-20
Area: Zuid, De Pijp
Address: Albert Cuypstraat 129 1072
CS Amsterdam The Netherlands
Phone: +31 20 4707875

#41
Foodism
Category: GastroPub, Food
Average price: €8-20
Area: West, Frederik Hendrikbuurt
Address: Nassaukade 122 1052 EC
Amsterdam The Netherlands
Phone: +31 20 4868137

#42
De Reiger
Category: Pub, Cafe
Average price: €8-20
Area: Centrum, Jordaan
Address: Nieuwe Leliestraat 34 1015 ST
Amsterdam The Netherlands
Phone: +31 20 6247426

#43
Hotel de Goudfazant
Category: Venues & Events
Average price: €21-40
Area: Noord
Address: Aambeeldstraat 10-H 1021 KB
Amsterdam The Netherlands
Phone: +31 20 6365170

#44
Restaurant PS
Category: Mediterranean
Average price: €21-40
Area: Centrum, Haarlemmerbuurt
Address: Planciusstraat 49 1013 ME
Amsterdam The Netherlands
Phone: +31 20 4215218

#45
Tempo Doeloe
Category: Indonesian
Average price: €21-40
Area: Centrum
Address: Utrechtsestraat 75 1017 VJ
Amsterdam The Netherlands
Phone: +31 20 6256718

#46
New King Mandarin Cuisine
Category: Chinese
Average price: €8-20
Area: Centrum
Address: Zeedijk 115-117 1012 AV
Amsterdam The Netherlands
Phone: +31 20 6252180

#47
La Oliva
Category: Tapas, Bagels
Average price: €21-40
Area: Centrum, Jordaan
Address: Egelantiersstraat 122-124
1015 PR Amsterdam The Netherlands
Phone: +31 20 3204316

#48
Wilde Zwijnen
Category: Diners
Average price: €21-40
Area: Oost, Indische Buurt
Address: Javaplein 23 hs 1095 CJ
Amsterdam The Netherlands
Phone: +31 20 4633043

#49
Wok to Walk
Category: Chinese
Average price: Under €7
Area: Centrum
Address: Kolksteeg 8 1012 PT
Amsterdam The Netherlands
Phone: +31 20 4276960

#50
Restaurant Incanto
Category: Italian
Average price: Above €41
Area: Centrum
Address: Amstel 2 1017 AA
Amsterdam The Netherlands
Phone: +31 20 4233681

#51
Tomaz
Category: Desserts, Diners
Average price: €8-20
Area: Centrum
Address: Begijnensteeg 6-8 1012 PN
Amsterdam The Netherlands
Phone: +31 20 3206489

#52
Van Kerkwijk
Category: Pub, GastroPub
Average price: €21-40
Area: Centrum, De Wallen
Address: Nes 41 1012 KC
Amsterdam The Netherlands
Phone: +31 20 6203316

#53
Restaurant Zaza's
Category: French
Average price: €21-40
Area: Zuid, De Pijp
Address: Daniel Stalpertstraat 103 1072
XD Amsterdam The Netherlands
Phone: +31 20 6736333

#54
Toos & Roos
Category: Cafe,
Breakfast & Brunch, European
Average price: €8-20
Area: Centrum
Address: Herengracht 309 1016 AV
Amsterdam The Netherlands
Phone: +31 641 366733

#55
Venkel
Category: Do-It-Yourself Food,
Organic Stores
Average price: €8-20
Area: Zuid, De Pijp
Address: Albert Cuypstraat 22 1072 CT
Amsterdam The Netherlands
Phone: +31 20 7723198

#56
Terra Zen Centre
Category: Japanese,
Caribbean, Vegan
Average price: €8-20
Area: Centrum
Address: 19 hs Sint Jacobstraat 1012
NC Amsterdam The Netherlands
Phone: +31 684 851848

#57
Singel 404
Category: Breakfast & Brunch
Average price: €8-20
Area: Centrum
Address: Singel 404 1016 AK
Amsterdam The Netherlands
Phone: +31 20 4280154

#58
&Samhoud Places
Category: Lounge, European
Average price: €8-20
Area: Centrum
Address: Oosterdokskade 5 1011 AD
Amsterdam The Netherlands
Phone: +31 20 2602094

#59
't Zwaantje
Category: Cafe
Average price: €8-20
Area: Centrum, Negen Straatjes
Address: Berenstraat 12 1016 GH
Amsterdam The Netherlands
Phone: +31 20 6232373

#60
Amstel Hotel
Category: Hotel, Restaurant
Average price: Above €41
Area: Plantagebuurt, Centrum
Address: Professor Tulpplein 1 1018 GX
Amsterdam The Netherlands
Phone: +31 20 6226060

#61
Pasta e Basta
Category: Italian
Average price: €21-40
Area: Centrum
Address: Nieuwe Spiegelstraat 8-BG
1017 DE Amsterdam The Netherlands
Phone: +31 20 4222222

#62
Sampurna
Category: Indonesian
Average price: €8-20
Area: Centrum
Address: Singel 498-HS 1017 AX
Amsterdam The Netherlands
Phone: +31 20 6253264

#63
Bar Boca's
Category: European, Tapas
Average price: Under €7
Area: Centrum, Jordaan
Address: Westerstraat 30 1015 MK
Amsterdam The Netherlands
Phone: +31 20 8203727

#64
Bar Spek
Category: GastroPub
Average price: €8-20
Area: West, De Baarsjes
Address: Admiraal de Ruijterweg 1 1057
JT Amsterdam The Netherlands
Phone: +31 20 6188102

#65
The Taco Shop
Category: Tex-Mex, Vegetarian
Average price: €8-20
Area: Zuid, De Pijp
Address: Tolstraat 200 1074 HZ
Amsterdam The Netherlands
Phone: +31 20 4703657

#66
De Biertuin
Category: Cafe, Breweries
Average price: €8-20
Area: Oost, Dapperbuurt
Address: Linnaeusstraat 29 1093 EE
Amsterdam The Netherlands
Phone: +31 20 6650956

#67
Burger-Bar
Category: Fast Food, Burgers
Average price: €8-20
Area: Centrum
Address: Reguliersbreestraat 9
1017 CL Amsterdam The Netherlands
Phone: +31 20 3305968

#68
Tomatillo Tex-Mex TO GO
Category: Mexican
Average price: €8-20
Area: West, Oud West
Address: Overtoom 261 1054 HW
Amsterdam The Netherlands
Phone: +31 20 6833086

#69
Little Collins
Category: Breakfast & Brunch,
Diners, Bar
Average price: €8-20
Area: Zuid, De Pijp
Address: 1e Sweelinckstraat 19 F 1073
CL Amsterdam The Netherlands
Phone: +31 20 6732293

#70
Wok to Walk
Category: Chinese
Average price: €8-20
Area: Centrum, De Wallen
Address: Warmoesstraat 85 1012 HZ
Amsterdam The Netherlands
Phone: +31 20 6250721

#71
Restaurant De Bolhoed
Category: Vegetarian
Average price: €8-20
Area: Centrum, Jordaan
Address: Prinsengracht 60-62 1015 DX
Amsterdam The Netherlands
Phone: +31 20 6261803

#72
The Seafood Bar
Category: Seafood
Average price: €21-40
Area: Zuid, Museumkwartier
Address: Van Baerlestraat 5 1071 AL
Amsterdam Oud Zuid The Netherlands
Phone: +31 20 6708355

#73
Hard Rock Cafe Amsterdam
Category: Pub, American, Food
Average price: €8-20
Area: Centrum
Address: Max Euweplein 57-61 1017
MA Amsterdam The Netherlands
Phone: +31 20 5237625

#74
Restaurant AS
Category: Diners, Wine Bar
Average price: Above €41
Area: Zuid, WTC
Address: Prinses Irenestraat 19 1077
WT Amsterdam The Netherlands
Phone: +31 20 6440100

#75
**Heavenly Made With
Love/Tagore**
Category: Indian, Cafe, Sandwiches
Average price: €8-20
Area: Centrum
Address: Utrechtsestraat 128 1017 VT
Amsterdam The Netherlands
Phone: +31 20 6241931

#76
The Dolphins Coffeeshop
Category: Cafe, Coffee & Tea
Average price: €8-20
Area: Centrum
Address: Kerkstraat 39 1017 GB
Amsterdam The Netherlands
Phone: +31 20 6259162

#77
Little Collins
Category: Breakfast & Brunch,
Diners, Bar
Average price: €8-20
Area: Zuid, De Pijp
Address: 1e Sweelinckstraat 19 F 1073
CL Amsterdam The Netherlands
Phone: +31 20 6732293

#78
Oriental City
Category: Dim Sum
Average price: €8-20
Area: Centrum, De Wallen
Address: Oudezijds Voorburgwal
177-179 1012 EV Amsterdam
The Netherlands
Phone: +31 20 6268352

#79
Thai Deum
Category: Thai
Average price: €8-20
Area: Zuid, De Pijp
Address: Ceintuurbaan 210-III BG
1072 GD Amsterdam The Netherlands
Phone: +31 20 3790705

#80
Red
Category: European
Average price: €21-40
Area: Centrum
Address: Keizersgracht 594 1017 EN
Amsterdam The Netherlands
Phone: +31 20 3202024

#81
Hannekes Boom
Category: GastroPub,
Jazz & Blues, Cafe, Pub
Average price: €8-20
Area: Centrum
Address: Dijksgracht 4 1019 BS
Amsterdam The Netherlands
Phone: +31 20 4199820

#82
d'Vijff Vlieghen
Category: European
Average price: Above €41
Area: Centrum
Address: Spuistraat 294-302
1012 VX Amsterdam The Netherlands
Phone: +31 20 5304060

#83
Bird Thais Restaurant
Category: Thai
Average price: €8-20
Area: Centrum, De Wallen
Address: Zeedijk 72- 74 1012 BA
Amsterdam The Netherlands
Phone: +31 20 6201442

#84
Burgermeester
Category: Burgers
Average price: €8-20
Area: Zuid, De Pijp
Address: Albert Cuypstraat 48
1072 CV Amsterdam The Netherlands
Phone: +31 20 6709339

#85
Harlem Soul Food
Category: Soul Food, Bar
Average price: €8-20
Area: Centrum, Haarlemmerbuurt
Address: Haarlemmerstraat 77 1013 EL
Amsterdam The Netherlands
Phone: +31 20 3301498

#86
Warung Mini Surinaams Eethuisje
Category: Diners, Ethnic Food,
Do-It-Yourself Food
Average price: €8-20
Area: Zuid, De Pijp
Address: Ceintuurbaan 205 1074 CV
Amsterdam The Netherlands
Phone: +31 20 6626804

#87
The Red Sun
Category: Japanese, Sushi Bar
Average price: Above €41
Area: Zuid, Stadionbuurt
Address: Olympiaplein 176 1076 AM
Amsterdam The Netherlands
Phone: +31 20 4707521

#88
Geisha
Category: Asian Fusion, Seafood
Average price: Above €41
Area: Centrum
Address: Prins Hendrikkade 106 A 1011
AJ Amsterdam The Netherlands
Phone: +31 20 6262410

#89
Envy
Category: European
Average price: €21-40
Area: Centrum, Negen Straatjes
Address: Prinsengracht 381 1016 HL
Amsterdam The Netherlands
Phone: +31 20 3446407

#90
Nam Kee
Category: Chinese
Average price: €8-20
Area: Centrum
Address: Geldersekade 117-HS 1011
EN Amsterdam The Netherlands
Phone: +31 20 6392848

#91
Brix Food 'n' Drinx
Category: Asian Fusion, Lounge
Average price: €8-20
Area: Centrum, Negen Straatjes
Address: Wolvenstraat 16 1016 EP
Amsterdam The Netherlands
Phone: +31 20 6390351

#92
l' Entrecôte et les Dames
Category: French
Average price: €21-40
Area: Zuid, Museumkwartier
Address: Van Baerlestraat 47 - 49 1071
AP Amsterdam The Netherlands
Phone: +31 20 6798888

#93
l' Entrecôte et les Dames
Category: French
Average price: €21-40
Area: Zuid, Museumkwartier
Address: Van Baerlestraat 47 - 49 1071
AP Amsterdam The Netherlands
Phone: +31 20 6798888

#94
Bazar
Category: Mediterranean, Arabian
Average price: €8-20
Area: Zuid, De Pijp
Address: Albert Cuypstraat 182 1073 BL
Amsterdam The Netherlands
Phone: +31 20 6750544

#95
Trouw Amsterdam
Category: Dance Club, Venues &
Events, Mediterranean
Average price: €8-20
Area: Oost, Oosterparkbuurt
Address: Wibautstraat 131 1091 GL
Amsterdam The Netherlands
Phone: +31 20 4637788

#96
Soup en Zo
Category: Do-It-Yourself Food
Average price: €8-20
Area: Centrum
Address: Nieuwe Spiegelstraat 54 1017
DG Amsterdam The Netherlands
Phone: +31 20 3307781

#97
Bridges
Category: Seafood, French
Average price: Above €41
Area: Centrum, De Wallen
Address: Oudezijds Voorburgwal 197
1012 EX Amsterdam The Netherlands
Phone: +31 20 5553560

#98
Cafe Kingfisher
Category: Pub, GastroPub
Average price: €8-20
Area: Zuid, De Pijp
Address: Ferdinand Bolstraat 24-II 1072
LK Amsterdam The Netherlands
Phone: +31 20 6712395

#99
Vinnies Deli
Category: Delis, Caterers
Average price: €8-20
Area: Centrum, Haarlemmerbuurt
Address: Haarlemmerstraat 46 1013 ES
Amsterdam The Netherlands
Phone: +31 20 7713086

#100
Burgermeester
Category: Burgers
Average price: €8-20
Area: Plantagebuurt, Centrum
Address: Plantage Kerklaan 37 1018 CV
Amsterdam The Netherlands
Phone: +31 20 4280211

#101
Letting
Category: Sandwiches
Average price: €8-20
Area: Centrum
Address: Prinsenstraat 3 1015 DA
Amsterdam The Netherlands
Phone: +31 20 6279393

#102
Restaurant Blauw Aan De Wal
Category: French, European,
Mediterranean
Average price: Above €41
Area: Centrum, De Wallen
Address: Oudezijds Achterburgwal 99
1012 DD Amsterdam The Netherlands
Phone: +31 20 3302257

#103
Elkaar
Category: French
Average price: €21-40
Area: Plantagebuurt, Centrum
Address: Alexanderplein 6 1018 CG
Amsterdam The Netherlands
Phone: +31 20 3307559

#104
Juice&Salad Café
Category: Salad, Vegetarian,
Sandwiches
Average price: €8-20
Area: Centrum
Address: Vijzelstraat 135 1017 HJ
Amsterdam The Netherlands
Phone: +31 20 3303114

#105
Roopram Roti
Category: Caribbean
Average price: Under €7
Area: Oost, Dapperbuurt
Address: Eerste van Swindenstraat 4
1093 GC Amsterdam The Netherlands
Phone: +31 20 6932902

#106
Pacific Parc
Category: GastroPub
Average price: €8-20
Area: West
Address: Polonceau-kade 23 1014 DA
Amsterdam The Netherlands
Phone: +31 20 4887778

#107
ManaMana
Category: Middle Eastern
Average price: €21-40
Area: Zuid, De Pijp
Address: Hemonystraat 66hs 1074 BT
Amsterdam The Netherlands
Phone: +31 641 631098

#108
Sluizer
Category: European, Seafood
Average price: €21-40
Area: Centrum
Address: Utrechtsestraat 45 1017 VH
Amsterdam The Netherlands
Phone: +31 20 6226376

#109
De Belhamel
Category: French
Average price: €21-40
Area: Centrum, Haarlemmerbuurt
Address: Brouwersgracht 60-C 1013 GX
Amsterdam The Netherlands
Phone: +31 20 6221095

#110
BUFFET Van Odette
Category: Mediterranean, Bistros
Average price: €8-20
Area: Centrum
Address: Prinsengracht 598 1017 KS
Amsterdam The Netherlands
Phone: +31 20 4236034

#111
Café 't Sluisje
Category: GastroPub
Average price: Under €7
Area: Noord
Address: Nieuwendammerdijk 297-HS
1025 LM Amsterdam The Netherlands
Phone: +31 20 6361712

#112
Lombardo's
Category: Specialty Food, Beer,
Wine & Spirits, Burgers
Average price: €8-20
Area: Centrum
Address: Nieuwe Spiegelstraat 50 1017
DG Amsterdam The Netherlands
Phone: +31 20 4205010

#113
Japanese Pancake World
Category: Japanese
Average price: €8-20
Area: Centrum, Jordaan
Address: Tweede
Egelantiersdwarsstraat 24a 1015 SC
Amsterdam The Netherlands
Phone: +31 20 3204447

#114
Panini
Category: Italian
Average price: €8-20
Area: Centrum
Address: Vijzelgracht 3-5 1017 HM
Amsterdam The Netherlands
Phone: +31 20 6264939

#115
Maoz
Category: Middle Eastern, Vegetarian
Average price: Under €7
Area: Centrum
Address: Leidsestraat 85 1017 NX
Amsterdam The Netherlands
Phone: +31 20 6253913

#116
Hutspot
Category: Art Gallery, Cafe
Average price: €21-40
Area: Zuid, De Pijp
Address: Van Woustraat 4 1073 LL
Amsterdam The Netherlands
Phone: +31 613 651566

#117
Villa Zeezicht
Category: GastroPub, Food
Average price: €8-20
Area: Centrum
Address: Torensteeg 7 1012 TH
Amsterdam The Netherlands
Phone: +31 20 6267433

#118
Café Kiebêrt
Category: French,
Breakfast & Brunch, Cafe
Average price: €21-40
Area: Zuid, Stadionbuurt
Address: Marathonweg 2 1076 TE
Amsterdam The Netherlands
Phone: +31 20 8458283

#119
Gebroeders Niemeijer
Category: Bakeries, French,
Breakfast & Brunch
Average price: €8-20
Area: Centrum
Address: Nieuwendijk 35 1012 MA
Amsterdam The Netherlands
Phone: +31 20 7076752

#120
Los Pilones
Category: Mexican
Average price: €21-40
Area: Centrum
Address: Kerkstraat 63 1017 GC
Amsterdam The Netherlands
Phone: +31 20 3204651

#121
Frenzi
Category: Italian, European
Average price: €21-40
Area: Centrum
Address: Zwanenburgwal 232 1011 JH
Amsterdam The Netherlands
Phone: +31 20 4235112

#122
Greetje
Category: Local Flavor, Restaurant
Average price: €21-40
Area: Centrum
Address: Peperstraat 23 1011 TJ
Amsterdam The Netherlands
Phone: +31 20 7797450

#123
Restaurant De Struisvogel
Category: French
Average price: €8-20
Area: Centrum, Negen Straatjes
Address: Keizersgracht 312 1016 EX
Amsterdam The Netherlands
Phone: +31 20 4233817

#124
Zuivere Koffie
Category: Breakfast & Brunch
Average price: €8-20
Area: Centrum
Address: Utrechtsestraat 39 1017 VH
Amsterdam The Netherlands
Phone: +31 20 6249999

#125
Cafe Kostverloren
Category: Coffee & Tea,
Breakfast & Brunch, Diners
Average price: €8-20
Area: West, Oud West, Kinkerbuurt
Address: Tweede Kostverlorenkade 70
1053 SB Amsterdam The Netherlands
Phone: +31 20 8203161

#126
Mata Hari
Category: Bar, Mediterranean
Average price: €8-20
Area: Centrum, De Wallen
Address: Oudezijds Achterburgwal 22
1012 DM Amsterdam The Netherlands
Phone: +31 20 2050919

#127
Restaurant Fraîche
Category: European,
Breakfast & Brunch
Average price: €8-20
Area: Centrum, Jordaan
Address: Westerstraat 264 1015 MT
Amsterdam The Netherlands
Phone: +31 20 6279932

#128
Koffiehuis De Hoek
Category: Breakfast & Brunch, Cafe
Average price: Under €7
Area: Centrum, Negen Straatjes
Address: Prinsengracht 341 1016 HK
Amsterdam The Netherlands
Phone: +31 20 6253872

#129
Restaurant Mantoe
Category: Afghan
Average price: Above €41
Area: Centrum, Jordaan
Address: Tweede Leliedwarsstraat
13-BG 1015 TB Amsterdam
The Netherlands
Phone: +31 20 4216374

#130
Bloem 36
Category: GastroPub
Average price: €8-20
Area: Centrum
Address: Entrepotdok 36 1018 AD
Amsterdam The Netherlands
Phone: +31 20 3300929

#131
Fyra
Category: Salad, Soup, French
Average price: Above €41
Area: Centrum
Address: Noorderstraat 19-23
1017 TR Amsterdam The Netherlands
Phone: +31 20 4283632

#132
Sie-Joe
Category: Indonesian
Average price: €8-20
Area: Centrum
Address: Gravenstraat 24A 1012 NM
Amsterdam The Netherlands
Phone: +31 20 6241830

#133
De Haven Van Texel
Category: GastroPub
Average price: €8-20
Area: Centrum, De Wallen
Address: Sint Olofssteeg 11 1012 AK
Amsterdam The Netherlands
Phone: +31 20 4270768

#134
Small World Catering
Category: Breakfast & Brunch
Average price: €8-20
Area: Centrum, Haarlemmerbuurt
Address: Binnen Oranjestraat 14 1013
JA Amsterdam The Netherlands
Phone: +31 20 4202774

#135
Van Dobben
Category: GastroPub
Average price: Under €7
Area: Centrum
Address: Korte Reguliersdwarsstraat 5
1017 BH Amsterdam The Netherlands
Phone: +31 20 6244200

#136
Maoz
Category: Middle Eastern
Average price: Under €7
Area: Centrum
Address: Damrak 40 1012 LK
Amsterdam The Netherlands
Phone: +31 20 4509987

#137
SLA
Category: Salad
Average price: €8-20
Area: Zuid, De Pijp
Address: Ceintuurbaan 149 1072 GB
Amsterdam The Netherlands
Phone: +31 20 7893080

#138
Brasserie Van Baerle
Category: Brasseries
Average price: €21-40
Area: Zuid, Museumkwartier
Address: Van Baerlestraat 158 1071 BG
Amsterdam The Netherlands
Phone: +31 20 6791532

#139
Café Reuring
Category: GastroPub,
French, European
Average price: €8-20
Area: Zuid, De Pijp
Address: Lutmastraat 99 1073 GR
Amsterdam The Netherlands
Phone: +31 20 7770996

#140
Wolvenstraat
Category: Asian Fusion
Average price: €8-20
Area: Centrum, Negen Straatjes
Address: Wolvenstraat 23 1016 EP
Amsterdam The Netherlands
Phone: +31 20 3200843

#141
Ciel Bleu
Category: French
Average price: Above €41
Area: Zuid, De Pijp
Address: Ferdinand Bolstraat 333 1072
LH Amsterdam The Netherlands
Phone: +31 20 6787450

#142
Café Kadijk
Category: Diners, GastroPub, Bar
Average price: €8-20
Area: Centrum
Address: Kadijksplein 5 1018 AB
Amsterdam The Netherlands
Phone: +31 617 744411

#143
Haesje Claes
Category: Salad, Seafood
Average price: €8-20
Area: Centrum
Address: Spuistraat 269-BG 1012 VR
Amsterdam The Netherlands
Phone: +31 20 6251535

#144
Caffè Toscanini
Category: Italian
Average price: €21-40
Area: Centrum, Jordaan
Address: Lindengracht 75 1015 KD
Amsterdam The Netherlands
Phone: +31 20 6232813

#145
Restaurant Bussia
Category: Italian
Average price: €21-40
Area: Centrum, Negen Straatjes
Address: Reestraat 28-32 1016 DN
Amsterdam The Netherlands
Phone: +31 20 6278794

#146
Mamouche
Category: Moroccan
Average price: €21-40
Area: Zuid, De Pijp
Address: Quellijnstraat 104 1072 XZ
Amsterdam The Netherlands
Phone: +31 20 6700736

#147
'Skek
Category: GastroPub
Average price: €8-20
Area: Centrum, De Wallen
Address: Zeedijk 4 - 8 1012 AX
Amsterdam The Netherlands
Phone: +31 20 4270551

#148
Bistro Bij Ons
Category: GastroPub
Average price: €8-20
Area: Centrum
Address: Prinsengracht 287 1016 GW
Amsterdam The Netherlands
Phone: +31 20 6279016

#149
Restaurant - Café In de Waag
Category: Diners, Breakfast & Brunch
Average price: €8-20
Area: Centrum, De Wallen
Address: Nieuwmarkt 4 1012 CR
Amsterdam The Netherlands
Phone: +31 20 4227772

#150
La Place, V&D Kalverstraat
Category: Buffets
Average price: €8-20
Area: Centrum
Address: Kalverstraat 201-203 1012 XC
Amsterdam The Netherlands
Phone: +31 20 6202364

#151
Sama Sebo
Category: Indonesian
Average price: €21-40
Area: Zuid, Museumkwartier
Address: P Cornelisz Hooftstr 27
1071 BL Amsterdam The Netherlands
Phone: +31 20 6628146

#152
Café-Restaurant Amsterdam
Category: Cafe
Average price: €8-20
Area: West, Bos en Lommer
Address: Watertorenplein 6 1051 PA
Amsterdam The Netherlands
Phone: +31 20 6822666

#153
Café Toussaint
Category: French, Cafe
Average price: €8-20
Area: West, Helmersbuurt
Address: Bosboom Toussaintstraat 26
1054 AS Amsterdam The Netherlands
Phone: +31 20 6850737

#154
Pata Negra
Category: Tapas, Spanish, Tapas Bar
Average price: €8-20
Area: Centrum
Address: Utrechtsestraat 124 1017 VT
Amsterdam The Netherlands
Phone: +31 20 4226250

#155
Bolenius
Category: European
Average price: Above €41
Area: Zuid, WTC, Buitenveldert
Address: George Gershwinlaan 30 1082
MT Amsterdam The Netherlands
Phone: +31 20 4044411

#156
Los Pilones
Category: Mexican
Average price: €21-40
Area: Centrum, Jordaan
Address: Eerste Anjeliersdwarsstraat 6
1015 NR Amsterdam The Netherlands
Phone: +31 20 6200323

#157
Brandstof
Category: Pub, Restaurant
Average price: €8-20
Area: Centrum, Jordaan
Address: Marnixstraat 341 1016 TD
Amsterdam The Netherlands
Phone: +31 20 4220813

#158
Sumo Amsterdam
Category: Sushi Bar, Japanese
Average price: €8-20
Area: Centrum
Address: Korte Leidsedwarsstraat
51-BG 1017 PW Amsterdam
The Netherlands
Phone: +31 20 4235131

#159
Café Schuim
Category: Pub, Sandwiches
Average price: €8-20
Area: Centrum
Address: Spuistraat 189 1012 VN
Amsterdam The Netherlands
Phone: +31 20 6389357

#160
Dynasty
Category: Chinese, Asian Fusion
Average price: Above €41
Area: Centrum
Address: Reguliersdwarsstraat 30 1017
BM Amsterdam The Netherlands
Phone: +31 20 6268400

#161
Petit Gateau
Category: Restaurant, Bakeries
Average price: €8-20
Area: Centrum, Haarlemmerbuurt
Address: Haarlemmerstraat 80 1013 EV
Amsterdam The Netherlands
Phone: +31 624 205631

#162
Thai & Co
Category: Thai
Average price: €8-20
Area: Centrum, Haarlemmerbuurt
Address: Haarlemmerstraat 54-BG 1013
ES Amsterdam The Netherlands
Phone: +31 20 6127324

#163
La Vallade
Category: French, Vegetarian
Average price: €21-40
Area: Oost, Oosterparkbuurt
Address: Ooster Ringdijk 23 1097 AB
Amsterdam The Netherlands
Phone: +31 20 6652025

#164
Vinkeles
Category: French
Average price: Above €41
Area: Centrum, Negen Straatjes
Address: Keizersgracht 384 1016 GB
Amsterdam The Netherlands
Phone: +31 20 5302010

#165
OCHA
Category: Thai
Average price: €8-20
Area: Centrum, De Wallen
Address: Binnen Bantammerstraat 1
1011 CH Amsterdam The Netherlands
Phone: +31 20 6259958

#166
Sushi Japans Eetcafé
Category: Japanese, Sushi Bar
Average price: €8-20
Area: Centrum
Address: Taksteeg 3-BG 1012 PB
Amsterdam The Netherlands
Phone: +31 20 4228978

#167
Lunchcafé Nielsen
Category: Breakfast & Brunch
Average price: €8-20
Area: Centrum, Negen Straatjes
Address: Berenstraat 19 1016 GG
Amsterdam The Netherlands
Phone: +31 20 3306006

#168
Golden Temple
Category: Vegetarian
Average price: €8-20
Area: Centrum
Address: Utrechtsestraat 126 1017 VT
Amsterdam The Netherlands
Phone: +31 20 6268560

#169
Burgermeester
Category: Burgers
Average price: €8-20
Area: Centrum, Jordaan
Address: Elandsgracht 130 1016 VB
Amsterdam The Netherlands
Phone: +31 20 6207437

#170
Xinh
Category: Vietnamese
Average price: €8-20
Area: Centrum, Jordaan
Address: Elandsgracht 2 1016 TV
Amsterdam The Netherlands
Phone: +31 20 6240308

#171
De Compagnon
Category: French, Diners
Average price: €21-40
Area: Centrum, De Wallen
Address: Guldehandsteeg 17 1012 RA
Amsterdam The Netherlands
Phone: +31 20 6204225

#172
Bar Moustache
Category: Bar, Italian
Average price: €8-20
Area: Centrum
Address: Utrechtsestraat 141 1017 VM
Amsterdam The Netherlands
Phone: +31 20 4281074

#173
Wok to Walk
Category: Chinese
Average price: Under €7
Area: Centrum
Address: Leidsestraat 96 1017 PE
Amsterdam The Netherlands
Phone: +31 20 6250721

#174
Café George
Category: French
Average price: €21-40
Area: Centrum, Jordaan
Address: Leidsegracht 84 1016 CR
Amsterdam The Netherlands
Phone: +31 20 6260802

#175
Rose's Cantina
Category: Mexican, Food
Average price: €8-20
Area: Centrum
Address: Reguliersdwarsstraat 38-40
1017 BM Amsterdam The Netherlands
Phone: +31 20 6259797

#176
Mi Sueno
Category: Argentine
Average price: €21-40
Area: Zuid, Rivierenbuurt
Address: Maasstraat 40 1078 HK
Amsterdam The Netherlands
Phone: +31 20 4711103

#177
Restaurant Utrechtsedwarstafel
Category: European, Salad
Average price: Above €41
Area: Centrum
Address: Utrechtsedwarsstraat 107-109
1017 WD Amsterdam The Netherlands
Phone: +31 20 6254189

#178
Meidi - Ya
Category: Japanese,
Grocery, Sushi Bar
Average price: €21-40
Area: Zuid, Apollobuurt
Address: Beethovenstraat 18-20 1077
HL Amsterdam The Netherlands
Phone: +31 20 4004370

#179
Grekas Griekse Traiterie
Category: Greek
Average price: €8-20
Area: Centrum
Address: Singel 311 1012 WJ
Amsterdam The Netherlands
Phone: +31 20 6203590

#180
Aan de Amstel
Category: French
Average price: €8-20
Area: Oost, Oosterparkbuurt
Address: Weesperzijde 42-A 1091 EE
Amsterdam The Netherlands
Phone: +31 20 6080077

#181
Stadscafe Van Mechelen
Category: Dive Bar, Restaurant
Average price: €8-20
Area: Zuid, Hoofddorppleinbuurt
Address: Sloterkade 96-97 1058 HK
Amsterdam The Netherlands
Phone: +31 20 2212348

#182
Brasserie Baton
Category: Sandwiches, Brasseries
Average price: €8-20
Area: Centrum
Address: Herengracht 82 1015 BS
Amsterdam The Netherlands
Phone: +31 20 6248195

#183
Blue
Category: Sandwiches, Bar, Cafe
Average price: €8-20
Area: Centrum
Address: Singel 457 1012 WP
Amsterdam The Netherlands
Phone: +31 20 4273901

#184
Studio/K
Category: Dance Club,
Cinema, GastroPub
Average price: €8-20
Area: Oost, Indische Buurt
Address: Timorplein 62 1094 CC
Amsterdam The Netherlands
Phone: +31 20 6920422

#185
Restaurant Shiva
Category: Indian
Average price: €21-40
Area: Centrum
Address: Reguliersdwarsstraat 72-III
1017 BN Amsterdam The Netherlands
Phone: +31 20 6248713

#186
Ethiopisch Eethuis Lalibela
Category: Ethiopian
Average price: €8-20
Area: West, Oud West, Helmersbuurt
Address: Eerste Helmersstraat 249
1054 DX Amsterdam The Netherlands
Phone: +31 20 6838332

#187
Feduzzi's Mercato Italiano
Category: Italian, Delis,
Do-It-Yourself Food
Average price: €8-20
Area: Zuid, Rivierenbuurt
Address: Scheldestraat 63 1078 GH
Amsterdam The Netherlands
Phone: +31 20 6646365

#188
De Pizzabakkers
Category: Italian, Pizza
Average price: €8-20
Area: Zuid, West
Address: Overtoom 501 1054 LH
Amsterdam The Netherlands
Phone: +31 20 6186554

#189
Restaurant Revan
Category: Turkish
Average price: €8-20
Area: Zuid, De Pijp
Address: Van Woustraat 206-212 1073
NA Amsterdam The Netherlands
Phone: +31 20 4700347

#190
De Bakkerswinkel West
Category: Bakeries, Restaurant
Average price: €21-40
Area: West
Address: 1 Polonceaukade 1014 DA
Amsterdam The Netherlands
Phone: +31 20 6880632

#191
Firma Pekelhaaring
Category: Italian
Average price: €21-40
Area: Zuid, De Pijp
Address: Van Woustraat 127-129 1074
AH Amsterdam The Netherlands
Phone: +31 20 6790460

#192
De Italiaan
Category: Italian, Pizza
Average price: €8-20
Area: West, Helmersbuurt
Address: Bosboom Toussaintstraat 29
1054 AN Amsterdam The Netherlands
Phone: +31 20 6836854

#193
Restaurant Jaspers
Category: European
Average price: €21-40
Area: Zuid, De Pijp
Address: Ceintuurbaan 196 1072 GC
Amsterdam The Netherlands
Phone: +31 20 4715233

#194
Japans Restaurant An
Category: Japanese
Average price: €21-40
Area: Centrum
Address: Weteringschans 76 1017 XR
Amsterdam The Netherlands
Phone: +31 20 6244672

#195
Warie's Thai food
Category: Thai
Average price: €8-20
Area: Centrum, Jordaan
Address: Rozengracht 235 1016 NA
Amsterdam The Netherlands
Phone: +31 20 6223638

#196
Struik
Category: Pub, Sandwiches
Average price: Under €7
Area: Centrum, Jordaan
Address: Rozengracht 160 1016 NJ
Amsterdam The Netherlands
Phone: +31 20 6254863

#197
Paso Doble
Category: Tapas
Average price: €8-20
Area: Centrum, Jordaan
Address: Westerstraat 86 1015 MN
Amsterdam The Netherlands
Phone: +31 20 4212670

#198
Novotel Amsterdam
Category: Hotel, Pub, Restaurant
Average price: €8-20
Area: Zuid, Buitenveldert
Address: Europaboulevard 10 1083 AD
Amsterdam The Netherlands
Phone: +31 20 5411123

#199
Bistrot Neuf
Category: French
Average price: €21-40
Area: Centrum, Haarlemmerbuurt
Address: Haarlemmerstraat 9
1013 EH Amsterdam The Netherlands
Phone: +31 20 4003210

#200
Restaurant Vapiano
Category: Italian, Bar, Pizza
Average price: €8-20
Area: Centrum
Address: Oosterdokskade 145
1011 DL Amsterdam The Netherlands
Phone: +31 20 4202025

#201
La Rive
Category: Ice Cream,Frozen Yogurt
Average price: €8-20
Area: Plantagebuurt, Centrum
Address: Professor Tupplein 1
1018 GX Amsterdam The Netherlands
Phone: +31 20 520364

#202
Yamazato Restaurant
Category: Japanese
Average price: Above €41
Area: Zuid, De Pijp
Address: Ferdinand Bolstraat 333
1072 LH Amsterdam The Netherlands
Phone: +31 20 6787

#203
Restaurant Vermeer
Category: European
Average price: Above €41
Area: Centrum, De Wallen
Address: Prins Hendrikkade 59 - 72
1012 AD Amsterdam The Netherlands
Phone: +31 20 5564885

#204
't Blauwe Theehuis
Category: GastroPub
Average price: €8-20
Area: Zuid, Museumkwartier
Address: Vondelpark 5 1071 AA
Amsterdam The Netherlands
Phone: +31 20 6620254

#205
Rijsel
Category: French
Average price: €21-40
Area: Oost, Oosterparkbuurt
Address: Marcusstraat 52 B 1091 TK
Amsterdam The Netherlands
Phone: +31 20 4632142

#206
Bella Storia
Category: Italian
Average price: €21-40
Area: West, Staatsliedenbuurt
Address: Bentinckstraat 28 1051 GL
Amsterdam The Netherlands
Phone: +31 20 4880599

#207
Lo Stivale D'oro
Category: Italian
Average price: €8-20
Area: Centrum
Address: Amstelstraat 49 1017 DA
Amsterdam The Netherlands
Phone: +31 20 6387307

#208
Eetcafe Van Beeren
Category: GastroPub, Pub, Brasseries
Average price: €21-40
Area: Centrum
Address: Koningsstraat 54 1011 EW
Amsterdam The Netherlands
Phone: +31 20 6222329

#209
Café Van Leeuwen
Category: GastroPub
Average price: €8-20
Area: Centrum
Address: Keizersgracht 711 1017 DX
Amsterdam The Netherlands
Phone: +31 20 6258215

#210
CAU Carne Argentina Unica
Category: Steakhouses, Argentine
Average price: €21-40
Area: Centrum, De Wallen
Address: Damstraat 5 1012 JL
Amsterdam The Netherlands
Phone: +31 20 6239632

#211
Cotton Cake
Category: Cafe
Average price: €21-40
Area: Zuid, De Pijp
Address: 1e Van Der Helstsrraat 76-hs
1072 NZ Amsterdam The Netherlands
Phone: +31 20 7895838

#212
Blue Pepper Indonesian
Category: Indonesian
Average price: Above €41
Area: West, Helmersbuurt
Address: Nassaukade 366 1054 AB
Amsterdam The Netherlands
Phone: +31 20 4897039

#213
Mashua
Category: Latin American
Average price: €21-40
Area: Centrum
Address: Prinsengracht 703 1017 JV
Amsterdam The Netherlands
Phone: +31 20 4200559

#214
't Vliegertje
Category: GastroPub
Average price: €21-40
Area: Zuid, Rivierenbuurt
Address: Scheldestraat 79 1078 GH
Amsterdam The Netherlands
Phone: +31 20 6798480

#215
Restaurant Fier
Category: Belgian
Average price: €8-20
Area: West, Oud West, Kinkerbuurt
Address: De Clerqstraat 79 1053 AG
Amsterdam The Netherlands
Phone: +31 20 2217449

#216
Caffe Il Momento
Category: Cafe, Coffee & Tea
Average price: €8-20
Area: Centrum
Address: Singel 180 1015 AJ
Amsterdam The Netherlands
Phone: +31 20 3316652

#217
Hoi Tin
Category: Chinese
Average price: €8-20
Area: Centrum, De Wallen
Address: Zeedijk 122-124 1012 BB
Amsterdam The Netherlands
Phone: +31 20 6256451

#218
Pompstation Bar&Grill
Category: Restaurant, Music Venues
Average price: €21-40
Area: Oost, Zeeburg
Address: Zeeburgerdijk 52 1094 AE
Amsterdam The Netherlands
Phone: +31 20 6922888

#219
De Fles
Category: GastroPub
Average price: €8-20
Area: Centrum
Address: Vijzelstraat 137-III 1017 HJ
Amsterdam The Netherlands
Phone: +31 20 6249644

#220
Eetcafe Het Pakhuis
Category: GastroPub
Average price: €8-20
Area: Centrum
Address: Voetboogstraat 10 1012 XL
Amsterdam The Netherlands
Phone: +31 20 6250856

#221
Dauphine Café
Category: Brasseries
Average price: €21-40
Area: Oost, Watergraafsmeer
Address: Prins Bernhardplein 175 1097
BL Amsterdam The Netherlands
Phone: +31 20 4621646

#222
Players Food & Drinks
Category: Pub, Restaurant
Average price: €8-20
Area: Centrum
Address: Kleine Gartmanplantsoen 25
1017 RP Amsterdam The Netherlands
Phone: +31 20 8888886

#223
Stork
Category: Seafood
Average price: €21-40
Area: Noord
Address: Bedrijventerrein de Overkant
1021 KR Amsterdam The Netherlands
Phone: +31 20 6344000

#224
Notting Hill Hotel
Category: Hotel, Nightlife, Restaurant
Average price: Above €41
Area: Centrum
Address: Westeinde 26 1017 ZP
Amsterdam The Netherlands
Phone: +31 20 5231030

#225
Le Fou Fow
Category: Chinese
Average price: €8-20
Area: Centrum, De Wallen
Address: Stormsteeg 9 1012 BD
Amsterdam The Netherlands
Phone: +31 20 2044528

#226
Marius
Category: French
Average price: €21-40
Area: Centrum, West
Address: Barentszstraat 173 1013 NM
Amsterdam The Netherlands
Phone: +31 20 4227880

#227
Nyonya Malasya Express
Category: Malaysian
Average price: €8-20
Area: Centrum, De Wallen
Address: Kloveniersburgwal 38-H 1012
CW Amsterdam The Netherlands
Phone: +31 20 4222447

#228
De Silveren Spiegel
Category: Seafood
Average price: €21-40
Area: Centrum
Address: Kattengat 4-6 1012 SZ
Amsterdam The Netherlands
Phone: +31 20 6246589

#229
Brasserie De Joffers
Category: Brasseries, Diners,
Breakfast & Brunch
Average price: €21-40
Area: Zuid, Museumkwartier
Address: Willemsparkweg 163 1071 GZ
Amsterdam The Netherlands
Phone: +31 20 6730360

#230
Chipsy King
Category: Fish & Chips
Average price: Under €7
Area: Centrum, De Wallen
Address: Damstraat 8 1012 JM
Amsterdam The Netherlands
Phone: +31 624 435003

#231
Café Vrijdag
Category: Cafe
Average price: €8-20
Area: Zuid, Rivierenbuurt
Address: Amsteldijk 137 1079 LE
Amsterdam The Netherlands
Phone: +31 20 7797793

#232
Café Gambrinus
Category: GastroPub, Pub, Dive Bar
Average price: €8-20
Area: Zuid, De Pijp
Address: Ferdinand Bolstraat 180 1072
LV Amsterdam The Netherlands
Phone: +31 20 6717389

#233
Beter & Leuk
Category: Coffee & Tea,
Breakfast & Brunch, GastroPub
Average price: €8-20
Area: Oost, Oosterparkbuurt
Address: Eerste Oosterparkstraat 91
1091 GW Amsterdam The Netherlands
Phone: +31 20 7670029

#234
Kyoto Café
Category: Japanese
Average price: €21-40
Area: Centrum
Address: Damrak 44 1012 LK
Amsterdam The Netherlands
Phone: +31 20 6255302

#235
Bo Cinq
Category: Bar, French, Desserts
Average price: €21-40
Area: Centrum
Address: Prinsengracht 494 1017 KH
Amsterdam The Netherlands
Phone: +31 20 6220682

#236
De Ysbreeker
Category: Cafe, Brasseries, French
Average price: €8-20
Area: Oost, Oosterparkbuurt
Address: Weesperzijde 23 1091 EC
Amsterdam The Netherlands
Phone: +31 20 4681808

#237
Ctaste
Category: Restaurant
Average price: Above €41
Area: Zuid, De Pijp
Address: Amsteldijk 54-55 1074 HX
Amsterdam The Netherlands
Phone: +31 20 6752831

#238
Cafe Restaurant Walem
Category: GastroPub
Average price: €8-20
Area: Centrum
Address: Keizersgracht 449 1017 DK
Amsterdam The Netherlands
Phone: +31 20 6253544

#239
Groot Melkhuis
Category: Breakfast & Brunch,
Playgrounds
Average price: €8-20
Area: Zuid, Museumkwartier
Address: Vondelpark 2 1071 AA
Amsterdam The Netherlands
Phone: +31 20 6129674

#240
Renzo's
Category: Sandwiches,
Specialty Food, Do-It-Yourself Food
Average price: €8-20
Area: Zuid, Museumkwartier
Address: Van Baerlestraat 67 1071 AR
Amsterdam The Netherlands
Phone: +31 20 6731673

#241
Marathonweg
Category: Cafe, Barbeque
Average price: €21-40
Area: Zuid, Stadionbuurt
Address: Marathonweg 1-3-5 1076 SW
Amsterdam The Netherlands
Phone: +31 20 3703731

#242
Lion Noir
Category: French
Average price: €21-40
Area: Centrum
Address: Reguliersdwarsstraat 28 1017
BM Amsterdam The Netherlands
Phone: +31 20 6276603

#243
Bierfabriek
Category: Barbeque, Pub
Average price: €8-20
Area: Centrum
Address: Rokin 75 1012 KL
Amsterdam The Netherlands
Phone: +31 20 5289910

#244
Wilhelmina-Dok
Category: Mediterranean
Average price: €8-20
Area: Noord
Address: Noordwal 1 1021 PX
Amsterdam The Netherlands
Phone: +31 20 6323701

#245
Japan Inn Yakitori
Category: Sushi Bar, Japanese
Average price: €8-20
Area: Centrum
Address: Leidsekruisstraat 4 1017 RH
Amsterdam The Netherlands
Phone: +31 20 6204989

#246
Wagamama
Category: Asian Fusion
Average price: €8-20
Area: Zuid, WTC
Address: Zuidplein 12 1077 XV
Amsterdam The Netherlands
Phone: +31 20 6203032

#247
De Koe
Category: Bar, Cafe
Average price: €8-20
Area: Centrum, Jordaan
Address: Marnixstraat 381 1016 XR
Amsterdam The Netherlands
Phone: +31 20 6254482

#248
Song Kwae Thai Food
Category: Thai
Average price: €8-20
Area: Centrum, De Wallen
Address: Kloveniersburgwal 14-A
1012 CT Amsterdam The Netherlands
Phone: +31 20 6242568

#249
De Waaghals
Category: Vegetarian
Average price: €21-40
Area: Zuid, De Pijp
Address: Frans Halsstraat 29 1072 BK
Amsterdam The Netherlands
Phone: +31 20 6799609

#250
Maurya Organic Indian Lounge
Category: Indian, Specialty Food
Average price: €8-20
Area: Centrum
Address: Korte Leidsedwarsstraat 49A
1017 PW Amsterdam The Netherlands
Phone: +31 20 6263809

#251
Boca's Park
Category: Tapas
Average price: €8-20
Area: Zuid, De Pijp
Address: Sarphatipark 4 1072 PA
Amsterdam The Netherlands
Phone: +31 20 6759945

#252
Café Wheels
Category: Dive Bar, GastroPub
Average price: €8-20
Area: Centrum, Negen Straatjes
Address: Wolvenstraat 4-III 1016 EP
Amsterdam The Netherlands
Phone: +31 20 6228673

#253
The Beef Chief
Category: Burgers
Average price: €8-20
Area: West, Oud West
Address: Jacob van Lennepkade
215 Amsterdam, Noord-Holland
The Netherlands
Phone: +31 619 997846

#254
Sari Citra
Category: Indonesian
Average price: Under €7
Area: Zuid, De Pijp
Address: Ferdinand Bolstraat 52
1072 LL Amsterdam The Netherlands
Phone: +31 20 6754102

#255
Daalder
Category: GastroPub
Average price: €8-20
Area: Centrum, Jordaan
Address: Lindengracht 90 1015 KK
Amsterdam The Netherlands
Phone: +31 20 6248864

#256
Yokiyo
Category: Korean
Average price: €21-40
Area: Centrum, De Wallen
Address: Oudezijds Voorburgwal 67
1012 EK Amsterdam The Netherlands
Phone: +31 20 3314562

#257
Pink Flamingo Pizza
Category: Pizza
Average price: €8-20
Area: Zuid, De Pijp
Address: Gerard Douplein 8 1072 VE
Amsterdam The Netherlands
Phone: +31 20 6703274

#258
Ron Gastrobar
Category: French, GastroPub
Average price: Above €41
Area: Zuid, Willemspark
Address: Sophialaan 55 1075 BP
Amsterdam The Netherlands
Phone: +31 20 4961943

#259
Tokyo Cafe
Category: Japanese, Sushi Bar
Average price: €21-40
Area: Centrum
Address: Spui 15 1012 WX
Amsterdam The Netherlands
Phone: +31 20 4897918

#260
Meuwese Espresso
Category: Coffee & Tea, Brasseries
Average price: €8-20
Area: Centrum, De Wallen
Address: Rokin 119 1012 KP
Amsterdam The Netherlands
Phone: +31 20 6241243

#261
Sonny
Category: Falafel, Vegan, Vegetarian
Average price: Under €7
Area: Zuid, De Pijp
Address: Eerste van der Helststraat 43
1073 AC Amsterdam The Netherlands
Phone: +31 20 6767612

#262
Olijfje
Category: Mediterranean
Average price: €8-20
Area: Centrum
Address: Valkenburgerstraat 223-D
1011 MJ Amsterdam The Netherlands
Phone: +31 20 3304444

#263
Gebr.
Category: Cafe
Average price: Above €41
Area: Centrum
Address: Peperstraat 10hs 1011 NX
Amsterdam The Netherlands
Phone: +31 20 4210699

#264
Surya
Category: Indian, Vegetarian
Average price: €21-40
Area: Zuid, De Pijp
Address: Ceintuurbaan 147 1072 GB
Amsterdam The Netherlands
Phone: +31 20 6767985

#265
Screaming Beans
Category: Pub, Wine Bar
Average price: €21-40
Area: West, Oud West, Helmersbuurt
Address: Eerste Constantijn
Huygensstraat 35 1054 BR
Amsterdam The Netherlands
Phone: +31 20 6160770

#266
Dragon i
Category: Japanese, Korean, Thai
Average price: €8-20
Area: Zuid
Address: Amstelveenseweg 154 1075
XM Amsterdam The Netherlands
Phone: +31 20 7706420

#267
**Belgisch Restaurant Lieve
Amsterdam**
Category: Belgian
Average price: €8-20
Area: Centrum
Address: Herengracht 88 1015 BS
Amsterdam The Netherlands
Phone: +31 20 6249635

#268
De Duvel Eetcafé
Category: GastroPub
Average price: €8-20
Area: Zuid, De Pijp
Address: 1e van der Helststraat 59-HS
1073 AD Amsterdam The Netherlands
Phone: +31 20 6757517

#269
Kam Yin
Category: Chinese, Indonesian
Average price: €8-20
Area: Centrum, De Wallen
Address: Warmoesstraat 6 1012 JD
Amsterdam The Netherlands
Phone: +31 20 6253115

#270
BAUT Amsterdam
Category: French,
Juice Bar& Smoothies, Italian
Average price: €21-40
Area: Oost, Oosterparkbuurt
Address: Wibautstraat 125 1091 GL
Amsterdam The Netherlands
Phone: +31 20 4659260

#271
Pilsvogel
Category: GastroPub, Tapas
Average price: €8-20
Area: Zuid, De Pijp
Address: Gerard Douplein 14
1072 VE Amsterdam The Netherlands
Phone: +31 20 6646483

#272
Bagels & Beans
Category: Bagels, Coffee & Tea,
Gluten-Free
Average price: €8-20
Area: Zuid, De Pijp
Address: Ferdinand Bolstraat 70
1072 LM Amsterdam The Netherlands
Phone: +31 20 6721610

#273
Dwaze Zaken
Category: Do-It-Yourself Food,
Cafe, Brasseries
Average price: €8-20
Area: Centrum, De Wallen
Address: Prins Hendrikkade 50
1012 AC Amsterdam The Netherlands
Phone: +31 20 6124175

#274
Balraj
Category: Indian
Average price: €8-20
Area: Centrum, Haarlemmerbuurt
Address: Haarlemmerdijk 28-II
1013 JD Amsterdam The Netherlands
Phone: +31 20 6251428

#275
China Sichuan
Category: Chinese
Average price: €21-40
Area: Centrum, De Wallen
Address: Warmoesstraat 17
1012 HT Amsterdam The Netherlands
Phone: +31 20 4207833

#276
Oliver's
Category: European
Average price: €8-20
Area: Zuid, WTC
Address: Claude Debussylaan 78
1082 MD Amsterdam The Netherlands
Phone: +31 20 6461626

#277
Zouk
Category: GastroPub, Pub
Average price: €8-20
Area: West, Oud West, Helmersbuurt
Address: 1e C Huygensstr 45 1054 BS
Amsterdam The Netherlands
Phone: +31 20 6891133

#278
Thai Tiger
Category: Thai
Average price: €8-20
Area: Oost, Indische Buurt
Address: Javaplein 7a 1095 CH
Amsterdam The Netherlands
Phone: +31 20 2210858

#279
Fuoco Vivo
Category: Pizza
Average price: €8-20
Area: West, Da Costabuurt
Address: De Clercqstraat 12-BG 1052
NC Amsterdam The Netherlands
Phone: +31 20 6124309

#280
NH Grand Hotel Krasnapolsky
Category: Hotel, Restaurant
Average price: €21-40
Area: Centrum, De Wallen
Address: Dam 9 1012 JS
Amsterdam The Netherlands
Phone: +31 20 5549111

#281
Bickers Aan De Werf
Category: Salad, Sandwiches
Average price: €21-40
Area: Centrum, Haarlemmerbuurt
Address: Bickerswerf 2 1013 KX
Amsterdam The Netherlands
Phone: +31 20 3202951

#282
Sazanka Restaurant
Category: Japanese
Average price: Above €41
Area: Zuid, De Pijp
Address: Ferdinand Bolstraat 333 1072
LH Amsterdam The Netherlands
Phone: +31 20 6787111

#283
Koffiehuis Van Den Volksbond
Category: GastroPub
Average price: €8-20
Area: Centrum
Address: Kadijksplein 4 1018 AB
Amsterdam The Netherlands
Phone: +31 20 6221209

#284
Gare de l'Est
Category: French
Average price: €21-40
Area: Oost, Zeeburg
Address: Cruqiusweg 9 1019 AT
Amsterdam The Netherlands
Phone: +31 20 4630620

#285
CrepeBar
Category: Creperies, Cafe
Average price: €8-20
Area: Centrum
Address: Martelaarsgracht 11
1012 TN Amsterdam The Netherlands
Phone: +31 20 4896262

#286
Kaiko
Category: Sushi Bar
Average price: Above €41
Area: Zuid, Rivierenbuurt
Address: Jekerstraat 114 1078 MJ
Amsterdam The Netherlands
Phone: +31 20 6625641

#287
Hugo's Bar & Kitchen
Category: Restaurant, Cocktail Bar
Average price: €8-20
Area: West, Frederik Hendrikbuurt
Address: Hugo de Grootplein 10 1052
KW Amsterdam The Netherlands
Phone: +31 20 7516633

#288
Japans Delicatessenhuis Zen
Category: Japanese, Diners
Average price: €21-40
Area: Zuid, De Pijp
Address: Frans Halsstraat 38 1072 BS
Amsterdam The Netherlands
Phone: +31 20 6270607

#289
The Lobby
Category: European
Average price: Above €41
Area: Centrum, De Wallen
Address: Nes 49 1012 KD
Amsterdam The Netherlands
Phone: +31 20 7585275

#290
Renato's Pizzeria
Category: Pizza, Italian
Average price: €21-40
Area: Zuid, De Pijp
Address: Karel du Jardinstraat 32
1072 SK Amsterdam The Netherlands
Phone: +31 20 6732300

#291
Sefa Grill-Shoarma
Category: Fast Food, Diners, Turkish
Average price: €8-20
Area: Centrum
Address: Westermarkt 25 1016 DJ
Amsterdam The Netherlands
Phone: +31 20 7739212

#292
Me Naam Naan
Category: Thai
Average price: €21-40
Area: Centrum
Address: Koningsstraat 29 1011 ET
Amsterdam The Netherlands
Phone: +31 20 4233344

#293
Comfort Caffè
Category: Italian
Average price: €21-40
Area: Oost, Indische Buurt
Address: Sumatrastraat 28-30 1094 ND
Amsterdam The Netherlands
Phone: +31 20 4630092

#294
Cafe Sonneveld
Category: Cafe
Average price: €8-20
Area: Centrum, Jordaan
Address: Egelantiersgracht 72-74 1015
RN Amsterdam The Netherlands
Phone: +31 20 4234287

#295
Spanjer En Van Twist
Category: GastroPub
Average price: €8-20
Area: Centrum
Address: Leliegracht 60 1015 DJ
Amsterdam The Netherlands
Phone: +31 20 6390109

#296
Le Pain Quotidien Oud Zuid
Category: Belgian,
Breakfast & Brunch, Sandwiches
Average price: €8-20
Area: Zuid, Museumkwartier
Address: Johannes Verhulststraat 104
1071 NL Amsterdam The Netherlands
Phone: +31 20 3795900

#297
Sushi Me
Category: Sushi Bar
Average price: €8-20
Area: Centrum
Address: Oude Leliestraat 7-BG 1016
BD Amsterdam The Netherlands
Phone: +31 20 6277043

#298
Restaurant Bidou
Category: French, Italian
Average price: €21-40
Area: Oost, Oosterparkbuurt
Address: Beukenplein 19-21 1092 BB
Amsterdam The Netherlands
Phone: +31 20 3624390

#299
Pizza Sotto
Category: Pizza
Average price: €8-20
Area: Zuid, Willemspark
Address: Amstelveenseweg 89 1075
VW Amsterdam The Netherlands
Phone: +31 20 2239000

#300
Café Schiller
Category: Cafe, Brasseries
Average price: €8-20
Area: Centrum
Address: Rembrandtplein 24 1017 CV
Amsterdam The Netherlands
Phone: +31 20 6249846

#301
De Smoeshaan
Category: Pub, GastroPub
Average price: €8-20
Area: West
Address: Leidsekade 90 1017 PN
Amsterdam The Netherlands
Phone: +31 20 6250368

#302
Febo
Category: Fast Food
Average price: Under €7
Area: Centrum
Address: Reguliersbreestraat 38 1017
CN Amsterdam The Netherlands
Phone: +31 20 6235304

#303
Vlaming
Category: GastroPub
Average price: €21-40
Area: Centrum, Jordaan
Address: Lindengracht 95 1015 KD
Amsterdam The Netherlands
Phone: +31 20 6222716

#304
Restaurant Chang-I
Category: Asian Fusion
Average price: €8-20
Area: Zuid, Museumkwartier
Address: Jan Willem Brouwersstr 7
1071 LH Amsterdam The Netherlands
Phone: +31 20 4701700

#305
Spare Rib Express
Category: Barbeque, Steakhouses
Average price: €8-20
Area: Oost, Zeeburg
Address: Veemarkt 76 1019 DD
Amsterdam The Netherlands
Phone: +31 20 4687647

#306
Na Siam
Category: Thai
Average price: €8-20
Area: Centrum
Address: Kerkstraat 332 1017 JA
Amsterdam The Netherlands
Phone: +31 20 4210505

#307
Maoz Falafel
Category: Vegetarian
Average price: Under €7
Area: Centrum
Address: Muntplein 1 1017 CM
Amsterdam The Netherlands
Phone: +31 20 6249290

#308
La Perla
Category: Pizza, Italian
Average price: €8-20
Area: Centrum, Jordaan
Address: Tweede Tuindwarsstraat 14,
Amsterdam The Netherlands
Phone: +31 20 6876230

#309
Bar Baarsch
Category: GastroPub
Average price: €8-20
Area: West, Hoofdweg en Omgeving
Address: Jan Evertsenstraat 91 1057
BS Amsterdam The Netherlands
Phone: +31 20 6181970

#310
NAM KEE
Category: Chinese
Average price: €8-20
Area: Centrum, De Wallen
Address: Zeedijk 111-113 1012 AV
Amsterdam The Netherlands
Phone: +31 20 6243470

#311
Café Thuys
Category: Pub, Food
Average price: €8-20
Area: West, Oud West, Kinkerbuurt
Address: De Clercqstraat 129 1053 AK
Amsterdam The Netherlands
Phone: +31 20 6120898

#312
Casa Di David
Category: Italian
Average price: €8-20
Area: Centrum
Address: Singel 426-BG 1017 AV
Amsterdam The Netherlands
Phone: +31 20 6262429

#313
O'reilly's
Category: Pub, GastroPub, Irish
Average price: €8-20
Area: Centrum
Address: Paleisstraat 103-105
1012 ZL Amsterdam The Netherlands
Phone: +31 20 6249498

#314
Nooch
Category: Asian Fusion
Average price: €8-20
Area: Centrum, Negen Straatjes
Address: Reestraat 11 1016 DM
Amsterdam The Netherlands
Phone: +31 20 6222105

#315
Barça
Category: Spanish, Pub, Tapas Bar
Average price: €8-20
Area: Zuid, De Pijp
Address: Marie Heinekenplein 30-31
1072 MH Amsterdam The Netherlands
Phone: +31 20 4704144

#316
Pompa
Category: Italian
Average price: €8-20
Area: Zuid, Museumkwartier
Address: Willemsparkweg 6 1071 HD
Amsterdam The Netherlands
Phone: +31 20 6626206

#317
Gollem's Proeflokaal
Category: Pub, GastroPub
Average price: €8-20
Area: West, Oud West, Helmersbuurt
Address: Overtoom 160-162 1054 HP
Amsterdam The Netherlands
Phone: +31 20 6129444

#318
Café Maxwell
Category: GastroPub
Average price: €8-20
Area: Oost, Oosterparkbuurt
Address: Beukenplein 27 1092 BB
Amsterdam The Netherlands
Phone: +31 20 7726748

#319
Pizzeria San Marco
Category: Do-It-Yourself Food, Italian
Average price: €8-20
Area: Zuid, De Pijp
Address: Amstelkade 148-A 1078 AW
Amsterdam The Netherlands
Phone: +31 20 6730884

#320
Eye Bar &Restaurant
Category: GastroPub
Average price: €8-20
Area: Noord
Address: IJpromenade 1 1031 KT
Amsterdam The Netherlands
Phone: +31 20 5891402

#321
Bagels & Beans
Category: Bagels, Coffee & Tea,
Breakfast & Brunch
Average price: €8-20
Area: Centrum
Address: Waterlooplein 2 1011 PG
Amsterdam The Netherlands
Phone: +31 20 4288906

#322
Izakaya
Category: Japanese, Asian Fusion
Average price: Above €41
Area: Zuid, De Pijp
Address: Albert Cuypstraat 2-6
1072 CT Amsterdam The Netherlands
Phone: +31 20 3053090

#323
Café De Blauwe Pan
Category: GastroPub
Average price: Under €7
Area: Centrum, Jordaan
Address: Westerstraat 200
1015 MS Amsterdam The Netherlands
Phone: +31 20 3207211

#324
Café Flinck
Category: GastroPub, Pub
Average price: €8-20
Area: Zuid, De Pijp
Address: 1e van der Helststraat 51 1073
AD Amsterdam The Netherlands
Phone: +31 20 8462101

#325
Momo
Category: Asian Fusion
Average price: €21-40
Area: Zuid, Museumkwartier
Address: Hobbemastraat 1 1071 XZ
Amsterdam The Netherlands
Phone: +31 20 6717474

#326
Café Kobalt
Category: GastroPub, Pub
Average price: €8-20
Area: Centrum, Haarlemmerbuurt
Address: Singel 2-A 1013 GA
Amsterdam The Netherlands
Phone: +31 20 3202059

#327
Loetje Oost
Category: Salad, Sandwiches
Average price: €21-40
Area: Oost, Oosterparkbuurt
Address: Ruyschstraat 15 1091 BR
Amsterdam The Netherlands
Phone: +31 20 3624709

#328
Sushi Time
Category: Japanese
Average price: €8-20
Area: Zuid, WTC
Address: Strawinskylaan 13
1077 XW Amsterdam The Netherlands
Phone: +31 20 5753200

#329
Spijshuys Versch
Category: Restaurant
Average price: €8-20
Area: Zuid, Museumkwartier
Address: Ruysdaelkade 183
1072 AT Amsterdam The Netherlands
Phone: +31 611 628545

#330
Cut Throat Barber & Coffee
Category: Barbers, Coffee & Tea
Average price: €21-40
Area: Centrum, De Wallen
Address: Warmoesstraat 155
1012 JC Amsterdam The Netherlands
Phone: +31 625 343769

#331
De Kaasboer
Category: Food, Sandwiches
Average price: Under €7
Area: Centrum, Jordaan
Address: Tweede Tuindwarsstraat 3
1015 RX Amsterdam The Netherlands
Phone: +31 20 6248802

#332
Betty's
Category: Vegetarian
Average price: €21-40
Area: Zuid, Rivierenbuurt
Address: Rijnstraat 75-HS 1079 GX
Amsterdam The Netherlands
Phone: +31 20 6445896

#333
Sane
Category: Do-It-Yourself Food,
Juice Bar& Smoothies, Soup
Average price: Under €7
Area: Centrum, Haarlemmerbuurt
Address: Haarlemmerdijk 136 1013 JJ
Amsterdam The Netherlands
Phone: +31 20 2237211

#334
Serre Restaurant
Category: French, European
Average price: €21-40
Area: Zuid, De Pijp
Address: Ferdinand Bolstraat 333 1072
LH Amsterdam The Netherlands
Phone: +31 20 6787450

#335
The Burrito Maker
Category: Tex-Mex
Average price: €8-20
Area: Centrum, Haarlemmerbuurt
Address: Haarlemmerplein 29 1013 HP
Amsterdam The Netherlands
Phone: +31 20 4208383

#336
Yam Yam Trattoria - Pizzeria
Category: Italian
Average price: €8-20
Area: West, Frederik Hendrikbuurt
Address: Frederik Hendrikstraat 90 1052
HZ Amsterdam The Netherlands
Phone: +31 20 6815097

#337
Ponte Arcari
Category: Italian
Average price: €21-40
Area: Centrum
Address: Herengracht 534 1017 CG
Amsterdam The Netherlands
Phone: +31 20 6250853

#338
Lucius Visrestaurant
Category: Fish & Chips
Average price: €21-40
Area: Centrum
Address: Spuistraat 247 1012 VP
Amsterdam The Netherlands
Phone: +31 20 6241831

#339
College Hotel
Category: Lounge, Hotel
Average price: €21-40
Area: Zuid, Museumkwartier
Address: Roelof Hartstraat 1
1071 VE Amsterdam The Netherlands
Phone: +31 20 5711511

#340
Sumo Sushi & Grill
Category: Japanese
Average price: €8-20
Area: Centrum
Address: Vijzelstraat 26 1017 HK
Amsterdam The Netherlands
Phone: +31 20 4207822

#341
Hemelse Modder
Category: European
Average price: €21-40
Area: Centrum
Address: Oude Waal 11 1011 BZ
Amsterdam The Netherlands
Phone: +31 20 6243203

#342
Tibet Restaurant
Category: Soup
Average price: €8-20
Area: Centrum, De Wallen
Address: Lange Niezel 24 1012 GT
Amsterdam The Netherlands
Phone: +31 20 6241137

#343
Restaurant Dubbel
Category: GastroPub
Average price: €8-20
Area: Centrum
Address: Lijnbaansgracht 256 1017 RK
Amsterdam The Netherlands
Phone: +31 20 6200909

#344
Ko Chang
Category: Thai
Average price: €8-20
Area: Centrum, Jordaan
Address: Westerstraat 91 1015 LX
Amsterdam The Netherlands
Phone: +31 20 6381039

#345
Frederique
Category: Specialty Food,
Sandwiches, Salad
Average price: Under €7
Area: Zuid, De Pijp
Address: Gerard Doustraat 224 1073
XC Amsterdam The Netherlands
Phone: +31 20 7740332

#346
Restaurant Spelt
Category: European,
Breakfast & Brunch
Average price: €21-40
Area: Centrum
Address: Nieuwe Spiegelstraat 5a
1017 DB Amsterdam The Netherlands
Phone: +31 20 4207022

#347
**Holland International
Canal Cruises**
Category: Nightlife,
Arts & Entertainment
Average price: €8-20
Area: Centrum
Address: Prins Hendrikkade 33a
1012 TM Amsterdam The Netherlands
Phone: +31 20 6253035

#348
Stoop & Stoop Eetcafé
Category: GastroPub
Average price: €8-20
Area: Centrum
Address: Lange Leidsedwarsstraat
82-HS 1017 NM Amsterdam
The Netherlands
Phone: +31 20 6200982

#349
Ciro Passami L'olio!
Category: Italian
Average price: Above €41
Area: West, Helmersbuurt
Address: Tweede Helmersstraat 3-BG
1054 CA Amsterdam The Netherlands
Phone: +31 615 699649

#350
Brasserie Blazer
Category: Brasseries
Average price: €8-20
Area: Centrum, Jordaan
Address: Lijnbaansgracht 190
1016 XA Amsterdam The Netherlands
Phone: +31 20 6209690

#351
Wijnbar Boelen & Boelen
Category: French, Wine Bar
Average price: €8-20
Area: Zuid, De Pijp
Address: 1e van der Helststraat 50
1072 NV Amsterdam The Netherlands
Phone: +31 20 6712242

#352
Dante Kitchen & Bar
Category: Pub, Italian
Average price: €8-20
Area: Centrum
Address: Spuistraat 320 1012 VX
Amsterdam The Netherlands
Phone: +31 20 6246266

#353
Ristorante Saturnino
Category: Italian
Average price: €21-40
Area: Centrum
Address: Reguliersdwarsstraat 3-5
1017 BJ Amsterdam The Netherlands
Phone: +31 20 6390102

#354
Khorat Top Thai
Category: Thai, Food Delivery Services
Average price: €8-20
Area: West, Oud West
Address: 2de C. Huygensstraat 64
Amsterdam, Noord-Holland
The Netherlands
Phone: +31 20 6831297

#355
Espressobar Puccini
Category: Coffee & Tea, Brasseries
Average price: €21-40
Area: Centrum
Address: Staalstraat 21 1011 JK
Amsterdam The Netherlands
Phone: +31 20 6208458

#356
Max
Category: French, Indonesian
Average price: €21-40
Area: Centrum
Address: Herenstraat 14 1015 CA
Amsterdam The Netherlands
Phone: +31 20 4200222

#357
Restaurant Caprese
Category: Italian
Average price: €8-20
Area: Centrum
Address: Spuistraat 261 1012 VR
Amsterdam The Netherlands
Phone: +31 20 6200059

#358
Lunchcafé Studio 2
Category: GastroPub
Average price: €8-20
Area: Centrum
Address: Singel 504 1017 AX
Amsterdam The Netherlands
Phone: +31 20 6239136

#359
CC Muziekcafé
Category: Jazz & Blues,
Music Venues, Cafe
Average price: Under €7
Area: Zuid, De Pijp
Address: Rustenburgerstraat 384
1072 HG Amsterdam The Netherlands
Phone: +31 624 236956

#360
Van Speyk
Category: Brasseries
Average price: €21-40
Area: Centrum
Address: Spuistraat 3a 1012 SP
Amsterdam The Netherlands
Phone: +31 20 4200117

#361
Pastis
Category: European
Average price: €8-20
Area: West, Oud West, Helmersbuurt
Address: 1e Constantijn Huygenstraat
15 1054 BP Amsterdam The Netherlands
Phone: +31 20 6166166

#362
Febo
Category: Fast Food
Average price: Under €7
Area: Centrum
Address: Leidsestraat 121 1017 NZ
Amsterdam The Netherlands
Phone: +31 20 4343556

#363
Caffe Milo
Category: Pub, Italian, GastroPub
Average price: €8-20
Area: Oost, Dapperbuurt
Address: Linnaeusstraat 71-H
1093 EJ Amsterdam The Netherlands
Phone: +31 20 4638027

#364
De Wasserette
Category: Sandwiches, Coffee & Tea
Average price: €8-20
Area: Zuid, De Pijp
Address: Eerste van der Helststraat
271073 AC Oud-Zuid
The Netherlands
Phone: +31 20 4638027

#365
Drovers Dog
Category: Do-It-Yourself Food,
Coffee & Tea, Australian
Average price: €8-20
Area: Oost, Indische Buurt
Address: Eerste Atjehstraat 62 1094 KP
Amsterdam The Netherlands
Phone: +31 20 3703784

#366
Toastable
Category: Breakfast & Brunch,
Juice Bar& Smoothies, Cafe
Average price: €8-20
Area: Centrum
Address: Singel 441 Sous 1012 WP
Amsterdam The Netherlands
Phone: +31 20 6262969

#367
Maoz Falafel
Category: Fast Food
Average price: Under €7
Area: Centrum
Address: Leidsestraat 85 1017 NX
Amsterdam The Netherlands
Phone: +31 20 4279720

#368
Hostaria
Category: Italian
Average price: €8-20
Area: Centrum, Jordaan
Address: 2e Egelantiersdwarsstraat 9
1015 SB Amsterdam The Netherlands
Phone: +31 20 6260028

#369
Café De Engelbewaarder
Category: Pub, GastroPub
Average price: €8-20
Area: Centrum
Address: Kloveniersburgwal 59-HS
1011 JZ Amsterdam The Netherlands
Phone: +31 20 6253772

#370
@ Seven
Category: Breakfast & Brunch
Average price: €8-20
Area: Zuid, Rivierenbuurt
Address: Scheldestraat 92 1078 GN
Amsterdam The Netherlands
Phone: +31 20 6709295

#371
Getto
Category: Gay Bar, GastroPub
Average price: €8-20
Area: Centrum, De Wallen
Address: Warmoesstraat 51-B
1012 HW Amsterdam The Netherlands
Phone: +31 20 4215151

#372
Café Restaurant Kapitein Zeppos
Category: Diners, Pub
Average price: €8-20
Area: Centrum, De Wallen
Address: Gebed Zonder End 5
1012 HS Amsterdam The Netherlands
Phone: +31 20 6242057

#373
Mazzo
Category: Beer, Wine & Spirits
Average price: €8-20
Area: Centrum, Jordaan
Address: Rozengracht 114 1016 NH
Amsterdam The Netherlands
Phone: +31 20 3446402

#374
Cafe Nassau
Category: Italian
Average price: €8-20
Area: West, Staatsliedenbuurt
Address: De Wittenkade 105-A
1052 AG Amsterdam The Netherlands
Phone: +31 20 6843562

#375
Charles Eten & Drinken
Category: Salad, Sandwiches
Average price: €8-20
Area: Oost, Oosterparkbuurt
Address: Linnaeuskade 3 1098 BC
Amsterdam The Netherlands
Phone: +31 20 6634359

#376
Think Soup
Category: Cafe, Soup
Average price: Under €7
Area: Centrum, Jordaan
Address: Kinkerstraat 83hs 1053 DH
Amsterdam The Netherlands
Phone: +31 20 2332150

#377
Wurst & Schnitzelhaus
Category: German
Average price: €8-20
Area: Centrum
Address: Prinsengracht 474 hs
1017 KG Amsterdam The Netherlands
Phone: +31 20 7371592

#378
Madrid
Category: Tapas Bar, Spanish
Average price: €8-20
Area: West, Oud West, Kinkerbuurt
Address: Bellamystraat 11 1053 BM
Amsterdam The Netherlands
Phone: +31 20 4899375

#379
De Pizzakamer
Category: Pizza
Average price: €8-20
Area: Zuid, De Pijp
Address: 2e van der Helststraat 16 1072
PD Amsterdam The Netherlands
Phone: +31 20 2211457

#380
Otaru
Category: Japanese
Average price: €8-20
Area: Zuid, De Pijp
Address: Frans Halsstraat 2 1072 BR
Amsterdam The Netherlands
Phone: +31 20 6708972

#381
LAB111
Category: Diners, Cafe
Average price: €8-20
Area: West, Oud West, Helmersbuurt
Address: Arie Biemondstraat 111 1054
PD Amsterdam The Netherlands
Phone: +31 20 6169994

#382
Nel
Category: Desserts, Diners, Cafe
Average price: €8-20
Area: Centrum
Address: Amstelveld 12 1017 JD
Amsterdam The Netherlands
Phone: +31 20 6261199

#383
Vapiano Rembrandtplein
Category: Italian, Mediterranean
Average price: €8-20
Area: Centrum
Address: Amstelstraat 2-4 1017 DA
Amsterdam The Netherlands
Phone: +31 20 7670800

#384
Humphrey's
Category: Brasseries
Average price: €21-40
Area: Centrum
Address: Nieuwezijds Kolk 23 1012 PV
Amsterdam The Netherlands
Phone: +31 20 4221234

#385
't Fornuis
Category: French
Average price: €21-40
Area: Centrum
Address: Utrechtsestraat 33 1017 VH
Amsterdam The Netherlands
Phone: +31 20 6269139

#386
Sapporo
Category: Japanese
Average price: Above €41
Area: Zuid, Rivierenbuurt
Address: Scheldestraat 99 1078 GJ
Amsterdam The Netherlands
Phone: +31 20 4710039

#387
Kobe House
Category: Japanese
Average price: €21-40
Area: Centrum
Address: Nieuwezijds Voorburgwal 77
1012 RE Amsterdam The Netherlands
Phone: +31 20 6226458

#388
Golden Brown Bar
Category: GastroPub, Bar, Thai
Average price: €8-20
Area: West, Oud West, Helmersbuurt
Address: Jan Pieter Heijestraat 146
1054 WT Amsterdam The Netherlands
Phone: +31 20 6124076

#389
Het Bosch
Category: Lounge, Seafood, French
Average price: €21-40
Area: Zuid, Buitenveldert
Address: Jollenpad 10 1081 KC
Amsterdam The Netherlands
Phone: +31 20 6445800

#390
Restaurant Luna
Category: Argentine,
Steakhouses, Latin American
Average price: €21-40
Area: Centrum, Jordaan
Address: Lindengracht 152 1015 KK
Amsterdam The Netherlands
Phone: +31 20 6274149

#391
Los Pilones
Category: Mexican
Average price: €8-20
Area: Centrum, De Wallen
Address: Geldersekade 111 1011 EN
Amsterdam The Netherlands
Phone: +31 20 7760210

#392
Thaicoon
Category: Thai
Average price: €8-20
Area: Oost, Oosterparkbuurt
Address: Beukenplein 10 1091 KG
Amsterdam The Netherlands
Phone: +31 20 3623302

#393
Dos
Category: Tapas Bar, Spanish
Average price: €21-40
Area: Centrum, Jordaan
Address: Nieuwe Willemsstraat 1 1015
JH Amsterdam The Netherlands
Phone: +31 620 429303

#394
Assaggi
Category: Italian
Average price: €8-20
Area: Centrum, Jordaan
Address: Tweede Egelantiersdwstr 4-6
1015 SC Amsterdam The Netherlands
Phone: +31 20 4205589

#395
Café de Gaeper
Category: Pub, GastroPub
Average price: €8-20
Area: Centrum
Address: Staalstraat 4-IV 1011 JL
Amsterdam The Netherlands
Phone: +31 20 6233895

#396
Louter
Category: Brasseries
Average price: €8-20
Area: West, Oud West, Da Costabuurt
Address: De Clercqstraat 82 1052 NK
Amsterdam The Netherlands
Phone: +31 20 3892623

#397
Casa Peru
Category: Peruvian
Average price: €21-40
Area: Centrum
Address: Leidsegracht 68-SOUS 1016
CP Amsterdam The Netherlands
Phone: +31 20 6203749

#398
Bosco
Category: GastroPub
Average price: €8-20
Area: West, Oud West, Helmersbuurt
Address: Eerste Constantijn
Huygensstraat 7-9 1054 BN Amsterdam
The Netherlands
Phone: +31 20 2213480

#399
Nomads
Category: Middle Eastern, Hookah Bar
Average price: €21-40
Area: Centrum, Jordaan
Address: Rozengracht 133 I 1016 LV
Amsterdam The Netherlands
Phone: +31 20 3446405

#400
Tasca Bellota
Category: Tapas, Spanish
Average price: €8-20
Area: Centrum
Address: Herenstraat 22 1015 CB
Amsterdam The Netherlands
Phone: +31 20 4202946

#401
Bistro Bonjour
Category: French
Average price: €8-20
Area: Centrum
Address: Keizersgracht 770 1017 EB
Amsterdam The Netherlands
Phone: +31 20 6266040

#402
Sa Seada
Category: Italian
Average price: €8-20
Area: Oost, Oosterparkbuurt
Address: Eerste Oosterparkstraat 3-5
1091 GT Amsterdam The Netherlands
Phone: +31 20 6633276

#403
Kok Kita
Category: Indonesian,
Do-It-Yourself Food
Average price: Under €7
Area: Zuid
Address: Amstelveenseweg 166
1075 XN Amsterdam The Netherlands
Phone: +31 20 6702933

#404
A la Ferme
Category: French
Average price: €8-20
Area: Zuid, De Pijp
Address: Govert Flinckstraat 251 1073
BX Amsterdam The Netherlands
Phone: +31 20 6798240

#405
Hutspot
Category: Cafe
Average price: Under €7
Area: Centrum, Jordaan
Address: Rozengracht 204-210 1016 NL
Amsterdam The Netherlands
Phone: +31 20 2231331

#406
Terang Boelan Afhaalcentrum
Category: Indonesian
Average price: €8-20
Area: Centrum, Jordaan
Address: Tweede Lindendwarsstraat
3-HS 1015 LH Amsterdam The
Netherlands
Phone: +31 20 6209974

#407
Daarbaand
Category: Persian/Iranian
Average price: €8-20
Area: West, Oud West, Helmersbuurt
Address: Overtoom 350 1054 JG
Amsterdam The Netherlands
Phone: +31 20 6185481

#408
De Ebeling
Category: Bar, GastroPub
Average price: €8-20
Area: West, Helmersbuurt
Address: Overtoom 50-54 1054 HK
Amsterdam The Netherlands
Phone: +31 20 6891218

#409
De Blauwe Engel
Category: GastroPub
Average price: €8-20
Area: Zuid, WTC
Address: Strawinskylaan 143 1077 XX
Amsterdam The Netherlands
Phone: +31 20 5752140

#410
Café Restaurant Van Puffelen
Category: Restaurant
Average price: €8-20
Area: Centrum, Negen Straatjes
Address: Prinsengracht 375-HS 1016
HL Amsterdam The Netherlands
Phone: +31 20 6246270

#411
Café de Doelen
Category: Pub, GastroPub
Average price: €8-20
Area: Centrum
Address: Kloveniersburgwal 125 1011
KC Amsterdam The Netherlands
Phone: +31 20 6249023

#412
Stacey's Pennywell
Category: GastroPub
Average price: €8-20
Area: Centrum
Address: Herengracht 558 1017 CG
Amsterdam The Netherlands
Phone: +31 20 6243506

#413
Bark
Category: Brasseries, Seafood, French
Average price: €21-40
Area: Zuid, Museumkwartier
Address: Van Baerlestraat 120 1071 BD
Amsterdam The Netherlands
Phone: +31 20 6750210

#414
Goodies
Category: Cafe
Average price: €8-20
Area: Centrum, Negen Straatjes
Address: Huidenstraat 9 1016 ER
Amsterdam The Netherlands
Phone: +31 20 6256122

#415
Bar Bukowski
Category: Cafe, Breakfast & Brunch
Average price: €8-20
Area: Oost, Oosterparkbuurt
Address: Oosterpark 10 1092 AE
Amsterdam The Netherlands
Phone: +31 20 6654893

#416
Febo
Category: Fast Food
Average price: Under €7
Area: Centrum
Address: Nieuwendijk 220 1012 MX
Amsterdam The Netherlands
Phone: +31 20 6259906

#417
Sea Palace
Category: Chinese
Average price: €8-20
Area: Centrum
Address: Oosterdokskade 8 1011 AE
Amsterdam The Netherlands
Phone: +31 20 6258672

#418
Bar Lempicka
Category: Brasseries, Cocktail Bar
Average price: €8-20
Area: Plantagebuurt, Centrum
Address: Sarphatistraat 23 1018 EV
Amsterdam The Netherlands
Phone: +31 20 6220209

#419
Café Het Molenpad
Category: GastroPub, Cafe
Average price: €8-20
Area: Centrum
Address: Prinsengracht 653 1016 HV
Amsterdam The Netherlands
Phone: +31 20 6259680

#420
Solo Eten & Drinken
Category: Diners
Average price: €8-20
Area: Zuid, Museumkwartier
Address: Van Baerlestraat 35-37 1071
AP Amsterdam The Netherlands
Phone: +31 20 6622655

#421
District 5
Category: Italian, Pizza
Average price: €8-20
Area: Zuid, De Pijp
Address: Van der Helstplein 17 1073 AR
Amsterdam The Netherlands
Phone: +31 20 7700884

#422
WestergasTerras
Category: Pub, Cafe
Average price: €8-20
Area: West
Address: Klönneplein 4-6 1014 DD
Amsterdam The Netherlands
Phone: +31 20 6848496

#423
Van Harte
Category: GastroPub
Average price: €8-20
Area: Centrum, Negen Straatjes
Address: Hartenstraat 24-BG 1016 CC
Amsterdam The Netherlands
Phone: +31 20 6258500

#424
Bouf
Category: French, European
Average price: €21-40
Area: Zuid, Museumkwartier
Address: Van Baerlestraat 51-I
1071 AP Amsterdam The Netherlands
Phone: +31 20 6736222

#425
Café de Vergulde Gaper
Category: GastroPub
Average price: €8-20
Area: Centrum
Address: Prinsenstraat 30 1015 DD
Amsterdam The Netherlands
Phone: +31 20 6248975

#426
Het Karbeel
Category: GastroPub
Average price: €8-20
Area: Centrum, De Wallen
Address: Warmoesstraat 16
1012 JD Amsterdam The Netherlands
Phone: +31 20 6274995

#427
St.
Category: Irish, GastroPub
Average price: €21-40
Area: Centrum
Address: Rembrandtplein 8-10
1017 CV Amsterdam The Netherlands
Phone: +31 20 4226886

#428
Kitchen & Bar Van Rijn
Category: Bar, Steakhouses
Average price: €8-20
Area: Centrum
Address: Rembrandtplein 17 1017 CT
Amsterdam The Netherlands
Phone: +31 20 4500555

#429
Café Zilt
Category: Dive Bar, Cafe
Average price: €8-20
Area: Centrum, De Wallen
Address: Zeedijk 49 1012 AR
Amsterdam The Netherlands
Phone: +31 20 4215416

#430
Kong Kha
Category: Thai
Average price: €8-20
Area: Zuid, Rivierenbuurt
Address: Rijnstraat 87 1079 GZ
Amsterdam The Netherlands
Phone: +31 20 6612578

#431
Senses restaurant
Category: French, Wine Bar
Average price: €8-20
Area: Centrum
Address: Vijzelstraat 45 1017 HE
Amsterdam The Netherlands
Phone: +31 20 5306266

#432
De Blauwe Hollander
Category: GastroPub
Average price: €8-20
Area: Centrum
Address: Leidsekruisstraat 28 1017 RJ
Amsterdam The Netherlands
Phone: +31 20 6270521

#433
Brasserie Harkema
Category: French, Brasseries
Average price: €21-40
Area: Centrum, De Wallen
Address: Nes 67-69 1012 KD
Amsterdam The Netherlands
Phone: +31 20 4281111

#434
Coco's Outback
Category: Bar, Dance Club, Australian
Average price: €8-20
Area: Centrum
Address: Thorbeckeplein 8 1017 CS
Amsterdam The Netherlands
Phone: +31 20 6272423

#435
D' Overkant
Category: Pub, GastroPub, Cafe
Average price: €8-20
Area: Zuid, Rivierenbuurt
Address: Scheldestraat 101-105 1078
GJ Amsterdam The Netherlands
Phone: +31 20 6797366

#436
Cafe Fonteyn
Category: Bar, GastroPub
Average price: €8-20
Area: Centrum
Address: Nieuwmarkt 13-BG 1011 JR
Amsterdam The Netherlands
Phone: +31 20 4227050

#437
Ganesha Indian
Category: Indian
Average price: €8-20
Area: Centrum, De Wallen
Address: Geldersekade 5-BG 1011 EH
Amsterdam The Netherlands
Phone: +31 20 3207302

#438
Côte Ouest Café
Category: French
Average price: €21-40
Area: Centrum
Address: Gravenstraat 20 1012 NM
Amsterdam The Netherlands
Phone: +31 20 3208998

#439
Rakang
Category: Thai
Average price: €8-20
Area: Centrum, Jordaan
Address: Elandsgracht 29-HS
1016 TM Amsterdam The Netherlands
Phone: +31 20 6275012

#440
Flinders Cafe
Category: Diners, Cafe, Sandwiches
Average price: €8-20
Area: West, Frederik Hendrikbuurt
Address: Frederik Hendrikplantsoen 36
1052 XS Amsterdam The Netherlands
Phone: +31 20 2231583

#441
Brasserie Klokspijs
Category: Brasseries
Average price: €8-20
Area: Zuid, De Pijp
Address: Hemonystraat 38 1074 BS
Amsterdam The Netherlands
Phone: +31 20 3642560

#442
Cafe de Zagerij
Category: GastroPub, Sandwiches
Average price: €8-20
Area: Centrum, Jordaan
Address: Westerstraat 182 1015 MR
Amsterdam The Netherlands
Phone: +31 20 4211155

#443
Roberto's Restaurant
Category: Italian
Average price: Above €41
Area: Zuid, Apollobuurt
Address: Apollolaan 138 1077 BG
Amsterdam The Netherlands
Phone: +31 20 7106025

#444
Chinees Specialiteiten Restaurant Oceania
Category: Chinese
Average price: Above €41
Area: Zuid, Rivierenbuurt
Address: Scheldestraat 77 1078 GH Amsterdam The Netherlands
Phone: +31 20 6738907

#445
De Hollandsche Manege
Category: Venues & Events, Horseback Riding, Cafe
Average price: €8-20
Area: Oud West
Address: Vondelstraat 140-I 1054 GT Amsterdam The Netherlands
Phone: +31 20 6180942

#446
Le Zinc...
Category: French
Average price: €8-20
Area: Centrum
Address: Prinsengracht 999 1017 KM Amsterdam The Netherlands
Phone: +31 20 6229044

#447
Oresti's Taverna
Category: Tapas, Mediterranean
Average price: €8-20
Area: Zuid, De Pijp
Address: Daniel Stalpertstraat 93 1072 XD Amsterdam The Netherlands
Phone: +31 20 4222742

#448
Hesp
Category: Nightlife, GastroPub
Average price: €8-20
Area: Oost, Oosterparkbuurt
Address: Weesperzijde 130-131 1091 ER Amsterdam The Netherlands
Phone: +31 20 6651202

#449
Starbucks
Category: Coffee & Tea, Cafe
Average price: €8-20
Area: Centrum
Address: Leidsestraat 101 1017 NZ Amsterdam The Netherlands
Phone: +31 20 6241592

#450
Cafe Marie
Category: GastroPub, European
Average price: €8-20
Area: Zuid, De Pijp
Address: Marie Heinekenplein 5 1072 MH Amsterdam The Netherlands
Phone: +31 20 2232096

#451
Café Thijssen
Category: Pub, Sandwiches
Average price: €8-20
Area: Centrum, Jordaan
Address: Brouwersgracht 107-II 1015 GD Amsterdam The Netherlands
Phone: +31 20 6238994

#452
Het Paardje
Category: GastroPub
Average price: €8-20
Area: Zuid, De Pijp
Address: Gerard Douplein 1 1073 XE Amsterdam The Netherlands
Phone: +31 20 6643539

#453
Uliveto traiteur
Category: Italian, Do-It-Yourself Food
Average price: €21-40
Area: Centrum
Address: Weteringschans 118 1017 XT Amsterdam The Netherlands
Phone: +31 20 4230099

#454
Boom
Category: European, French
Average price: €8-20
Area: Oost, Dapperbuurt
Address: Linnaeusstraat 63 1093 EJ Amsterdam The Netherlands
Phone: +31 20 6655224

#455
MC Theater
Category: Caribbean
Average price: €8-20
Area: West
Address: Polonceaukade 5 1014 DA Amsterdam The Netherlands
Phone: +31 20 4750425

#456
BIHP
Category: Art Gallery, French
Average price: €21-40
Area: Centrum, Negen Straatjes
Address: Keizersgracht 335 1016 EG
Amsterdam The Netherlands
Phone: +31 20 4282609

#457
Mercat
Category: Spanish
Average price: €21-40
Area: Oost
Address: Oostelijke Handelskade 4
1019 BM Amsterdam The Netherlands
Phone: +31 20 3446424

#458
L'Express
Category: French
Average price: €21-40
Area: Centrum
Address: Utrechtsestraat 29-4
1017 VH Amsterdam The Netherlands
Phone: +31 20 6205129

#459
Café 't Hooischip
Category: Dive Bar, GastroPub
Average price: €8-20
Area: Centrum
Address: Amstel 31 1011 PT
Amsterdam The Netherlands
Phone: +31 20 6238733

#460
Tapas Café Duende
Category: Spanish, Tapas
Average price: €8-20
Area: Centrum, Jordaan
Address: Lindengracht 62-BG
1015 KJ Amsterdam The Netherlands
Phone: +31 20 4206692

#461
Casa Del Gusto
Category: Italian, Do-It-Yourself Food,
Ethnic Food
Average price: Under €7
Area: Centrum
Address: Kerkstraat 121 1017 GE
Amsterdam The Netherlands
Phone: +31 20 3308330

#462
Restaurant Freud
Category: Mediterranean
Average price: €8-20
Area: West
Address: Spaarndammerstraat 424
1013 SZ Amsterdam The Netherlands
Phone: +31 20 6885548

#463
Saskia's Huiskamer
Category: Portuguese
Average price: €8-20
Area: Zuid, De Pijp
Address: Albert Cuypstraat 203 C
1073 BE Amsterdam The Netherlands
Phone: +31 628 629839

#464
Café Saloon
Category: Cafe
Average price: €8-20
Area: Centrum
Address: Lijnbaansgracht 271
1017 RL Amsterdam The Netherlands
Phone: +31 20 6230466

#465
Quattro Gatti
Category: Italian
Average price: €21-40
Area: Centrum, Negen Straatjes
Address: Hartenstraat 3-1 1016 BZ
Amsterdam The Netherlands
Phone: +31 20 4214585

#466
Tjin's Exotische Broodjes
Category: Bakeries, Food Delivery
Services, Sandwiches
Average price: Under €7
Area: Zuid, De Pijp
Address: Van Woustraat 17 1074 AA
Amsterdam The Netherlands
Phone: +31 20 6793758

#467
Hakata Senpachi
Category: Japanese
Average price: €21-40
Area: Zuid, Rivierenbuurt
Address: Wielingenstraat 16-HS 1078
KK Amsterdam The Netherlands
Phone: +31 20 6625823

#468
Himalaya New Age Shop
Category: Books, Mags,
Music & Video, Breakfast & Brunch
Average price: €8-20
Area: Centrum, De Wallen
Address: Warmoesstraat 56 1012 JG
Amsterdam The Netherlands
Phone: +31 20 6260899

#469
Eau de Vie
Category: Mediterranean, French
Average price: €21-40
Area: Zuid, Rivierenbuurt
Address: Maasstraat 20 1078 HK
Amsterdam The Netherlands
Phone: +31 20 6629588

#470
Di Sale
Category: Italian
Average price: €21-40
Area: Zuid, Museumkwartier
Address: Willemsparkweg 155 1071 GX
Amsterdam The Netherlands
Phone: +31 20 6623853

#471
Midtown Grill
Category: Steakhouses
Average price: €21-40
Area: West
Address: Stadhouderskade 12 1054 ES
Amsterdam The Netherlands
Phone: +31 20 6075529

#472
Beulings
Category: Restaurant
Average price: €21-40
Area: Centrum
Address: Beulingstraat 9-HS 1017 BA
Amsterdam The Netherlands
Phone: +31 20 3206100

#473
Restaurant Orontes
Category: Turkish
Average price: €8-20
Area: Zuid, De Pijp
Address: Albert Cuypstraat 40-BG 1072
CV Amsterdam The Netherlands
Phone: +31 20 6796225

#474
Roem
Category: Do-It-Yourself Food,
GastroPub
Average price: €8-20
Area: Centrum, Jordaan
Address: Prinsengracht 126 1015 EA
Amsterdam The Netherlands
Phone: +31 20 4277955

#475
Asian Kitchen
Category: Chinese
Average price: €8-20
Area: Centrum
Address: Vijzelstraat 5 a 1017 HD
Amsterdam The Netherlands
Phone: +31 20 6202016

#476
De Blaffende Vis
Category: GastroPub
Average price: €8-20
Area: Centrum, Jordaan
Address: Westerstraat 118 1015 MN
Amsterdam The Netherlands
Phone: +31 20 6251721

#477
Proust
Category: GastroPub
Average price: €8-20
Area: Centrum, Jordaan
Address: Noordermarkt 4 1015 MV
Amsterdam The Netherlands
Phone: +31 20 6239145

#478
Eetcafé de Staalmeesters
Category: GastroPub
Average price: €8-20
Area: Centrum
Address: Kloveniersburgwal 127-HS
1011 KD Amsterdam The Netherlands
Phone: +31 20 6234218

#479
Mappa
Category: Italian
Average price: €21-40
Area: Centrum, De Wallen
Address: Nes 59 1012 KD Amsterdam
The Netherlands
Phone: +31 20 5289170

#480
L'invité le Restaurant
Category: French, Vegetarian,
Do-It-Yourself Food
Average price: Above €41
Area: Centrum, Jordaan
Address: Bloemgracht 47 1016 KD
Amsterdam The Netherlands
Phone: +31 20 5702010

#481
Orloff
Category: GastroPub
Average price: €8-20
Area: Centrum
Address: Kadijksplein 10-12 1018 AC
Amsterdam The Netherlands
Phone: +31 20 3203347

#482
Het Paleis
Category: GastroPub
Average price: €8-20
Area: Centrum
Address: Paleisstraat 16 1012 RB
Amsterdam The Netherlands
Phone: +31 20 6260600

#483
Fifteen
Category: Italian
Average price: €8-20
Area: Oost
Address: Jollemanhof 9 1019 GW
Amsterdam The Netherlands
Phone: +31 20 5095015

#484
Café Goos
Category: GastroPub
Average price: €8-20
Area: Zuid, Rivierenbuurt
Address: Maasstraat 74-BG 1078 HL
Amsterdam The Netherlands
Phone: +31 20 6793443

#485
Braque
Category: Cafe, French
Average price: €21-40
Area: Zuid, De Pijp
Address: Albert Cuypstraat 29-31 1072
CK Amsterdam The Netherlands
Phone: +31 20 6707357

#486
Stout
Category: Cafe
Average price: €8-20
Area: Centrum, Haarlemmerbuurt
Address: Haarlemmerstraat 73
1013 EL Amsterdam The Netherlands
Phone: +31 20 6163664

#487
Gent aan de Schinkel
Category: GastroPub
Average price: €8-20
Area: Zuid, Hoofddorppleinbuurt
Address: Theophile de Bockstraat 1
1058 TV Amsterdam The Netherlands
Phone: +31 20 3882851

#488
VandeMarkt
Category: French, Mediterranean
Average price: €21-40
Area: Oost
Address: Weesperzijde 144-147
1091 EZ Amsterdam The Netherlands
Phone: +31 20 4686958

#489
Het Badhuis
Category: French
Average price: €8-20
Area: Oost, Indische Buurt
Address: Javaplein 21 1095 CJ
Amsterdam The Netherlands
Phone: +31 20 6651226

#490
La Place Openbare Bibliotheek
Category: Restaurant
Average price: €8-20
Area: Centrum
Address: Oosterdokskade 143
1011 AD Amsterdam The Netherlands
Phone: +31 20 5230870

#491
Miss Korea
Category: Korean, Japanese
Average price: €8-20
Area: Zuid, De Pijp
Address: Albert Cuypstraat 66-70 1072
CW Amsterdam The Netherlands
Phone: +31 20 6790606

#492
Thrill Grill
Category: American, Burgers
Average price: €8-20
Area: Centrum, De Wallen
Address: Wolvenstraat 22 1016 EP
Amsterdam The Netherlands
Phone: +31 20 3033968

#493
Café de Groene Vlinder
Category: GastroPub
Average price: €8-20
Area: Zuid, De Pijp
Address: Albert Cuypstraat 130 1072 EA
Amsterdam The Netherlands
Phone: +31 20 4702500

#494
Eetcafé de Hut
Category: GastroPub
Average price: €8-20
Area: Zuid, Stadionbuurt
Address: Olympiaplein 132 1076 AK
Amsterdam The Netherlands
Phone: +31 20 6718426

#495
De Ponteneur
Category: GastroPub
Average price: €8-20
Area: Oost, Dapperbuurt
Address: Eerste van Swindenstraat 581
1093 LC Amsterdam The Netherlands
Phone: +31 20 6680680

#496
The Tara
Category: Bar, Irish, GastroPub
Average price: €8-20
Area: Centrum, De Wallen
Address: Rokin 89 1012 KL Amsterdam
The Netherlands
Phone: +31 20 4274657

#497
Café Van Zuylen
Category: GastroPub, European
Average price: €8-20
Area: Centrum
Address: Torensteeg 8-BG 1012 TH
Amsterdam The Netherlands
Phone: +31 20 6391055

#498
Starbikes Rental
Category: Breakfast & Brunch
Average price: Under €7
Area: Centrum
Address: De Ruyterkade 127 1011 AC
Amsterdam The Netherlands
Phone: +31 20 6203215

#499
Bombay Inn
Category: Pakistani, Indian
Average price: Under €7
Area: Centrum
Address: Lange Leidsedwarsstraat 46
1017 NL Amsterdam The Netherlands
Phone: +31 20 6241784

#500
Billy Thai
Category: Thai
Average price: Under €7
Area: Centrum, Jordaan
Address: Prinsengracht 358,
1016 JA Amsterdam The Netherlands
Phone: +31 20 3304220

TOP 500 ATTRACTIONS

Recommended by Locals & Trevelers
(From #1 to #500)

#1
Anne Frank Huis
Category: Museum
Area: Centrum
Address: Prinsengracht 267 1016 GV
Amsterdam The Netherlands
Phone: +31 20 5567105

#2
Van Gogh Museum
Category: Museum
Area: Zuid, Museumkwartier
Address: Paulus Potterstraat 7
1071 CX Amsterdam The Netherlands
Phone: +31 20 5705200

#3
De Melkweg
Category: Dance Club, Art Gallery
Area: Centrum
Address: Lijnbaansgracht 234
1017 PH Amsterdam The Netherlands
Phone: +31 20 5318181

#4
Pathé Tuschinski
Category: Cinema
Area: Centrum
Address: Reguliersbreestraat 26
1017 CN Amsterdam The Netherlands
Phone: +31 900 1458

#5
Het Rijksmuseum
Category: Museum
Area: Zuid, Museumkwartier
Address: Museumtraat 1 1071 CZ
Amsterdam The Netherlands
Phone: +31 20 6747000

#6
Bar Oldenhof
Category: Wine Bar, Jazz & Blues,
Cocktail Bar
Area: Centrum, Jordaan
Address: Elandsgracht 84 1016 TZ
Amsterdam The Netherlands
Phone: +31 20 7513273

#7
House of Bols
Category: Museum, Venues & Events
Area: Zuid, Museumkwartier
Address: Paulus Potterstraat 14 1071
CZ Amsterdam The Netherlands
Phone: +31 20 5708575

#8
The Movies
Category: Cinema
Area: Centrum, Haarlemmerbuurt
Address: Haarlemmerdijk 161 1013 KH
Amsterdam The Netherlands
Phone: +31 20 6245790

#9
Heineken Experience
Category: Museum, Venues & Events
Area: Zuid, De Pijp
Address: Stadhouderskade 78 1072 AE
Amsterdam The Netherlands
Phone: +31 20 5239222

#10
Verzetsmuseum
Category: Museum
Area: Plantagebuurt, Centrum
Address: Plantage Kerklaan 61 1018 CX
Amsterdam The Netherlands
Phone: +31 20 6202535

#11
Grachtenrundfahrten
Category: Transportation
Area: Phone number
Address: Prins Hendrikkade 33a
Amsterdam, Noord-Holland The
Netherlands

#12
Hermitage Aan de Amstel
Category: Museum
Area: Plantagebuurt, Centrum
Address: Nieuwe Herengracht 18 1018
DP Amsterdam The Netherlands
Phone: +31 20 4715257

#13
Het Concertgebouw
Category: Landmark& Historical
Buildings, Music Venues
Area: Zuid, Museumkwartier
Address: Concertgebouwplein 2-6 1071
LN Amsterdam The Netherlands
Phone: +31 20 5730573

#14
De Albert Cuypmarkt
Category: Arts & Entertainment
Area: Zuid, De Pijp
Address: Albert Cuypstraat 1072 CX
Amsterdam The Netherlands

#15
Tassenmuseum Hendrikje
Category: Museum
Area: Centrum
Address: Herengracht 573 1017 CD
Amsterdam The Netherlands
Phone: +31 20 5246452

#16
Foam Fotografiemuseum
Category: Museum, Art Gallery
Area: Centrum
Address: Keizersgracht 609 1017 DS
Amsterdam The Netherlands
Phone: +31 20 5516500

#17
Vondelpark Openluchttheater
Category: Jazz & Blues, Performing
Arts, Music Venues
Area: Zuid, Museumkwartier
Address: Vondelpark 1071 AA
Amsterdam The Netherlands

#18
Hannekes Boom
Category: GastroPub, Jazz & Blues,
Cafe, Pub
Area: Centrum
Address: Dijksgracht 4 1019 BS
Amsterdam The Netherlands
Phone: +31 20 4199820

#19
EYE Filminstituut
Category: Cinema, Museum
Area: Noord
Address: IJpromenade 1 1031 KT
Amsterdam The Netherlands
Phone: +31 20 5891400

#20
Het Kattenkabinet
Category: Museum
Area: Centrum
Address: Herengracht 499 1017 BT
Amsterdam The Netherlands
Phone: +31 20 6811378

#21
The Amsterdam Dungeon
Category: Museum
Area: Centrum
Address: Rokin 78 1012 KW
Amsterdam The Netherlands
Phone: +31 20 5308530

#22
Hollandsche Schouwburg
Category: Performing Arts, Museum
Area: Plantagebuurt, Centrum
Address: Plantage Middenlaan 24 1018
DE Amsterdam The Netherlands
Phone: +31 20 5310340

#23
Erik's Delicatessen
Category: Wineries
Area: Oost, Oosterparkbuurt
Address: Beukenplein 16 1091 KH
Amsterdam The Netherlands
Phone: +31 20 6943077

#24
Science Center NEMO
Category: Museum
Area: Centrum
Address: Oosterdok 2 1011 VX
Amsterdam The Netherlands
Phone: +31 20 5313233

#25
Het Begijnhof
Category: Botanical Garden, Church
Area: Centrum
Address: Nieuwezijds Voorburgwal 373
1012 RM Amsterdam The Netherlands
Phone: +31 20 6233565

#26
Koninklijk Paleis Amsterdam
Category: Museum, Landmark&
Historical Buildings
Area: Centrum
Address: Nieuwezijds Voorburgwal 147
1012 RJ Amsterdam The Netherlands
Phone: +31 20 6204060

#27
Muziektheater
Category: Landmark& Historical
Buildings, Music Venues, Opera & Ballet,
Performing Arts
Area: Centrum
Address: Waterlooplein 22 1011 PG
Amsterdam The Netherlands
Phone: +31 20 6255455

#28
Tropenmuseum
Category: Museum
Area: Oost, Oosterparkbuurt
Address: Linnaeusstraat 2 1092 CK
Amsterdam The Netherlands
Phone: +31 20 5688215

#29
Amsterdam Museum
Category: Museum
Area: Centrum
Address: Nieuwezijds Voorburgwal 359
1012 RM Amsterdam The Netherlands
Phone: +31 20 5231822

#30
Stichting de Poezenboot
Category: Animal Shelters,
Social Club, Local Flavor
Area: Centrum
Address: Singel 38-G 1015 AB
Amsterdam The Netherlands
Phone: +31 20 6258794

#31
Café Alto
Category: Jazz & Blues
Area: Centrum
Address: Korte Leidsedwarsstraat 115
1017 PX Amsterdam The Netherlands
Phone: +31 20 6263249

#33
Leidseplein
Category: Landmark& Historical
Buildings
Area: Centrum
Address: Leidseplein 1-35 1017 PR
Amsterdam The Netherlands
Phone: +31 20 6842090

#32
Fashion Week Amsterdam
Category: Festival, Fashion
Area: West, Bos en Lommer
Address: Haarlemmerweg 317-D 1051
LG Amsterdam The Netherlands
Phone: +31 20 6842878

#34
Huis Marseille
Category: Museum
Area: Centrum
Address: Keizersgracht 401 1016 EK
Amsterdam The Netherlands
Phone: +31 20 5318989

#35
DeLaMar Theater
Category: Performing Arts
Area: Centrum
Address: Marnixstraat 402 1071 DR
Amsterdam The Netherlands
Phone: +31 20 5552627

#36
Kriterion
Category: Cinema, Pub, Music Venues
Area: Plantagebuurt, Centrum
Address: Roetersstraat 170 1018 WE
Amsterdam The Netherlands
Phone: +31 20 6231708

#37
Woonbootmuseum
Category: Museum
Area: Centrum, Jordaan
Address: Prinsengracht 296-TO 1016
HW Amsterdam The Netherlands
Phone: +31 20 4270750

#38
Museumnacht Amsterdam
Category: Museum
Area: Oost
Address: Piet Heinkade 11 1019 BR
Amsterdam The Netherlands
Phone: +31 20 5270785

#39
Museum Willet-Holthuysen
Category: Museum
Area: Centrum
Address: Herengracht 605 1017 CE
Amsterdam The Netherlands
Phone: +31 20 5231822

#40
Amsterdam Museum
Category: Museum
Area: Phone number
Address: Kalverstraat 92 1001 AC
Amsterdam The Netherlands

#41
Museum Het Rembrandthuis
Category: Museum
Area: Centrum
Address: Jodenbreestraat 4 1011 NK
Amsterdam The Netherlands
Phone: +31 20 5200400

#42
Bourbon Street
Category: Jazz & Blues
Area: Centrum
Address: Leidsekruisstraat 6-8 1017 RH
Amsterdam The Netherlands
Phone: +31 20 6233440

#43
Atelier Molenpad
Category: Art Gallery, Local Flavor
Area: Centrum
Address: Molenpad 17d 1016 GL
Amsterdam The Netherlands
Phone: +31 610 915544

#44
Gay Canal Parade
Category: Festival
Area: Centrum, Negen Straatjes
Address: Prinsengracht Amsterdam,
Noord-Holland The Netherlands

#45
Studio/K
Category: Dance Club,
Cinema, GastroPub
Area: Oost, Indische Buurt
Address: Timorplein 62 1094 CC
Amsterdam The Netherlands
Phone: +31 20 6920422

#46
Amsterdam Tulip Museum
Category: Museum, Flowers & Gifts
Area: Centrum, Jordaan
Address: Prinsengracht 112 1015 EA
Amsterdam The Netherlands
Phone: +31 20 4210095

#47
Pompstation Bar&Grill
Category: Restaurant, Music Venues
Area: Oost, Zeeburg
Address: Zeeburgerdijk 52 1094 AE
Amsterdam The Netherlands
Phone: +31 20 6922888

#48
De Oude Kerk
Category: Museum, Church
Area: Centrum, De Wallen
Address: Oudekerksplein 23 1012 GX
Amsterdam The Netherlands
Phone: +31 20 6258284

#49
Café de Dokter
Category: Pub, Jazz & Blues
Area: Centrum
Address: Rozenboomsteeg 4 1012 PR
Amsterdam The Netherlands
Phone: +31 20 6264427

#50
IDFA
Category: Festival
Area: Centrum
Address: Frederiksplein 52 1017 XN
Amsterdam The Netherlands
Phone: +31 20 4220348

#51
De Kleine Komedie
Category: Arts & Entertainment
Area: Centrum
Address: Amstel 56-58 1017 AC
Amsterdam The Netherlands
Phone: +31 20 6240534

#52
Pathé de Munt
Category: Cinema
Area: Centrum
Address: Vijzelstraat 15 1017 HD
Amsterdam The Netherlands
Phone: +31 900 2357284

#53
Madame Tussauds Museum
Category: Museum
Area: Centrum
Address: Dam square Amsterdam,
Noord-Holland The Netherlands
Phone: +31 622 9949

#54
Tolhuistuin
Category: Music Venues,
Performing Arts
Area: Noord
Address: Tolhuisweg 2 1031 CL
Amsterdam The Netherlands
Phone: +31 20 7630650

#55
**Holland International
Canal Cruises**
Category: Restaurant
Area: Centrum
Address: Prins Hendrikkade 33a 1012
TM Amsterdam The Netherlands
Phone: +31 20 6253035

#56
CC MuziekCafé
Category: Jazz & Blues,
Music Venues, Cafe
Area: Zuid, De Pijp
Address: Rustenburgerstraat 384 1072
HG Amsterdam The Netherlands
Phone: +31 624 236956

#57
Lomography
Category: Photography Stores, Art
Gallery
Area: Centrum, Negen Straatjes
Address: Herengracht 298 1016 BX
Amsterdam The Netherlands

#58
Circus Elleboog
Category: Performing Arts
Area: Centrum, Jordaan
Address: Passeerdersgracht 32 1016
XH Amsterdam The Netherlands
Phone: +31 20 6235326

#59
Het Sexmuseum Amsterdam
Category: Museum, Adult Entertainment
Area: Centrum
Address: Damrak 18 1012 LH
Amsterdam The Netherlands
Phone: +31 20 6228376

#60
Kaashuis Tromp
Category: Cheese Shops, Wineries
Area: Centrum
Address: Utrechtsestraat 90 1017 VS
Amsterdam The Netherlands
Phone: +31 20 6241399

#61
De Parade
Category: Performing Arts
Area: Zuid
Address: Martin Luther Kingpark
Amsterdam, Noord-Holland
The Netherlands
Phone: +31 33 4654555

#62
Rialto
Category: Cinema
Area: Zuid, De Pijp
Address: Ceintuurbaan 338 1072 GN
Amsterdam The Netherlands
Phone: +31 20 6623488

#63
Joods Historisch Museum
Category: Museum
Area: Centrum
Address: Nieuwe Amstelstraat 1
1011 PL Amsterdam The Netherlands
Phone: +31 20 5310310

#64
Gashouder
Category: Music Venues
Area: Westerpark, West
Address: Haarlemmerweg 8-10
1014 BE Amsterdam The Netherlands
Phone: +31 20 5974458

#65
De Nieuwe Anita
Category: Pub, Performing Arts,
Music Venues
Area: West, Frederik Hendrikbuurt
Address: Frederik Hendrikstraat 111
1052 HN Amsterdam The Netherlands
Phone: +31 641 503512

#66
Pathe City
Category: Cinema
Area: Centrum
Address: Kleine-Gartmanplantsoen
15-19 1017 RP Amsterdam
The Netherlands
Phone: +31 900 2357284

#67
Het Scheepvaartmuseum
Category: Museum
Area: Centrum
Address: Kattenburgerplein 1
1018 KK Amsterdam The Netherlands
Phone: +31 20 5232222

#68
Amsterdam Light Festival
Category: Festival, Local Flavor
Area: Centrum
Address: Amstel 1 1011 PN Amsterdam
The Netherlands

#69
Theater Carré
Category: Opera & Ballet, Music
Venues, Performing Arts
Area: Plantagebuurt, Centrum
Address: Amstel 115-125 1018 EM
Amsterdam The Netherlands

#70
Hutspot
Category: Art Gallery, Cafe
Area: Zuid, De Pijp
Address: Van Woustraat 4 1073 LL
Amsterdam The Netherlands
Phone: +31 613 651566

#71
Compagnietheater
Category: Performing Arts
Area: Centrum
Address: Kloveniersburgwal 50
1012 CX Amsterdam The Netherlands
Phone: +31 20 5205310

#72
De Looier
Category: Arts & Entertainment
Area: Centrum, Jordaan
Address: Elandsgracht 109 1016 TT
Amsterdam The Netherlands
Phone: +31 20 6249038

#73
Prinsengrachtconcert
Category: Festival, Opera & Ballet
Area: Centrum, Negen Straatjes
Address: Prinsengracht 1016 DN
Amsterdam The Netherlands

#74
Sugarfactory
Category: Dance Club, Performing Arts,
Music Venues
Area: Centrum
Address: Lijnbaansgracht 238 1017 ph
Amsterdam The Netherlands
Phone: +31 20 6265006

#75
Moooi
Category: Interior Design,
Home Decor, Art Gallery
Area: Centrum, Jordaan
Address: Westerstraat 187 1015 MA
Amsterdam The Netherlands
Phone: +31 20 5287760

#76
Allard Pierson Museum
Category: Museum
Area: Centrum, De Wallen
Address: Oude Turfmarkt 127
1012 GC Amsterdam The Netherlands
Phone: +31 20 5252556

#77
B.J.
Category: Beer, Wine & Spirits,
Wineries, Wholesale Stores
Area: Zuid, Apollobuurt
Address: Beethovenstraat 27 1077 HM
Amsterdam The Netherlands
Phone: +31 20 6626208

#78
De Vredespijp
Category: Coffee & Tea, Art Gallery
Area: Zuid, De Pijp
Address: Eerste van der Helststraat 11a
1073 AA Amsterdam The Netherlands
Phone: +31 20 6764855

#79
Kermis Op De Dam
Category: Festival
Area: Centrum
Address: Dam Amsterdam, Noord-
Holland The Netherlands

#80
Ketelhuis
Category: Venues & Events, Cinema
Area: West
Address: Pazzanistraat 4 1014 DB
Amsterdam The Netherlands
Phone: +31 20 6840090

#81
Museum van Loon
Category: Museum, Venues & Events
Area: Centrum
Address: Keizersgracht 672 1017 ET
Amsterdam The Netherlands
Phone: +31 20 6245255

#82
Museum Het Grachtenhuis
Category: Museum, Local Flavor
Area: Centrum
Address: Herengracht 386 1016 CJ
Amsterdam The Netherlands
Phone: +31 20 4211656

#83
Last Minute Ticket Shop
Category: Arts & Entertainment
Area: Centrum
Address: Leidseplein 26 1017 PT
Amsterdam The Netherlands
Phone: +31 20 7959950

#84
Brug9
Category: Jazz & Blues
Area: Centrum
Address: Singel 161 1001 EJ
Amsterdam The Netherlands
Phone: +31 654 954358

#85
Café The Cotton Club
Category: Jazz & Blues
Area: Centrum
Address: Nieuwmarkt 5 1011 JP
Amsterdam The Netherlands
Phone: +31 20 6266192

#86
Amsterdam Cheese Museum
Category: Museum, Cheese Shops
Area: Centrum, Jordaan
Address: Prinsengracht 112 1015 EA
Amsterdam The Netherlands
Phone: +31 55 4787111

#87
Reederij P.
Category: Tours
Area: Centrum, De Wallen
Address: Rokin t/o nr. 125 1012 KK
Amsterdam The Netherlands
Phone: +31 20 6233810

#88
Toomler
Category: Performing Arts,
Comedy Club, Pub
Area: Zuid, Apollobuurt
Address: Breitnerstraat 2 1077 BL
Amsterdam The Netherlands
Phone: +31 20 6707400

#89
De Duivel
Category: Music Venues, Pub
Area: Centrum
Address: Reguliersdwarsstraat 87
1017 BK Amsterdam The Netherlands
Phone: +31 20 6266184

#90
Friday Night Skate
Category: Social Club
Area: Zuid, Museumkwartier
Address: Vondelpark Amsterdam,
Noord-Holland The Netherlands

#91
Café de Buurvrouw
Category: Pub, Botanical Garden
Area: Centrum, De Wallen
Address: Sint Pieterspoortsteeg 29-1
1012 HM Amsterdam The Netherlands
Phone: +31 20 6259654

#92
P.C.
Category: Shopping, Arts &
Entertainment, Restaurant
Area: Zuid, Museumkwartier
Address: Pieter Cornelisz Hooftstraat
1071 BR Amsterdam The Netherlands
Phone: +31 20 6702606

#93
CineCenter
Category: Cinema
Area: Centrum
Address: Lijnbaansgracht 236
1017 PH Amsterdam The Netherlands
Phone: +31 20 6236615

#94
Filmtheater De Uitkijk
Category: Cinema
Area: Centrum
Address: Prinsengracht 452
1017 KE Amsterdam The Netherlands
Phone: +31 20 6237460

#95
Pakhuis De Zwijger
Category: Performing Arts,
Brasseries, Venues & Events
Area: Oost
Address: Piet Heinkade 179
1019 HC Amsterdam The Netherlands
Phone: +31 20 6246380

#96
GO Gallery
Category: Art Gallery
Area: Centrum, Jordaan
Address: Prinsengracht 64-BG
1015 DX Amsterdam The Netherlands
Phone: +31 20 4229580

#97
De Nieuwe Kerk
Category: Church, Museum
Area: Centrum
Address: Dam 1012 NL
Amsterdam The Netherlands
Phone: +31 20 6268168

#98
Hart's Wijnhandel
Category: Wineries
Area: Centrum
Address: Vijzelgracht 27 1017 HN
Amsterdam The Netherlands
Phone: +31 20 6238350

#99
Restaurant Barrique
Category: Wine Bar, Wineries, French
Area: Zuid, De Pijp
Address: 1072 VW 1072 VW
Amsterdam The Netherlands
Phone: +31 20 2218162

#100
**Moya & Van Der Laag
Galerie & Atelier**
Category: Jewelry, Art Gallery
Area: Centrum
Address: Spiegelgracht 36 SOUS 1017
JS Amsterdam The Netherlands
Phone: +31 20 7370679

#101
Muziekgebouw Aan 't IJ
Category: Music Venues
Area: Centrum
Address: Piet Heinkade 1 1019 BR
Amsterdam The Netherlands
Phone: +31 20 7882010

#102
**Stichting Koninklijk
Concertgebouworkest**
Category: Performing Arts
Area: Zuid, Museumkwartier
Address: Jacob Obrechtstraat 51 1071
KJ Amsterdam The Netherlands
Phone: +31 20 3051010

#103
Comedy Café
Category: Arts & Entertainment
Area: Centrum
Address: Max Euweplein 43
1017 MA Amsterdam The Netherlands
Phone: +31 20 6383971

#104
Torture Museum
Category: Museum
Area: Centrum
Address: Singel 449 1012 WP
Amsterdam The Netherlands
Phone: +31 20 3206642

#105
Wijnkoperij de Gouden Ton
Category: Wineries
Area: Zuid, Museumkwartier
Address: Willemsparkweg 158 1071 HS
Amsterdam The Netherlands
Phone: +31 20 6796231

#106
Quartier Putain
Category: Coffee & Tea, Art Gallery
Area: Centrum, De Wallen
Address: Oudekerksplein 4a 1012 GZ
Amsterdam The Netherlands

#107
Wilhelmina Huiskamer Festival
Category: Festival
Area: West, Oud West
Address: J.J. Cremerplein 34
Amsterdam, Noord-Holland The
Netherlands
Phone: +31 20 6851553

#108
Peter Donkersloot Galerie
Category: Art Gallery
Area: Centrum
Address: Spiegelgracht 14 - 16
1017 JR Amsterdam The Netherlands
Phone: +31 20 6236538

#109
Sociëteit De Kring
Category: Arts & Entertainment
Area: Centrum
Address: Kleine-Gartmanplantsoen 7-9
1017 RP Amsterdam The Netherlands
Phone: +31 20 6236985

#110
London Calling
Category: Festival
Area: Centrum
Address: Weteringschans 6-8 1017 SG
Amsterdam The Netherlands
Phone: +31 20 6264521

#111
Stadsschouwburg Amsterdam
Category: Performing Arts
Area: Centrum
Address: Leidseplein 26 1017 PT
Amsterdam The Netherlands
Phone: +31 20 6242311

#112
Last Minute Ticketshop
Category: Arts & Entertainment
Area: Centrum
Address: Leidseplein 26 1017 PT
Amsterdam The Netherlands
Phone: +31 20 7959950

#113
Amsterdam Dance Event
Category: Music Venues
Area: Centrum, Negen Straatjes
Address: Keizersgracht 324 Amsterdam,
Noord-Holland The Netherlands

#114
Vrijmarkt
Category: Festival
Area: Phone number
Address: Amsterdam, Noord-Holland
The Netherlands

#115
Madame Tussauds
Category: Museum
Area: Centrum
Address: Dam 20 1012 NP
Amsterdam The Netherlands
Phone: +31 20 5221010

#116
UVA Bijzondere Collecties
Category: Museum
Area: Centrum, De Wallen
Address: Oude Turfmarkt 129 1012 GC
Amsterdam The Netherlands
Phone: +31 20 5257300

#117
Club Dauphine
Category: Music Venues, Dance Club
Area: Oost, Watergraafsmeer
Address: Prins Bernhardplein 175 1097
BL Amsterdam The Netherlands
Phone: +31 20 4621646

#118
Theater Bellevue
Category: Performing Arts,
Music Venues
Area: West
Address: Leidsekade 90-AHS 1017 PN
Amsterdam The Netherlands
Phone: +31 20 5305300

#119
Brilmuseum/Brillenwinkel
Category: Museum
Area: Centrum
Address: Gasthuismolensteeg 7 1016
AM Amsterdam The Netherlands
Phone: +31 20 4212414

#120
Christie's
Category: Art Gallery
Area: Zuid, Museumkwartier
Address: Cornelis Schuytstraat 57 1071
JG Amsterdam The Netherlands
Phone: +31 20 5755255

#121
OT301
Category: Music Venues
Area: Oud West
Address: Overtoom 301 1054 HW
Amsterdam The Netherlands

#122
Amsterdam Canal Cruises
Category: Venues & Events,
Arts & Entertainment
Area: Zuid, De Pijp
Address: Stadhouderskade 550
1072 AE Amsterdam The Netherlands
Phone: +31 20 6265636

#123
Sail Amsterdam
Category: Arts & Entertainment
Area: Centrum
Address: Kattenburgerstraat 7
1018 JA Amsterdam The Netherlands
Phone: +31 20 6811804

#124
Monega
Category: Wineries
Area: Oost, Dapperbuurt
Address: Pieter Vlamingstraat 40
1093 AE Amsterdam The Netherlands
Phone: +31 20 4634902

#125
Amsterdam Convention Factory
Category: Venues & Events,
Arts & Entertainment
Area: Centrum
Address: Czaar Peterstraat 213
1018 PL Amsterdam The Netherlands
Phone: +31 20 5356940

#126
Salsa4Fun Salsaschool
Category: Performing Arts
Area: West
Address: Spaarndammerstraat 460
1013 SZ Amsterdam The Netherlands
Phone: +31 652 473047

#127
Badcuyp
Category: Restaurant, Music Venues
Area: Zuid, De Pijp
Address: Eerste Sweelinckstraat 10
1073 CM Amsterdam The Netherlands
Phone: +31 20 6759669

#128
The Affordable Art Fair Amsterdam
Category: Festival
Area: Centrum
Address: Prinsengracht 715 BG 1017
JW Amsterdam The Netherlands
Phone: +31 20 6227728

#129
Cave Rokin' Wine & Liquor Shop
Category: Wineries
Area: Centrum
Address: Rokin 60-E 1012 KV
Amsterdam The Netherlands
Phone: +31 20 6250628

#130
Garrity Fine Wines
Category: Wineries
Area: Oost, Zeeburg
Address: C. van Eesterenlaan 31-33
1019 JK Amsterdam The Netherlands
Phone: +31 20 4199792

#131
De Bazel
Category: Museum, Venues & Events
Area: Centrum
Address: Vijzelstraat 32 1017 HL
Amsterdam The Netherlands
Phone: +31 20 2511800

#132
De Balie Theater
Category: Performing Arts
Area: Centrum
Address: Kleine-Gartmanplantsoen 10
1017 RR Amsterdam The Netherlands
Phone: +31 20 5535100

#133
De Wijnwinkel Renalda
Category: Wineries
Area: Centrum, Negen Straatjes
Address: Runstraat 23 1016 GJ
Amsterdam The Netherlands
Phone: +31 20 6380157

#134
Reflex New Art Gallery
Category: Art Gallery
Area: Centrum
Address: Weteringschans 83 1017 RZ
Amsterdam The Netherlands
Phone: +31 20 4235423

#135
Bijbels Museum
Category: Landmark& Historical
Buildings, Museum
Area: Centrum, Negen Straatjes
Address: Herengracht 366 1016 CH
Amsterdam The Netherlands
Phone: +31 20 6242436

#136
'Skek
Category: Restaurant, Pub, Music
Venues
Area: Centrum, De Wallen
Address: Zeedijk 4-8 1012 AX
Amsterdam The Netherlands
Phone: +31 20 4270551

#137
Pluk de Nacht
Category: Festival
Area: Centrum, Haarlemmerbuurt
Address: Westerdoksdijk/s100
Amsterdam, Noord-Holland The
Netherlands
Phone: +31 20 6392170

#138
Diamant Museum Amsterdam
Category: Museum
Area: Zuid, Museumkwartier
Address: Paulus Potterstraat 8 1071 CZ
Amsterdam The Netherlands
Phone: +31 20 3055300

#139
Movie Center
Category: Arts & Entertainment
Area: Zuid, De Pijp
Address: Ferdinand Bolstraat 32-III
1072 LK Amsterdam The Netherlands
Phone: +31 20 6790576

#140
The Wine Cellar
Category: Wineries
Area: Centrum
Address: Nieuwezijds Voorburgwal 137
1012 RJ Amsterdam The Netherlands
Phone: +31 654 712201

#141
World Press Photo
Category: Festival, Art Gallery
Area: Centrum, De Wallen
Address: Oudekerksplein 23 1012 GX
Amsterdam The Netherlands
Phone: +31 20 6766096

#142
Boekie Woekie Books BY Artists
Category: Arts & Entertainment
Area: Centrum, Negen Straatjes
Address: Berenstraat 16-WKL 1016 GH
Amsterdam The Netherlands
Phone: +31 20 6390507

#143
Artis Planetarium
Category: Cinema
Area: Plantagebuurt, Centrum
Address: Artis 1018 CZ
Amsterdam The Netherlands
Phone: +31 900 2784796

#144
Holland Village Amsterdam
Category: Music Venues, European
Area: Centrum
Address: Entrepotdok 7-8 1018 AD
Amsterdam The Netherlands
Phone: +31 20 6241876

#145
Café 16cc
Category: Music Venues, Pub, Cinema
Area: Centrum
Address: Kadijksplein 16 1018 AC
Amsterdam The Netherlands
Phone: +31 20 6270236

#146
Wijnimport Jean Defize
Category: Wineries
Area: Centrum
Address: Entrepotdok 82-82A
1018 AD Amsterdam The Netherlands
Phone: +31 20 6263058

#147
Meneer de Wit
Category: Art Gallery
Area: West, De Baarsjes
Address: Postjesweg 2 1057 EA
Amsterdam The Netherlands

#148
Meubel Stukken
Category: Festival
Area: Centrum, Haarlemmerbuurt
Address: Tussen de Bogen 24
1013 JB Amsterdam The Netherlands
Phone: +31 20 4221888

#149
Roode Bioscoop
Category: Music Venues, Performing
Arts, Venues & Events
Area: Centrum, Haarlemmerbuurt
Address: Haarlemmerplein 7 1013 HP
Amsterdam The Netherlands
Phone: +31 20 6257500

#150
Cavia
Category: Cinema
Area: West, Staatsliedenbuurt
Address: Van Hallstraat 52 1051 HH
Amsterdam The Netherlands
Phone: +31 20 6811419

#151
Live at Westerpark
Category: Music Venues
Area: Westerpark, West
Address: Westerpark Amsterdam,
Noord-Holland The Netherlands

#152
De Schreeuw
Category: Arts & Entertainment,
Landmark& Historical Buildings
Area: Oost, Oosterparkbuurt
Address: Oosterpark 1092 AS
Amsterdam The Netherlands

#153
OCCII
Category: Music Venues
Area: Zuid
Address: Amstelveenseweg 134
1075 XL Amsterdam The Netherlands
Phone: +31 20 6717778

#154
Sopranos Pianobar
Category: Bar, Jazz & Blues
Area: Centrum
Address: Paardenstraat 11-15
1017 CX Amsterdam The Netherlands
Phone: +31 20 4288211

#155
Het Veem
Category: Performing Arts
Area: Centrum, West
Address: Van Diemenstraat 410-412
1013 CR Amsterdam The Netherlands
Phone: +31 20 6278714

#156
Museum Het Schip
Category: Museum
Area: West
Address: Spaarndammerplantsoen 140
1013 XT Amsterdam The Netherlands
Phone: +31 20 4182885

#157
Il Sogno
Category: Art Gallery,
Specialty Food, Italian
Area: Centrum
Address: Koningsstraat 19 1011 ET
Amsterdam The Netherlands
Phone: +31 20 3200611

#158
Het Smalste Huis Ter Wereld
Category: Museum
Area: Centrum
Address: Singel 7 Amsterdam,
Noord-Holland The Netherlands
Phone: +31 20 5512512

#159
Coster Diamonds
Category: Jewelry, Museum
Area: Zuid, Museumkwartier
Address: Paulus Potterstraat 2-8
1071 CZ Amsterdam The Netherlands
Phone: +31 20 3055555

#160
FunX
Category: Professional Services,
Arts & Entertainment
Area: Centrum
Address: Herengracht 545 1017 BW
Amsterdam The Netherlands
Phone: +31 20 5304960

#161
Cinekid Festival
Category: Festival
Area: Centrum
Address: Kleine Gartmanplantsoen 21
1017 RP Amsterdam The Netherlands
Phone: +31 20 5317890

#162
Kunstmarkt Spui
Category: Art Gallery
Area: Centrum
Address: Spui 1012 XK
Amsterdam The Netherlands
Phone: +31 35 5416078

#163
Bols Distillery
Category: Beer, Wine & Spirits, Museum
Area: Zuid, Museumkwartier
Address: Paulus Potterstraat 14 1071
CZ Amsterdam The Netherlands
Phone: +31 20 5708575

#164
Erotic Museum Amsterdam
Category: Museum
Area: Centrum, De Wallen
Address: O.Z. Achterburgwal 54 1012
DP Amsterdam The Netherlands
Phone: +31 20 6200630

#165
Buurtboerderij Ons Genoegen
Category: Local Flavor, Social Club
Area: West, Westpoort
Address: Spaarndammerdijk 319 1014
AA Amsterdam The Netherlands
Phone: +31 20 3376820

#166
Zuiveringshal West
Category: Arcades
Area: Phone number
Address: Westergastfabriek Amsterdam,
Noord-Holland The Netherlands

#167
Stichting Smart Project Space
Category: Cinema, Museum
Area: West, Oud West, Helmersbuurt
Address: Arie Biemondstraat 111 1054
PD Amsterdam The Netherlands
Phone: +31 654 765894

#168
Comedy Theater in de Nes
Category: Performing Arts
Area: Centrum, De Wallen
Address: Nes 110 1012 KE
Amsterdam The Netherlands
Phone: +31 20 4220033

#169
NOU MOE
Category: Arts & Entertainment
Area: Centrum, Jordaan
Address: Lindenstraat 1 1015 KV
Amsterdam The Netherlands
Phone: +31 20 6936345

#170
Museum Tot Zover
Category: Museum
Area: Oost, Watergraafsmeer
Address: Kruislaan 124 1097 GA
Amsterdam The Netherlands
Phone: +31 20 6940482

#171
V!P's International Art Gallery
Category: Art Gallery
Area: Centrum
Address: Spiegelgracht 8 1017 JR
Amsterdam The Netherlands
Phone: +31 20 7737656

#172
**Koninklijk Instituut
Voor de Tropen**
Category: Museum
Area: Oost, Oosterparkbuurt
Address: Mauritskade 63 1092 AD
Amsterdam The Netherlands
Phone: +31 20 5688711

#173
Veilinggebouw de Zwaan
Category: Art Gallery
Area: Centrum
Address: Keizersgracht 474-I
1017 EG Amsterdam The Netherlands
Phone: +31 20 6220447

#174
Amsterdams Uitburo
Category: Arts & Entertainment
Area: Centrum
Address: Leidseplein 26 1017 PT
Amsterdam The Netherlands
Phone: +31 20 7959950

#175
de Krakeling Jeugdtheater,
Category: Arts & Entertainment
Area: Centrum, Jordaan
Address: Nieuwe Passeerdersstraat 1
1016 XP Amsterdam The Netherlands
Phone: +31 20 6245123

#176
De Toverknol
Category: Performing Arts
Area: Centrum
Address: Kerkstraat 174 1017 GT
Amsterdam The Netherlands
Phone: +31 623 851032

#177
Zaal 100
Category: Performing Arts,
Music Venues
Area: West, Staatsliedenbuurt
Address: De Wittenstraat 100-1 1052
BA Amsterdam The Netherlands
Phone: +31 20 6880127

#178
Friends of Art
Category: Art Gallery
Area: Centrum
Address: Keizersgracht 510
1017 EJ Amsterdam The Netherlands
Phone: +31 20 6248419

#179
**Hash, Marihuana
& Hemp Museum**
Category: Tobacco Shops, Museum
Area: Centrum, De Wallen
Address: Oudezijds Achterburgwal 148
1012 DV Amsterdam The Netherlands
Phone: +31 20 6248926

#180
Amsterdam Photo Club
Category: Social Club
Address: ABC Treehouse,
Voetboogstraat 11 1012 XK
Amsterdam The Netherlands
Phone: +31 627 334331

#181
The ABC Treehouse
Category: Art Gallery
Area: Centrum
Address: Voetboogstraat 11
1012 XK Amsterdam The Netherlands
Phone: +31 20 4230967

#182
Het Spiegelkwartier
Category: Local Flavor, Art Gallery
Area: Centrum
Address: Spiegelstraat Amsterdam,
Noord-Holland The Netherlands

#183
OHAF
Category: Festival
Area: Centrum
Address: Weteringschans 6-8
1017 SG Amsterdam The Netherlands
Phone: +31 20 6264521

#184
Total Football Festival
Category: Festival, Soccer
Area: Centrum
Address: Kleine Gartmanplantsoen 10
1017 RR Amsterdam The Netherlands

#185
SLAA
Category: Performing Arts
Area: Centrum
Address: Kleine-Gartmanplantsoen 10
1017 RR Amsterdam The Netherlands
Phone: +31 20 5535137

#186
3D Hologrammen
Category: Souvenir Shops, Art Gallery
Area: Centrum, De Wallen
Address: Grimburgwal 2 1012 GA
Amsterdam The Netherlands
Phone: +31 20 6247225

#187
Movie Center
Category: Arts & Entertainment
Area: West
Address: Overtoom 73 1054 HC
Amsterdam The Netherlands
Phone: +31 20 4120573

#188
Cinéart
Category: Cinema
Area: Centrum, Negen Straatjes
Address: Herengracht 328-3 1016 CE
Amsterdam The Netherlands
Phone: +31 20 5308840

#189
Stichting Perdu
Category: Performing Arts
Area: Centrum, De Wallen
Address: Kloveniersburgwal 86 1012 CZ
Amsterdam The Netherlands
Phone: +31 20 4220542

#190
Het Bethaniënklooster
Category: Venues & Events,
Music Venues
Area: Centrum, De Wallen
Address: Barndesteeg 4-C 1012 BV
Amsterdam The Netherlands
Phone: +31 20 6250078

#191
Het Burgerweeshuis
Category: Museum
Area: Centrum
Address: Kalverstraat 92 1012 PH
Amsterdam The Netherlands

#192
Romeo Vetro
Category: Art Gallery
Area: Zuid, Museumkwartier
Address: Hobbemastraat 11 1071 XZ
Amsterdam The Netherlands
Phone: +31 20 4702705

#193
Wonderwood
Category: Home Decor, Furniture
Stores, Art Gallery
Area: Centrum, De Wallen
Address: Rusland 3 1012 CK
Amsterdam The Netherlands
Phone: +31 20 6253738

#194
Blauwbrug
Category: Arts & Entertainment
Area: Centrum
Address: Blauwbrug 1011 Amsterdam
The Netherlands

#195
Torpedo Theater
Category: Performing Arts
Area: Centrum, De Wallen
Address: Sint Pieterspoortsteeg 33 1012
HM Amsterdam The Netherlands
Phone: +31 653 977456

#196
Muziekhandel Saul B.
Category: Musical Instruments &
Teachers, Music Venues
Area: Zuid, De Pijp
Address: Ferdinand Bolstraat 8
1072 LJ Amsterdam The Netherlands
Phone: +31 20 6762240

#197
Body Worlds
Category: Museum
Area: Centrum
Address: Damrak 66 1012 LM
Amsterdam The Netherlands
Phone: +31 900 8411

#198
Gedempte Begijnensloot
Category: Arts & Entertainment
Area: Centrum
Address: Gedempte begijnensloot
Amsterdam, Noord-Holland
The Netherlands

#199
Oldschool Amsterdam
Category: Salad, Barbeque,
Arts & Entertainment
Area: Zuid
Address: Gaasterlandstraat 3-5 1079
RH Amsterdam The Netherlands

#200
Stichting GRAP
Category: Music Venues
Area: Centrum, De Wallen
Address: Oudebrugsteeg 11-III
1012 JN Amsterdam The Netherlands
Phone: +31 20 4208160

#201
Koninginnedag
Category: Festival
Area: Centrum, De Wallen
Address: Centrum Amsterdam, Noord-
Holland The Netherlands

#202
Galerie Plein 7
Category: Art Gallery
Area: West, Da Costabuurt
Address: Da Costaplein 7 1053 ZV
Amsterdam The Netherlands
Phone: +31 20 6183388

#203
Grachten Festival
Category: Festival
Area: Centrum, Negen Straatjes
Address: Prinsengracht 583 IV
1016 GZ Amsterdam The Netherlands

#204
Paleis van de Weemoed
Category: Performing Arts,
Venues & Events, Music Venues
Area: Centrum, De Wallen
Address: Oudezijds Voorburgwal 15
1012 EH Amsterdam The Netherlands
Phone: +31 20 6256964

#205
College-Club
Category: Social Club
Area: Centrum
Address: Prinsengracht 301b
1016 GX Amsterdam The Netherlands
Phone: +31 20 8944291

#206
Waag Society
Category: Social Club
Area: Centrum, De Wallen
Address: Nieuwmarkt 4 1012 CR
Amsterdam The Netherlands
Phone: +31 20 6240973

#207
Ten Haaf Projects
Category: Art Gallery
Area: Centrum, Jordaan
Address: Laurierstraat 248 1016 PT
Amsterdam The Netherlands
Phone: +31 20 4285885

#208
Ostadetheater
Category: Performing Arts
Area: Zuid, De Pijp
Address: Van Ostadestraat 233-D 1073
TN Amsterdam The Netherlands
Phone: +31 20 6712417

#209
Peritus Network
Category: Social Club
Area: Centrum
Address: Westermarkt 2G 1016 DK
Amsterdam The Netherlands
Phone: +31 20 7371710

#210
Het Perron
Category: Performing Arts, Music
Venues
Area: Centrum, Jordaan
Address: Egelantiersstraat 130 1015 PR
Amsterdam The Netherlands
Phone: +31 20 3307035

#211
Sagra dell'Uva
Category: Wineries
Area: Plantagebuurt, Centrum
Address: Plantage Kerklaan 24 1018 TB
Amsterdam The Netherlands
Phone: +31 20 3206195

#212
Nationaal Comité 4 & 5 Mei
Category: Festival, Local Flavor
Area: Plantagebuurt, Centrum
Address: Nieuwe Prinsengracht 89 1011
VL Amsterdam The Netherlands
Phone: +31 20 7183500

#213
Het Houtzagertje
Category: Arts & Entertainment
Area: Centrum
Address: Leidseplein, Leidsebosje 1017
PR Amsterdam The Netherlands

#214
Grimm Fine Art
Category: Art Gallery
Area: Centrum
Address: Keizersgracht 82-BG 1015 CT
Amsterdam The Netherlands
Phone: +31 20 4227227

#215
Stichting Nutsateliers Artis
Category: Performing Arts
Area: Plantagebuurt, Centrum
Address: Plantage Kerklaan 40-2 1018
CZ Amsterdam The Netherlands
Phone: +31 20 6220467

#216
Wizards of Art
Category: Art Gallery
Area: West, Oud West, Da Costabuurt
Address: de Clercqstraat 73 1053 AE
Amsterdam The Netherlands

#217
Café Clandestien
Category: Music Venues
Area: Oost, Oosterparkbuurt
Address: Sajetplein 39 1091 DB
Amsterdam The Netherlands
Phone: +31 641 024098

#218
Wolkentheater
Category: Performing Arts
Area: Oost, Oosterparkbuurt
Address: Tweede Boerhaavestraat 49
1091 AL Amsterdam The Netherlands
Phone: +31 20 6157233

#219
De bloeiende Victoria
Category: Botanical Garden, Landmark&
Historical Buildings
Area: Plantagebuurt, Centrum
Address: Hortus Botanicus Amsterdam
1018 DD Amsterdam The Netherlands
Phone: +31 20 6259021

#220
Amsterdam Tattoo Museum
Category: Museum
Area: Plantagebuurt, Centrum
Address: Plantage Middenlaan 62 1018
DH Amsterdam The Netherlands
Phone: +31 20 7009320

#221
Het Fijnhout
Category: Performing Arts
Area: West, Oud West
Address: Lootsstraat 39 1053 NV
Amsterdam The Netherlands
Phone: +31 20 6184768

#222
Fotogram Centrum Voor Fotografie
Category: Arts & Entertainment
Area: Centrum, Haarlemmerbuurt
Address: Korte Prinsengracht 33 1013 GN Amsterdam The Netherlands
Phone: +31 20 5309250

#223
Muziekschool Amsterdam
Category: Performing Arts
Area: Zuid, Apollobuurt
Address: Bachstraat 5 1077 GD Amsterdam The Netherlands
Phone: +31 20 5787373

#224
Muziekgebouw Aan 't IJ
Category: Music Venues
Area: Centrum
Address: Piet Heinkade 1 1019 BR Amsterdam The Netherlands
Phone: +31 20 7882000

#225
De Verhalenman
Category: Performing Arts
Area: West, Oud West
Address: Lootsstraat 31-33 1053 NV Amsterdam The Netherlands
Phone: +31 20 6755535

#226
Het Sieraad
Category: Venues & Events, Arts & Entertainment
Area: West
Address: Postjesweg 1 1057 DT Amsterdam The Netherlands
Phone: +31 20 8200928

#227
Serieuze Zaken Studioos
Category: Art Gallery
Area: West, De Baarsjes
Address: Postjesweg 2 1057 EA Amsterdam The Netherlands
Phone: +31 20 4275770

#228
ART Centre
Category: Restaurant, Art Gallery
Area: West, De Baarsjes
Address: Witte de Withstraat 128 1057 ZH Amsterdam The Netherlands
Phone: +31 20 6166222

#229
IJDock
Category: Arts & Entertainment
Area: Centrum, Haarlemmerbuurt
Address: De Ruyterkade 11A-11D 1013 Amsterdam The Netherlands

#230
Filmhuis Cavia
Category: Cinema
Area: West, Staatsliedenbuurt
Address: Van Hallstraat 52 1051 HH Amsterdam The Netherlands
Phone: +31 20 6811419

#231
Beelden in het Oosterpark
Category: Arts & Entertainment
Area: Oost, Oosterparkbuurt
Address: Oosterpark 1092 AS Amsterdam The Netherlands

#232
Art Unlimited
Category: Art Gallery
Area: Centrum
Address: Keizersgracht 510 1017 EJ Amsterdam The Netherlands
Phone: +31 20 6248419

#233
De Titaantjes
Category: Arts & Entertainment
Area: Oost, Oosterparkbuurt
Address: Oosterpark 1092 AS Amsterdam The Netherlands

#234
Nationaal Monument Slavernijverleden
Category: Arts & Entertainment
Area: Oost, Oosterparkbuurt
Address: Oosterpark 1092 AS Amsterdam The Netherlands

#235
Stuifmeel Ideeën Boom
Category: Arts & Entertainment
Area: Oost, Oosterparkbuurt
Address: Oosterpark 1092 AS Amsterdam The Netherlands

#236
**Vlaams Cultuurhuis
de Brakke Grond**
Category: Performing Arts,
Venues & Events, Belgian
Area: Centrum, De Wallen
Address: Nes 45 1012 KD
Amsterdam The Netherlands
Phone: +31 20 6229014

#237
W.
Category: Art Gallery
Area: Centrum, De Wallen
Address: Warmoesstraat 139
1012 JB Amsterdam The Netherlands
Phone: +31 20 6229434

#238
Mezrab
Category: Art Gallery
Area: Oost
Address: Veemkade 572d 1019 BL
Amsterdam The Netherlands
Phone: +31 614 775777

#239
Het Verhalen Festival
Category: Festival
Area: West
Address: westergasfabriek Amsterdam,
Noord-Holland The Netherlands

#240
Centrum voor Beeldende Kunst
Category: Art Gallery
Area: Oost, Oosterparkbuurt
Address: Oranje-vrijstaatkade 71
1093 KS Amsterdam The Netherlands
Phone: +31 20 2535456

#241
GZG Amsterdam
Category: Festival
Area: Oost, Java Eiland
Address: Sumatrakade 951 1019 RC
Amsterdam The Netherlands
Phone: +31 20 4194028

#242
Persmuseum
Category: Museum
Area: Oost, Zeeburg
Address: Zeeburgerkade 10 1019 HA
Amsterdam The Netherlands
Phone: +31 20 6928810

#243
De Bijentafels
Category: Local Flavor,
Arts & Entertainment
Area: Oost, Zeeburg
Address: Rietlandpark, naast de
tramhalte 1019 DR
Amsterdam The Netherlands

#244
Pleasure Island
Category: Festival
Area: Phone number
Address: Java eiland 1 Amsterdam,
Noord-Holland The Netherlands

#245
**Levant
Kunstenaarsbenodigdheden**
Category: Shopping, Arts &
Entertainment
Area: Oost, Java Eiland
Address: Levantkade 85 1019 MJ
Amsterdam The Netherlands
Phone: +31 20 4199618

#246
Casino City
Category: Casinos
Area: Phone number
Address: Ceintuurbaan 286 1071GK
Amsterdam, Noord-Holland The
Netherlands

#247
Het boomzagertje
Category: Arts & Entertainment
Area: Phone number
Address: In een boom op het
Leidsebosje Amsterdam, Noord-Holland
The Netherlands

#248
Maison Descartes
Category: Performing Arts,
Adult Education
Area: Centrum
Address: Vijzelgracht 2a 1017 HR
Amsterdam The Netherlands
Phone: +31 20 5319501

#249
Fringe Festival
Category: Festival, Performing Arts
Area: West
Address: Leidsebosje 1054 ES
Amsterdam The Netherlands

#250
Videoland
Category: Arts & Entertainment
Area: Centrum, Jordaan
Address: Westerstraat 84 1015 ML
Amsterdam The Netherlands
Phone: +31 20 6248283

#251
Mercato Centrale
Category: Do-It-Yourself Food, Specialty
Food, Wineries
Area: Oost, Oosterparkbuurt
Address: Eerste Oosterparkstraat 73
1091 GW Amsterdam The Netherlands
Phone: +31 20 4682851

#252
Museum Geelvinck
Category: Museum
Area: Centrum
Address: Keizersgracht 633 1017 DS
Amsterdam The Netherlands
Phone: +31 20 6390747

#253
Hollywood Mark Tattooshop
Category: Performing Arts
Area: Centrum, Jordaan
Address: Elandsgracht 65 1016 TP
Amsterdam The Netherlands
Phone: +31 20 4284860

#254
Elzinga Wijnen
Category: Wineries, Beer,
Wine & Spirits, Thrift Stores
Area: Centrum
Address: Frederiksplein 1 1017 XK
Amsterdam The Netherlands
Phone: +31 20 6237270

#255
Tricky Theater
Category: Creperies,
Music Venues, Venues & Events
Area: Centrum
Address: Oosterdoksdade 10
1011 AE Amsterdam The Netherlands
Phone: +31 20 6269383

#256
RAI Theater
Category: Performing Arts
Area: Zuid, Rivierenbuurt
Address: Europaplein 22 Amsterdam,
Noord-Holland The Netherlands
Phone: +31 20 5491212

#257
North Sea Jazz Club
Category: Jazz & Blues,
Restaurant, Dance Club
Area: West
Address: Pazzanistraat 1 1014 DB
Amsterdam The Netherlands
Phone: +31 20 7220980

#258
Stichting Open Monumentendag
Category: Arts & Entertainment
Area: Centrum
Address: Herengracht 474
1017 CA Amsterdam The Netherlands
Phone: +31 20 4222118

#259
Gertrud D.
Category: Art Gallery
Area: Centrum
Address: Keizersgracht 493
1017 DM Amsterdam The Netherlands
Phone: +31 20 6247681

#260
Art Unlimited
Category: Art Gallery
Area: Centrum
Address: Keizersgracht 510
1017 EJ Amsterdam The Netherlands
Phone: +31 20 6248419

#261
Atelier Open
Category: Art Gallery
Area: Centrum
Address: Keizersgracht 429
1017 DJ Amsterdam The Netherlands
Phone: +31 654 755454

#262
Merkur Casino
Category: Casinos
Area: Centrum
Address: Rembrandtplein 2
1017 CV Amsterdam The Netherlands

#263
El Punto Latino
Category: Bar, Music Venues
Area: Centrum
Address: Lange Leidsedwarsstraat 35
1017 NG Amsterdam The Netherlands
Phone: +31 20 4202235

#264
NIOD
Category: Landmark& Historical
Buildings, Museum
Area: Centrum, Negen Straatjes
Address: Herengracht 380 1016 CJ
Amsterdam The Netherlands
Phone: +31 20 5233800

#265
Nederlandse Dansdagen
Category: Festival
Area: Centrum
Address: Reguliersgracht 70 1017 LV
Amsterdam The Netherlands
Phone: +31 20 6262062

#266
Stichting Lezen
Category: Arts & Entertainment
Area: Centrum
Address: Nieuwezijds Voorburgwal 328-
G 1012 RW Amsterdam The Netherlands
Phone: +31 20 6230566

#267
Idfa Festival
Category: Festival
Area: Centrum
Address: Kleine-Gartmanplantsoen 10
1017 RR Amsterdam The Netherlands
Phone: +31 20 6273329

#268
Muziek Centrum Nederland
Category: Performing Arts
Area: Centrum, De Wallen
Address: Rokin 111 1012 KN
Amsterdam The Netherlands
Phone: +31 20 3446000

#269
Galerie Mokum
Category: Art Gallery
Area: Centrum, De Wallen
Address: Oudezijds Voorburgwal 334-I
1012 GM Amsterdam The Netherlands
Phone: +31 20 6243958

#270
Roze Filmdagen
Category: Festival
Area: Centrum
Address: Weteringschans 38-3
Amsterdam, Noord-Holland The
Netherlands

#271
Gemengd Zwemmen
Category: Music Venues
Area: Centrum
Address: Lijnbaansgracht 234A
1017 PH Amsterdam The Netherlands
Phone: +31 20 5318181

#272
Stichting Grachtenfestival
Category: Festival, Music Venues
Area: Centrum
Address: Prinsengracht 583-2 1016 HT
Amsterdam The Netherlands
Phone: +31 20 4214542

#273
Betty Asfalt Complex
Category: Performing Arts
Area: Centrum
Address: Nieuwezijds Voorburgwal
282-HS 1012 RT Amsterdam
The Netherlands
Phone: +31 20 6204748

#274
NAP Paal
Category: Arts & Entertainment
Area: Centrum
Address: Amstel 1 1011 PN
Amsterdam The Netherlands

#275
Modern Art Market
Category: Arts & Entertainment
Area: Centrum
Address: Thorbeckeplein 1017 CS
Amsterdam The Netherlands
Phone: +31 527 202059

#276
WM Gallery
Category: Art Gallery
Area: Centrum, Jordaan
Address: Elandsgracht 35 Amsterdam,
Noord-Holland The Netherlands
Phone: +31 20 4211113

#277
Hannah's 'Tooi'
Category: Shopping,
Arts & Entertainment
Area: Centrum
Address: Gasthuismolensteeg 3 1016
AM Amsterdam The Netherlands
Phone: +31 20 3206027

#278
Tiller Galerie
Category: Art Gallery
Area: Zuid, De Pijp
Address: 1e Jacob van Campenstr 1
1072 BB Amsterdam The Netherlands
Phone: +31 20 6622725

#279
Het Nationale Ballet
Category: Opera & Ballet
Area: Centrum
Address: Waterlooplein 22 1011 PG
Amsterdam The Netherlands
Phone: +31 20 5518225

#280
Jouw Stoute Schoenen
Category: Performing Arts, Shoe Stores
Area: Centrum, De Wallen
Address: Oudezijds Achterburgwal 133
1012 DG Amsterdam The Netherlands
Phone: +31 644 728319

#281
Mozes en Aäronkerk
Category: Performing Arts, Art Gallery
Area: Centrum
Address: Waterlooplein 205 1011 PG
Amsterdam The Netherlands
Phone: +31 20 6221305

#282
Toro Art
Category: Arts & Entertainment
Area: Centrum, De Wallen
Address: Sintjansstraat 35 1012 HG
Amsterdam The Netherlands

#283
Poppentheater Zenda's Wereld
Category: Music Venues
Area: Zuid, De Pijp
Address: Gerard Doustraat 71
1072 VM Amsterdam The Netherlands
Phone: +31 654 367881

#284
De Vondelbunker
Category: Music Venues
Area: Zuid, Museumkwartier
Address: Vondelpark 8 Amsterdam,
Noord-Holland The Netherlands

#285
Sid Lee Collective
Category: Art Gallery
Area: Zuid, De Pijp
Address: Gerard Doustraat 74
1072 VV Amsterdam The Netherlands
Phone: +31 20 4707277

#286
Megalodon Amsterdam
Category: Coffee & Tea, Art Gallery,
Concept Shops
Area: Centrum, De Wallen
Address: Oudezijds Voorburgwal 96a
1012 GH Amsterdam The Netherlands
Phone: +31 638 308732

#287
Vleck Wijnen
Category: Wineries
Area: West, Oud West, Helmersbuurt
Address: Eerste Helmersstraat 63-hs
1054 DC Amsterdam The Netherlands
Phone: +31 20 6835980

#288
Stepping-Menno
Category: Arts & Entertainment
Area: Zuid, De Pijp
Address: Govert Flinckstraat 188
1073 CD Amsterdam The Netherlands
Phone: +31 20 4115650

#289
Stichting Virtueel Platform
Category: Arts & Entertainment
Area: Centrum
Address: Damrak 70 1012 LM
Amsterdam The Netherlands
Phone: +31 20 6273758

#290
Stichting Rozentheater
Category: Performing Arts,
Music Venues
Area: Centrum, Jordaan
Address: Rozengracht 117
1016 LV Amsterdam The Netherlands
Phone: +31 20 6276162

#291
Galerie NU
Category: Art Gallery
Area: Centrum, Jordaan
Address: Rozengracht 58hs 1016 ND
Amsterdam The Netherlands
Phone: +31 20 8464613

#292
NLTracks
Category: Music Venues
Area: Centrum
Address: Singel 146 1015 AG
Amsterdam The Netherlands
Phone: +31 20 7787266

#293
Michaël Ferron
Category: Photographers, Art Gallery
Area: Zuid, Museumkwartier
Address: Van Baerlestraat 41 1071 AP
Amsterdam The Netherlands
Phone: +31 615 145053

#294
Cinemien
Category: Performing Arts
Area: Zuid, De Pijp
Address: Amsteldijk 10-BG 1074 HP
Amsterdam The Netherlands
Phone: +31 20 6643792

#295
**Stichting Schrijvers School
en Samenleving**
Category: Performing Arts
Area: Plantagebuurt, Centrum
Address: Huddestraat 7 1018 HB
Amsterdam The Netherlands
Phone: +31 20 6234923

#296
La Cave Insolite
Category: Wineries
Area: West, Da Costabuurt
Address: Da Costaplein 15 1053 ZV
Amsterdam The Netherlands
Phone: +31 20 4752068

#297
Festival De Pijp
Category: Festival
Area: Zuid, De Pijp
Address: Eerste Sweelinckstraat 1073
CK Amsterdam The Netherlands

#298
**Asian Food Festival
Xmast Edition**
Category: Festival
Area: Centrum, De Wallen
Address: Nieuwmarkt Amsterdam,
Noord-Holland The Netherlands

#299
Jazzcafé 't Geveltje
Category: Jazz & Blues, Pub
Area: Centrum, Jordaan
Address: Bloemgracht 170-HS
1015 TV Amsterdam The Netherlands
Phone: +31 20 6239983

#300
VriendvanBavink
Category: Art Gallery
Area: Centrum, De Wallen
Address: Geldersekade 58 1012 BK
Amsterdam The Netherlands

#301
Dans-Dansen
Category: Active Life, Social Club
Area: Zuid, De Pijp
Address: Ceintuurbaan 73 1072 EW
Amsterdam The Netherlands
Phone: +31 20 7796770

#302
Frascati WG
Category: Performing Arts
Area: West, Oud West, Helmersbuurt
Address: Marius van Bouwdijk
Bastiaansestraat 54 1054 SP Amsterdam
The Netherlands
Phone: +31 20 6832304

#303
Rockarchive
Category: Hobby Shops, Photography
Stores, Art Gallery
Area: Centrum, Jordaan
Address: Prinsengracht 110-BG 1015
EA Amsterdam The Netherlands
Phone: +31 20 4230489

#304
Kunstuitleen / Galerie 59
Category: Art Gallery
Area: Zuid, Museumkwartier
Address: Van Eeghenstraat 59
1071 EW Amsterdam The Netherlands
Phone: +31 20 6732640

#305
Filmfreaks
Category: Cinema
Area: Centrum
Address: Schippersstraat 7 1011 AZ
Amsterdam The Netherlands
Phone: +31 20 4864940

#306
De Appel Arts Centre
Category: Arts & Entertainment
Area: Centrum
Address: Prins Hendrikkade 142 1011
AT Amsterdam The Netherlands
Phone: +31 20 6255651

#307
Storm Space
Category: Art Gallery,
Department Stores
Area: Oost, Oosterparkbuurt
Address: Swammerdamstraat 44-54
1091 RV Amsterdam The Netherlands
Phone: +31 20 4865561

#308
Filmclub Videotheek Cinema
Category: Arts & Entertainment
Area: Zuid, De Pijp
Address: Ferdinand Bolstraat 149
1072 LH Amsterdam The Netherlands
Phone: +31 20 6717111

#309
ZOOmeravonden Artis
Category: Festival,
Venues & Events, Local Flavor
Area: Plantagebuurt, Centrum
Address: Plantage Kerklaan 40
1018 CZ Amsterdam The Netherlands
Phone: +31 900 278479

#310
EasyLaughs
Category: Performing Arts
Area: Plantagebuurt, Centrum
Address: Nieuwe Achtergracht 168 1018
WV Amsterdam The Netherlands
Phone: +31 20 5251400

#311
Salon 29
Category: Art Gallery
Area: Centrum
Address: Herengracht 29 1015 BB
Amsterdam The Netherlands
Phone: +31 623 438639

#312
G.
Category: Museum
Area: Centrum, Jordaan
Address: Westerstraat 119 1015 LZ
Amsterdam The Netherlands
Phone: +31 20 6249310

#313
Exit Art Amsterdam
Category: Art Gallery
Area: West, Oud West, Da Costabuurt
Address: De Clerqstraat 66-68
Amsterdam, Noord-Holland The
Netherlands

#314
Pianola Museum
Category: Music Venues
Area: Centrum, Jordaan
Address: Westerstraat 106-1
1015 MN Amsterdam The Netherlands
Phone: +31 20 6279624

#315
Het Mobiele Naaiatelier
Category: Performing Arts, Sewing &
Alterations, Party & Event Planning
Area: Centrum, Haarlemmerbuurt
Address: Binnen Wieringerstraat 25
1013 EA Amsterdam The Netherlands
Phone: +31 624 917436

#316
John Adams Institute
Category: Performing Arts
Area: Centrum, Haarlemmerbuurt
Address: Herenmarkt 95 1013 EC
Amsterdam The Netherlands
Phone: +31 20 6200358

#317
Theater Van Het Woord
Category: Performing Arts
Area: Centrum
Address: Oba 1011 DL
Amsterdam The Netherlands
Phone: +31 20 5230801

#318
Podium Mozaïek
Category: Music Venues,
Venues & Events
Area: West, Bos en Lommer
Address: Bos en Lommerweg 191
1055 DT Amsterdam The Netherlands
Phone: +31 20 5800381

#319
Kahmann Gallery
Category: Art Gallery
Area: Centrum, Jordaan
Address: Lindengracht 35 1015 KB
Amsterdam The Netherlands
Phone: +31 20 5158589

#320
Cri Cri
Category: Arts & Crafts, Art Gallery
Area: Oud West
Address: Overtoom 303 1054 JL
Amsterdam The Netherlands
Phone: +31 20 6162886

#321
Videotheek Starworld
Category: Local Services,
Arts & Entertainment
Area: West, Oud West, Helmersbuurt
Address: Jan Pieter Heijestraat 168-3
1054 ML Amsterdam The Netherlands
Phone: +31 20 6831788

#322
**Rijksakademie Van
Beeldende Kunsten**
Category: Adult Education, Art Gallery
Area: Plantagebuurt, Centrum
Address: Sarphatistraat 470 1018 GW
Amsterdam The Netherlands
Phone: +31 20 5270300

#323
Klankspeeltuin
Category: Venues & Events,
Music Venues
Area: Centrum
Address: Piet Heinkade 1 1019 BR
Amsterdam The Netherlands
Phone: +31 20 7882000

#324
Werfmuseum 't Kromhout
Category: Museum
Area: Centrum
Address: Hoogte Kadijk 147 1018 BJ
Amsterdam The Netherlands
Phone: +31 20 6276777

#325
The Wine Spot
Category: Beer, Wine & Spirits, Wineries
Area: West, De Baarsjes
Address: Admiraal de Ruyterweg 43hs
1057 JV Amsterdam The Netherlands
Phone: +31 20 7372212

#326
Tropentheater
Category: Performing Arts
Area: Oost, Oosterparkbuurt
Address: Mauritskade 63 1092 AD
Amsterdam The Netherlands
Phone: +31 20 5699500

#327
Arti et Amicitiae
Category: Social Club
Area: Centrum
Address: Rokin 112 1012 LB
Amsterdam The Netherlands
Phone: +31 20 6233508

#328
Club Lite
Category: Dance Club,
Venues & Events, Music Venues
Area: West, Bos en Lommer
Address: Van Galenstraat 24
1051 KM Amsterdam The Netherlands
Phone: +31 625 456518

#329
The Movies Filmdiner
Category: European, Cinema
Area: Centrum, Haarlemmerbuurt
Address: Haarlemmerdijk 161 1013 KH
Amsterdam The Netherlands
Phone: +31 20 6267069

#330
Tamara Jongsma
Category: Arts & Entertainment, Fashion
Area: Centrum, Haarlemmerbuurt
Address: Touwslagerstraat 19 1013 DL
Amsterdam The Netherlands
Phone: +31 20 4204969

#331
In Vino Momentum
Category: Wineries
Area: Centrum
Address: Oostenburgervoorstraat 188
1018 MR Amsterdam The Netherlands
Phone: +31 642 044472

#332
Wine Wijn
Category: Wineries
Area: Oost
Address: Schollenbrugstraat 7
1091 EX Amsterdam The Netherlands
Phone: +31 20 4686958

#333
**Museum of Medieval Torture
Instruments**
Category: Museum
Area: Centrum
Address: Damrak 33 1012 LK
Amsterdam The Netherlands
Phone: +31 20 5285482

#334
Volta
Category: Music Venues
Area: Westerpark, West
Address: Houtmankade 336
1013 RR Amsterdam The Netherlands
Phone: +31 20 6826429

#335
De Valk
Category: Music Venues
Area: Noord
Address: IJplein 3 1021 LA
Amsterdam The Netherlands
Phone: +31 20 6372155

#336
Veilinghuis AAG
Category: Arts & Entertainment
Area: Zuid, Rivierenbuurt
Address: Lekstraat 63 1079 EM
Amsterdam The Netherlands
Phone: +31 20 3012950

#337
Galerie Onrust
Category: Art Gallery
Area: Centrum, Haarlemmerbuurt
Address: Planciusstraat 9 1013 MD
Amsterdam The Netherlands
Phone: +31 20 4202219

#338
Mitra
Category: Wineries, Beer, Wine & Spirits
Area: Oost, Dapperbuurt
Address: Eerste van Swindenstraat 391
1093 GB Amsterdam The Netherlands
Phone: +31 20 6651732

#339
Filmlsreal
Category: Festival
Area: West
Address: Pazzanistraat 4
1014 DB Amsterdam The Netherlands

#340
Ton de Boer
Category: Art Gallery
Area: Centrum
Address: Czaar Peterstraat 139
1018 PH Amsterdam The Netherlands
Phone: +31 616 610195

#341
Hot Tub Movie Club
Category: Festival, Local Flavor
Area: West
Address: Pazzanistraat 8 1014 DB
Amsterdam The Netherlands

#342
Sotheby's
Category: Art Gallery
Area: Zuid, Buitenveldert
Address: De Boelelaan 30 1083 HJ
Amsterdam The Netherlands
Phone: +31 20 5502200

#343
MovieMax Zeeburg
Category: Arts & Entertainment
Area: Oost, Zeeburg
Address: Oostelijke Handelskade 1051
1019 BW Amsterdam The Netherlands
Phone: +31 20 4191009

#344
Sprocket Sounds
Category: Cinema
Area: Oud West
Address: OT301 1054 HW
Amsterdam The Netherlands

#345
De Buurtboerderij
Category: Performing Arts, GastroPub
Area: West, Westpoort
Address: Spaarndammerdijk 319
1014 AA Amsterdam The Netherlands
Phone: +31 20 3376820

#346
Kunstuitleen / Galerie 23
Category: Arts & Entertainment
Area: Oost, Java Eiland
Address: KNSM-laan 307-309
1019 LE Amsterdam The Netherlands
Phone: +31 20 6201321

#347
Open Tuinen Dagen
Category: Botanical Garden
Area: Phone number
Address: grachtenmusea Amsterdam,
Noord-Holland The Netherlands

#348
Symfonieorkest de Philharmonie
Category: Performing Arts
Area: Phone number
Address: M.F.C. Binnenhof Amsterdam,
Noord-Holland The Netherlands

#349
De Fluisterbank
Category: Arts & Entertainment
Area: Phone number
Address: Westergasfabriek 1014 BE
Amsterdam The Netherlands

#350
Bimhuis
Category: Music Venues
Area: Centrum
Address: Piet Heinkade 3 1019 BR
Amsterdam The Netherlands
Phone: +31 20 7882188

#351
Gallery Delaive
Category: Art Gallery
Area: Centrum
Address: Spiegelgracht 23-BG
1017 JP Amsterdam The Netherlands
Phone: +31 20 6260940

#352
Gallery Godá
Category: Art Gallery
Area: Centrum
Address: Weteringschans 69
1017 RX Amsterdam The Netherlands
Phone: +31 653 283989

#353
Museum Cafe Mokum
Category: Pub, Coffee & Tea
Area: Centrum
Address: Kalverstraat 92 1012 PH
Amsterdam The Netherlands
Phone: +31 20 6236736

#354
Galerie Artacasa
Category: Art Gallery
Area: Centrum
Address: Kerkstraat 411 Amsterdam,
Noord-Holland The Netherlands
Phone: +31 20 6393213

#355
People's Place
Category: Venues & Events,
Music Venues, Bar
Area: West
Address: Stadhouderskade 5/6
1054 ES Amsterdam The Netherlands
Phone: +31 20 5895467

#356
Diamant Museum
Category: Museum
Area: Zuid, Museumkwartier
Address: Paulus Potterstraat 8
1071 CZ Amsterdam The Netherlands
Phone: +31 20 3055300

#357
Don Mimmo
Category: Do-It-Yourself Food, Wineries
Area: Zuid, De Pijp
Address: Gerard Doustraat 252-A 1073
XD Amsterdam The Netherlands
Phone: +31 20 6898549

#358
Spinoza-Monument
Category: Arts & Entertainment
Area: Centrum
Address: Zwanenburgwal Amsterdam,
Noord-Holland The Netherlands

#359
Museum Of Prostitution
Category: Adult Entertainment, Museum
Area: Centrum, De Wallen
Address: Oudezijds Achterburgwal 60 H
1012 DS Amsterdam The Netherlands

#360
Casablanca Muziek
Category: Pub, Music Venues, Karaoke
Area: Centrum, De Wallen
Address: Zeedijk 26E 1012 AZ
Amsterdam The Netherlands
Phone: +31 612 200519

#361
100 Highlights Cruise
Category: Arts & Entertainment
Area: Centrum
Address: Prins Hendrikkade 33a
Amsterdam, Noord-Holland
The Netherlands

#362
Oostblok
Category: Performing Arts
Area: Oost, Oosterparkbuurt
Address: Sajetplein 39 1091 DB
Amsterdam The Netherlands
Phone: +31 20 6654568

#363
Percussiexpress
Category: Arts & Entertainment
Area: Centrum, Haarlemmerbuurt
Address: Studio PXP - Tussen de
Bogen 69 1013 JB Amsterdam
The Netherlands
Phone: +31 20 8943449

#364
Café de Nieuwe Vaart
Category: Pub, Music Venues
Area: Centrum
Address: Oostenburgergracht 187
1018 ND Amsterdam The Netherlands
Phone: +31 20 6279457

#365
Stichting ArtOlive
Category: Art Gallery
Area: West
Address: Polonceau-kade 17
1014 DA Amsterdam The Netherlands
Phone: +31 20 6758504

#366
Appelsap
Category: Festival
Area: Oost, Oosterparkbuurt
Address: Oosterpark 1091 HH
Amsterdam The Netherlands

#367
Amsterdam EXPO
Category: Art Gallery
Area: Zuid, WTC, Buitenveldert
Address: Gustav Mahlerlaan 24 1082
MC Amsterdam The Netherlands
Phone: +31 20 7630599

#368
Libbe Venema
Category: Arts & Entertainment
Area: Oost, Watergraafsmeer
Address: Hogeweg 2a 1098 CB
Amsterdam The Netherlands
Phone: +31 20 6922215

#369
**Amsterdam Fantastic
Film Festival**
Category: Festival
Area: Oost, Indische Buurt
Address: Timorplein 52 1094 CC
Amsterdam The Netherlands
Phone: +31 20 6794875

#370
Universal Studios
Category: Arts & Entertainment,
Video/Film Production
Area: Slotervaart
Address: Koningin Wilhelminaplein 2-4
1062 HK Amsterdam The Netherlands
Phone: +31 20 6177575

#371
Stopera
Category: Arts & Entertainment
Area: Centrum
Address: Waterlooplein 1011
Amsterdam The Netherlands

#372
Rederij Plas Rondvaarten
Category: Arts & Entertainment
Area: Centrum
Address: Damrak 28A 1012
Amsterdam The Netherlands

#373
Bitterzoet
Category: Music Venues
Area: Centrum
Address: Spuistraat 2-HS 1012 TS
Amsterdam The Netherlands
Phone: +31 20 4212318

#374
Club DNA
Category: Dance Club,
Cocktail Bar, Music Venues
Area: Oost
Address: H.J.E. Wenckebachweg 180
1096 AS Amsterdam The Netherlands
Phone: +31 20 6633322

#375
Kinderboerderij Westerpark
Category: Arts & Entertainment
Area: West
Address: Overbrakerpad 10
1014 AZ Amsterdam The Netherlands
Phone: +31 20 6822193

#376
**Le Musée du Haschich
et de la Marijuana**
Category: Museum
Area: Phone number
Address: Oudezijds achterbur 148
Amsterdam, Noord-Holland The
Netherlands

#377
Wonderbread
Category: Art Gallery, Bookstores
Area: Centrum
Address: Wijdesteeg 3a 1012 RN
Amsterdam The Netherlands
Phone: +31 625 104383

#378
Chabrol Wines & Spirits
Category: Wineries
Area: Centrum, Haarlemmerbuurt
Address: Haarlemmerstraat 7 1013 EH
Amsterdam The Netherlands
Phone: +31 20 6222781

#379
Dokzaal
Category: Music Venues
Area: Plantagebuurt, Centrum
Address: Plantage Doklaan 8-12 1018
CM Amsterdam The Netherlands

#380
Stadsboekwinkel
Category: Shopping,
Arts & Entertainment
Area: Centrum
Address: Vijzelstraat 32 1017 HL
Amsterdam The Netherlands
Phone: +31 20 6250950

#381
Walls
Category: Art Gallery
Area: Centrum
Address: Prinsengracht 737
1017 JX Amsterdam The Netherlands
Phone: +31 20 6169597

#382
Jack's Casino
Category: Casinos
Area: Centrum
Address: Korte Leidsedwarsstraat
38-42 1017 RC Amsterdam
The Netherlands

#383
Vrijdagmiddag Live
Category: Radio Stations,
Arts & Entertainment
Area: Centrum
Address: Rembrandtplein 17 1017 CT
Amsterdam The Netherlands
Phone: +31 20 6252011

#384
Willem Kerseboom gallery
Category: Art Gallery
Area: Centrum
Address: Leidsegracht 38-40 1016 CM
Amsterdam The Netherlands
Phone: +31 72 5895018

#385
Galerie de Passie
Category: Art Gallery
Area: Centrum, Jordaan
Address: Prinsengracht 408 1016 JB
Amsterdam The Netherlands
Phone: +31 20 6267250

#386
The Art Shop Amsterdam
Category: Art Gallery
Area: Centrum, Jordaan
Address: Leidsegracht 104 1072 GM
Amsterdam The Netherlands
Phone: +31 20 4221259

#387
Galerie Bart
Category: Art Gallery
Area: Centrum, Jordaan
Address: Elandsgracht 16 1016 TW
Amsterdam The Netherlands
Phone: +31 20 3206208

#388
Battalion
Category: Art Gallery, Books,
Mags, Music & Video
Area: Centrum, Jordaan
Address: Lijnbaansgracht 206
1016 XA Amsterdam The Netherlands

#389
Amsterdam Outsider Art
Category: Art Gallery
Area: Plantagebuurt, Centrum
Address: Nieuwe Keizersgracht 1a
1018 DR Amsterdam The Netherlands
Phone: +31 20 3302083

#390
Ultra De La Rue
Category: Art Gallery
Area: Centrum, De Wallen
Address: Oudekerksplein 30 1012 GZ
Amsterdam The Netherlands

#391
Wine Supply
Category: Wineries, Beer, Wine & Spirits
Area: Zuid, Museumkwartier
Address: van Baerlestraat 118hs 1071
BC Amsterdam The Netherlands

#392
Rockarchive
Category: Art Gallery
Area: Centrum, Jordaan
Address: 110 Prinsengracht bg
1015 EA Amsterdam The Netherlands
Phone: +31 20 4230489

#393
Ramses Shaffy - Dr.
Category: Retirement Homes,
Arts & Entertainment
Area: Plantagebuurt, Centrum
Address: Roetersstraat 2 1018 WC
Amsterdam The Netherlands
Phone: +31 20 5540404

#394
Tijd/Ruimte
Category: Arts & Entertainment
Area: Zuid, Museumkwartier
Address: Van Breestraat 72/1
1071 ZS Amsterdam The Netherlands
Phone: +31 624 217678

#395
Becker Antiques V.O.F.
Category: Art Gallery
Area: Zuid, Museumkwartier
Address: Willemsparkweg 117
1071 GW Amsterdam The Netherlands
Phone: +31 20 6629865

#396
**Kunstuitleen Beeldend
Gesproken**
Category: Art Gallery
Area: West, Oud West
Address: 1053 PW 1053 PW
Amsterdam The Netherlands
Phone: +31 20 5904500

#397
Urban Augmented Reality
Category: Arts & Entertainment
Area: Centrum
Address: Prins Hendrikkade 600
1011 VX Amsterdam The Netherlands
Phone: +31 20 6204878

#398
Café Water
Category: Dive Bar, Pub
Area: Zuid
Address: Ruysdaelkade 251
1072 AX Amsterdam The Netherlands
Phone: +31 20 3416024

#399
Oostblok
Category: Performing Arts
Area: Oost, Dapperbuurt
Address: Tweede van Swindenstraat 26
1093 VS Amsterdam The Netherlands
Phone: +31 20 6654568

#400
ParKt Presents
Category: Art Gallery
Area: Centrum
Address: Reguliersdwarsstraat 18
Amsterdam, Noord-Holland
The Netherlands
Phone: +31 623 284954

#401
Tóth - Ikonen
Category: Art Gallery
Area: Centrum
Address: Nieuwe Spiegelstraat 68-III
1017 DH Amsterdam The Netherlands
Phone: +31 20 4207359

#402
Jeroen Bechtold Keramiek
Category: Art Gallery
Area: Centrum
Address: Korte Leidsedwarsstraat 159
1017 RA Amsterdam The Netherlands
Phone: +31 20 6249871

#403
Galerie de Opsteker
Category: Art Gallery
Area: Centrum
Address: Noorderstraat 61 1017 TS
Amsterdam The Netherlands
Phone: +31 20 6386904

#404
The Tearat Theepottenmuseum
Category: Museum
Area: Centrum
Address: Raamsteeg 5 1012 VZ
Amsterdam The Netherlands
Phone: +31 20 6715500

#405
Studio 13
Category: Art Gallery
Area: Centrum
Address: Utrechtsedwarsstraat 13-2
1017 WB Amsterdam The Netherlands
Phone: +31 20 6206484

#406
Red Stamp
Category: Art Gallery
Area: Centrum, De Wallen
Address: Rusland 22 1012 CL
Amsterdam The Netherlands
Phone: +31 20 4208684

#407
Het Berlagehuis
Category: Art Gallery
Area: Zuid, De Pijp
Address: Van Woustraat 235
1074 AR Amsterdam The Netherlands
Phone: +31 20 4004787

#408
Stichting De Appel
Category: Art Gallery
Area: Zuid, De Pijp
Address: Eerste Jacob van
Campenstraat 59 1072 BD Amsterdam
The Netherlands
Phone: +31 20 6255651

#409
De Nederlandse Opera
Category: Opera & Ballet
Area: Centrum
Address: Waterlooplein 22 1011 PG
Amsterdam The Netherlands
Phone: +31 20 5518922

#410
Keramiek Centrum
Category: Arts & Entertainment
Area: West, Helmersbuurt
Address: Overtoom 10 1054 HH
Amsterdam The Netherlands
Phone: +31 20 6853533

#411
CNCPT13
Category: Art Gallery
Area: Centrum, Jordaan
Address: Prinsengracht 266 1016 HH
Amsterdam The Netherlands
Phone: +31 20 7527338

#412
Ververs
Category: Art Gallery
Area: Centrum, Jordaan
Address: Hazenstraat 54 1016 SR
Amsterdam The Netherlands
Phone: +31 624 202055

#413
Bv Expl.
Category: Performing Arts
Area: Plantagebuurt, Centrum
Address: Amstel 115 125 1018 EM
Amsterdam The Netherlands
Phone: +31 20 5249494

#414
Poppentheater Koos Kneus
Category: Arts & Entertainment
Area: Oost, Oosterparkbuurt
Address: Iepenplein 40 1091 JR
Amsterdam The Netherlands
Phone: +31 20 6928532

#415
College-Club
Category: Social Club
Area: Centrum
Address: Prinsengracht 301b 1016 GX
Amsterdam The Netherlands
Phone: +31 20 8944291

#416
GAIA Amsterdam
Category: Art Gallery
Area: Centrum
Address: Torensteeg 3 Amsterdam,
Noord-Holland The Netherlands
Phone: +31 20 6206403

#417
Piastrelle
Category: Performing Arts
Area: Zuid, Museumkwartier
Address: Van Baerlestraat 14
1071 AW Amsterdam The Netherlands
Phone: +31 20 6716475

#418
Meneer Malasch
Category: Art Gallery
Area: West, De Baarsjes
Address: Postjesweg 2 1057 EA
Amsterdam The Netherlands
Phone: +31 20 4275770

#419
Ten Haaf Projects
Category: Art Gallery
Area: Centrum, Jordaan
Address: Laurierstraat 248 1016 PT
Amsterdam The Netherlands
Phone: +31 312 04285885

#420
Exposure Photo Tours
Category: Tours, Performing Arts
Area: Centrum
Address: Korte Koningsstraat 33-1
1011 EZ Amsterdam The Netherlands
Phone: +31 648 476081

#421
Cherry Juice Recordings
Category: Music Venues
Area: Centrum, Haarlemmerbuurt
Address: Zeilmakerstraat 2 1013 DJ
Amsterdam The Netherlands
Phone: +31 681 935125

#422
Chinese Vereniging Fa Yin
Category: Music Venues
Area: Centrum
Address: Recht Boomssloot 5 1011 CR
Amsterdam The Netherlands
Phone: +31 20 6233191

#423
Cinema Venus
Category: Cinema
Area: Centrum, De Wallen
Address: Oudekerksplein 18 20 1012
GZ Amsterdam The Netherlands
Phone: +31 347 320528

#424
Ballonfeest
Category: Festival
Area: Centrum
Address: Paradiso 1017 SG
Amsterdam The Netherlands
Phone: +31 20 6264521

#425
Basil de Visser Strijkstokken
Category: Music Venues
Area: Centrum
Address: Binnen Bantammerstraat 10A
1011 CK Amsterdam The Netherlands
Phone: +31 20 6235614

#426
Kunstkopie
Category: Arts & Entertainment
Area: Zuid, De Pijp
Address: Ceintuurbaan 326 1072 GM
Amsterdam The Netherlands
Phone: +31 20 6765876

#427
ArTicks Gallery & Consultancy
Category: Art Gallery, Marketing
Area: Centrum
Address: Singel 88 1015 AD
Amsterdam The Netherlands
Phone: +31 20 7371505

#428
Gallery Victoria Kovalenchikova
Category: Art Gallery
Area: Zuid, De Pijp
Address: Ceintuurbaan 264
1072 GJ Amsterdam The Netherlands
Phone: +31 625 552538

#429
Supperclub Cruise
Category: Tapas,
Nightlife, Social Club
Area: Centrum
Address: De Ruiterkade 1012 PL
Amsterdam The Netherlands
Phone: +31 20 3446403

#430
Upstream Gallery
Category: Art Gallery
Area: Zuid, De Pijp
Address: Van Ostadestraat 294
1073 TW Amsterdam The Netherlands
Phone: +31 20 4284284

#431
Galerie Moon
Category: Art Gallery
Area: Centrum, Haarlemmerbuurt
Address: Grote Bickersstraat 71
1013 KP Amsterdam The Netherlands
Phone: +31 622 210481

#432
Hartjesdagen
Category: Festival
Area: Centrum, De Wallen
Address: Zeedijk 1012 AN
Amsterdam The Netherlands
Phone: +31 614 430451

#433
KochxBos Gallery
Category: Graphic Design,
Arts & Entertainment
Area: Centrum, Jordaan
Address: Eerste Anjeliersdwarsstraat 36
1015 NR Amsterdam The Netherlands
Phone: +31 20 6814567

#434
Scheepvaart Museum
Category: Museum
Area: Centrum
Address: Prins Hendrikkade 169-1
1011 TC Amsterdam The Netherlands
Phone: +31 20 6237222

#435
NiNsee
Category: Landmark& Historical
Buildings, Museum
Area: Oost, Dapperbuurt
Address: Linnaeusstraat 35-F
1093 EE Amsterdam The Netherlands
Phone: +31 20 5688568

#436
Island International Bookstore
Category: Arts & Entertainment
Area: Centrum, Jordaan
Address: 1015 LT 1015 LT
Amsterdam The Netherlands
Phone: +31 20 6389243

#437
Bezoekerscentrum De Dageraad
Category: Venues & Events, Art Gallery
Area: Zuid, De Pijp
Address: Burgemeester Tellegenstraat
128 1073 KG Amsterdam The
Netherlands
Phone: +31 20 4182885

#438
Stichting Mediamatic
Category: Art Gallery
Area: Centrum
Address: VOC-kade 10 1018 LG
Amsterdam The Netherlands
Phone: +31 20 6389901

#439
Wijnimport Jean Defize
Category: Wineries
Area: Centrum
Address: Entrepotdok 82 1018 AD
Amsterdam The Netherlands
Phone: +31 20 6263058

#440
Galerie Kunst is Kunst
Category: Art Gallery
Area: Centrum
Address: Nieuwevaart 200 1018 ZN
Amsterdam The Netherlands
Phone: +31 20 6264487

#441
Fiets & Wandelbeurs
Category: Festival
Area: Zuid
Address: Europaplein 20 1078 GZ
Amsterdam The Netherlands
Phone: +31 20 6002579

#442
Gallery Cultural Speech
Category: Art Gallery
Area: West, De Baarsjes
Address: Postjesweg 6-8 1057 EA
Amsterdam The Netherlands
Phone: +31 20 4121741

#443
Tropenmuseum Junior
Category: Arts & Entertainment
Area: Oost, Oosterparkbuurt
Address: Linnaeusstraat 2 1092 CK
Amsterdam The Netherlands
Phone: +31 20 5688300

#444
Glow Studio
Category: Performing Arts
Area: Centrum, Haarlemmerbuurt
Address: Tussen de Bogen 87 1013 JB
Amsterdam The Netherlands
Phone: +31 20 6239217

#445
If I Can't Dance
Category: Performing Arts
Area: Centrum, Haarlemmerbuurt
Address: Westerdok 606-608 1013 BV
Amsterdam The Netherlands
Phone: +31 20 3378711

#446
Video Plaza
Category: Arts & Entertainment
Area: West, Staatsliedenbuurt
Address: Van Limburg Stirumstraat 38
1051 BC Amsterdam The Netherlands
Phone: +31 20 6844395

#447
Galerie Ei
Category: Art Gallery
Area: West, De Baarsjes
Address: Admiraal de Ruijterweg 154
1056 GW Amsterdam The Netherlands
Phone: +31 20 6163961

#448
Theater de Cameleon
Category: Performing Arts
Area: Zuid, West
Address: Derde Kostverlorenkade 35
1054 TS Amsterdam The Netherlands
Phone: +31 20 4894656

#449
Tosti Fabriek
Category: Arts & Entertainment
Area: Centrum
Address: Voc-kade 1018 LG Amsterdam
The Netherlands
Phone: +31 20 6389901

#450
Dansschool Oostveen
Category: Social Club
Area: Zuid
Address: Amstelveenseweg 132-1 1075
XL Amsterdam The Netherlands
Phone: +31 20 6795331

#451
Salsa Club Mystique
Category: Music Venues
Area: West
Address: Spaarndammerstraat 460
1013 SZ Amsterdam The Netherlands
Phone: +31 20 7162479

#452
Karin Vromen atelier
Category: Performing Arts
Area: Centrum, West
Address: Van Linschotenstraat 32
1013 PN Amsterdam The Netherlands
Phone: +31 20 6812643

#453
Pakt
Category: Art Gallery
Area: Oost, Zeeburg
Address: Zeeburgerpad 53 1019 AB
Amsterdam The Netherlands
Phone: +31 20 4688395

#454
Schram Film Studio's
Category: Dance Club
Area: Noord
Address: Grasweg 50 1031 HX
Amsterdam The Netherlands
Phone: +31 20 6345123

#455
Ons Lieve Heer op Solder
Category: Museum
Area: Centrum, De Wallen
Address: Oudezijds Voorburgwal 40
1012 GE Amsterdam The Netherlands
Phone: +31 20 6246604

#456
A.V.V.
Category: Professional Sports Team
Area: Oost
Address: Kruislaan 4 1097 EC
Amsterdam The Netherlands
Phone: +31 20 6920810

#457
Ton Overmars
Category: Beer, Wine & Spirits, Wineries
Area: Zuid, Hoofddorppleinbuurt
Address: Hoofddorpplein 11 1059 CV
Amsterdam The Netherlands
Phone: +31 20 6157142

#458
BIHP
Category: Art Gallery, French
Area: Centrum, Negen Straatjes
Address: Keizersgracht 335 1016 EG
Amsterdam The Netherlands
Phone: +31 20 4282609

#459
Aronson Antiquairs
Category: Art Gallery
Area: Centrum
Address: Nieuwe Spiegelstraat 39-III
1017 DC Amsterdam The Netherlands
Phone: +31 20 6233103

#460
Kunsthandel Artist
Category: Antiques, Art Gallery
Area: Centrum
Address: Kerkstraat 159 1017 GG
Amsterdam The Netherlands
Phone: +31 20 4281360

#461
Mayadam
Category: Jewelry, Arts & Entertainment
Area: Centrum
Address: Vijzelstraat 133 1017 HJ
Amsterdam The Netherlands
Phone: +31 20 6946864

#462
Anneke Schat
Category: Art Gallery
Area: Centrum
Address: Spiegelgracht 20-A 1017 JR
Amsterdam The Netherlands
Phone: +31 20 6251608

#463
Spiegeling ART
Category: Art Gallery
Area: Centrum
Address: Spiegelgracht 26 1017 JS
Amsterdam The Netherlands
Phone: +31 20 4211406

#464
Silkwood Antiques
Category: Art Gallery
Area: Centrum
Address: Spiegelgracht 30 1017 JS
Amsterdam The Netherlands
Phone: +31 653 862270

#465
Het Muziektheater
Category: Performing Arts
Area: Centrum
Address: Waterlooplein 22 1011 PN
Amsterdam The Netherlands
Phone: +31 20 5518117

#466
Van Gogh Museum Library
Category: Museum
Area: Zuid, Museumkwartier
Address: Museumplein 4 1070 AJ
Amsterdam The Netherlands
Phone: +31 20 5705978

#467
Galerie Canvas International Art
Category: Art Gallery
Area: Zuid, De Pijp
Address: Gerard Doustraat 142-144
1073 VX Amsterdam The Netherlands
Phone: +31 20 4286040

#468
Harry Van Gestel
Category: Art Gallery
Area: Centrum
Address: Torensteeg 3 1012 TH
Amsterdam The Netherlands
Phone: +31 645 622607

#469
Erotisch Museum
Category: Museum, Adult Entertainment
Area: Centrum, De Wallen
Address: Oudezijds Achterburgwal 54
1012 DV Amsterdam The Netherlands
Phone: +31 20 6278954

#470
Club Underground
Category: Dance Club, Music Venues
Area: Centrum, Jordaan
Address: Rozengracht 133 1016 LV
Amsterdam The Netherlands
Phone: +31 20 4162211

#471
Argan
Category: Social Club
Area: West, Oud West
Address: Overtoom 141 1054 HG
Amsterdam The Netherlands
Phone: +31 20 6389966

#472
Concertgebouw
Category: Music Venues
Area: Zuid, Museumkwartier
Address: Concertgebouwplein 10 1071
LN Amsterdam The Netherlands
Phone: +31 20 5730400

#473
Amsterdamse Vereniging DE Zondagsschilders
Category: Social Club
Area: Centrum, De Wallen
Address: Geldersekade 101-3 1011 EM
Amsterdam The Netherlands
Phone: +31 20 6243933

#474
Bodill Lamain
Category: Arts & Entertainment
Area: Zuid, De Pijp
Address: Eerste Jan van der
Heijdenstraat 84-HS 1072 TZ Amsterdam
The Netherlands
Phone: +31 20 7717898

#475
Gallery PR2
Category: Art Gallery
Area: Centrum, De Wallen
Address: Zeedijk 73 1012 AS
Amsterdam The Netherlands
Phone: +31 685 16885

#476
De Erfenis Store
Category: Art Gallery
Area: Zuid, De Pijp
Address: Ceintuurbaan 384 1073 EM
Amsterdam The Netherlands
Phone: +31 653 647184

#477
Galerie Rob Koudijs
Category: Art Gallery
Area: Centrum, Jordaan
Address: Elandsgracht 12-HUIS 1016
TV Amsterdam The Netherlands
Phone: +31 20 3318796

#478
ART District
Category: Art Gallery
Area: Centrum, Jordaan
Address: Westerstraat 230 1015 MS
Amsterdam The Netherlands
Phone: +31 20 3302370

#479
Maggi Giles
Category: Art Gallery
Area: Centrum, Haarlemmerbuurt
Address: Korte Prinsengracht 660 1017
KW Amsterdam The Netherlands
Phone: +31 20 6247443

#480
LL World Wide
Category: Art Gallery
Area: Zuid, Willemspark
Address: Koninginneweg 83 1075 CJ
Amsterdam The Netherlands
Phone: +31 20 6720989

#481
Holland Festival
Category: Festival
Area: Centrum
Address: Piet Heinkade 5 1019 BR
Amsterdam The Netherlands
Phone: +31 20 7882100

#482
De Afrika Centrale
Category: Performing Arts,
Venues & Events
Area: West, De Baarsjes
Address: Witte de Withstraat 52-HS
1057 ZB Amsterdam The Netherlands
Phone: +31 20 6854197

#483
Meubel Stukken
Category: Festival
Area: Centrum, Haarlemmerbuurt
Address: Tussen de Bogen 24 1013 JB
Amsterdam The Netherlands
Phone: +31 20 6267305

#484
Stichting Theaterstraat
Category: Performing Arts
Area: Oost, Oosterparkbuurt
Address: Derde Oosterparkstraat 178
1092 EG Amsterdam The Netherlands
Phone: +31 20 4976076

#485
De Verbinding
Category: Social Club
Area: Oost, Oosterparkbuurt
Address: Joubertstraat 15 1091 XN
Amsterdam The Netherlands
Phone: +31 20 4609300

#486
Kim Sutherland
Category: Arts & Entertainment
Area: Centrum, Haarlemmerbuurt
Address: Tussen de Bogen 65 1052 AX
Amsterdam The Netherlands
Phone: +31 643 858811

#487
Harry Lakenman
Category: Performing Arts,
Event Planning & Services
Area: Zuid, Rivierenbuurt
Address: Rijnstraat 162-3 1079 HR
Amsterdam The Netherlands
Phone: +31 20 6427359

#488
EL Hema Tentoonstelling
Category: Art Gallery
Area: Centrum
Address: Blankenstraat 410 1018 SK
Amsterdam The Netherlands
Phone: +31 20 6655001

#489
M-Lab
Category: Performing Arts,
Venues & Events, Music Venues
Address: Aambeeldstraat 24 1021 KB
Amsterdam The Netherlands
Phone: +31 20 4350940

#490
Frascati
Category: Performing Arts
Area: Centrum, De Wallen
Address: Nes 63 1012 KD
Amsterdam The Netherlands
Phone: +31 20 6266866

#491
Titus Brein Fotografie
Category: Photographers, Art Gallery
Area: Centrum, Jordaan
Address: raamplein 1 Jordaan,
Noord-Holland The Netherlands
Phone: +31 624 209192

#492
331 West
Category: Art Gallery, Coffee & Tea
Area: West, Bos en Lommer
Address: Admiraal de Ruijterweg 331
Bos en Lommer, Noord-Holland
The Netherlands
Phone: +31 20 6828362

#493
Heremijntijd
Category: Art Gallery
Area: Centrum, Jordaan
Address: Eerste Bloemdwarsstraat 15
1016 KR Jordaan The Netherlands
Phone: +31 629 000609

#494
Meia Wippoo Video en Concept
Category: Performing Arts
Area: Zuid, De Pijp
Address: Eerste Jan Steenstraat 44E
1072 NL De Pijp The Netherlands
Phone: +31 651 250198

#495
**Eduard Planting Gallery
Fine Art Photographs**
Category: Art Gallery
Area: Centrum, De Wallen
Address: Eerste Bloemdwarsstraat 2
links 1013 KS Jordaan The Netherlands
Phone: +31 20 3206705

#496
Casa Rosso
Category: Arts & Entertainment
Area: Centrum, De Wallen
Address: 1001 RH 7833 AC
Amsterdam The Netherlands
Phone: +31 20 6278954

#497
John Winckel Music
Category: Performing Arts
Area: West, Hoofdweg en Omgeving
Address: Andreas Schelfhoutstraat 25
1058 HR 1Amsterdam The Netherlands
Phone: +31 645 320607

#498
Alina D.
Category: Venues & Events,
Performing Arts
Area: Centrum, De Wallen
Address: Prins Hendrikkade 48 k 1012
AC Amsterdam The Netherlands
Phone: +31 20 4687950

#499
Stedelijk Museum Amsterdam
Category: Museum
Area: Zuid, Museumkwartier
Address: Museumplein 10 1071 DJ
Amsterdam The Netherlands
Phone: +31 20 5732911

#500
Jaski Art Gallery
Category: Art Gallery
Area: Centrum
Address: Nieuwe Spiegelstraat 29 1017
DB Amsterdam The Netherlands
Phone: +31 20 6203939

#1
Paradiso Amsterdam
Category: Dance Club
Average price: Modest
Area: Centrum
Address: Weteringschans 6-8 1017 SG
Amsterdam The Netherlands
Phone: +31 20 6264521

#2
Proeflokaal Arendsnest
Category: Pub
Average price: Modest
Area: Centrum
Address: Herengracht 90 1015 BS
Amsterdam The Netherlands
Phone: +31 20 4212057

#3
De Melkweg
Category: Dance Club, Art Galleries
Average price: Modest
Area: Centrum
Address: Lijnbaansgracht 234 1017 PH
Amsterdam The Netherlands
Phone: +31 20 5318181

#4
Door 74
Category: Cocktail Bar
Average price: Expensive
Area: Centrum
Address: Reguliersdwarsstraat 74I 1017
BN Amsterdam The Netherlands
Phone: +31 634 045122

#5
Cafe Brecht
Category: Bar, Cafe
Average price: Modest
Area: Centrum
Address: Weteringschans 157 1017 SE
Amsterdam The Netherlands
Phone: +31 20 6272211

#6
Mystique
Category: Bar, Diners
Average price: Expensive
Area: Centrum
Address: Utrechtsestraat 30a 1017 VN
Amsterdam The Netherlands
Phone: +31 20 3302994

#7
Bierproeflokaal in de Wildeman
Category: Pub
Average price: Modest
Area: Centrum
Address: Kolksteeg 3-HS 1012 PT
Amsterdam The Netherlands
Phone: +31 20 6382348

#8
HPS
Category: Lounge
Average price: Expensive
Area: Centrum
Address: Rapenburg 18 1011 TX
Amsterdam The Netherlands
Phone: +31 625 293620

#9
Whisky Café L&B
Category: Pub
Average price: Modest
Area: Centrum
Address: Korte Leidsedwarsstraat 82-84
1017 RD Amsterdam The Netherlands
Phone: +31 624 554162

#10
Vesper Bar
Category: Bar
Average price: Expensive
Area: Centrum, Haarlemmerbuurt
Address: Vinkenstraat 57 1013 JM
Amsterdam The Netherlands
Phone: +31 20 4286888

#11
Beer Temple
Category: Pub
Average price: Modest
Area: Centrum
Address: Nieuwezijds Voorburgwal 250
1012 RR Amsterdam The Netherlands
Phone: +31 20 6271427

#12
Café Hoppe
Category: Pub
Average price: Modest
Area: Centrum
Address: Spui 18-20 1012 XA
Amsterdam The Netherlands
Phone: +31 20 4204420

#13
Café Belgique
Category: Beer, Wine & Spirits, Pub
Average price: Modest
Area: Centrum
Address: Gravenstraat 2 1012 NM
Amsterdam The Netherlands
Phone: +31 20 6251974

#14
De Reiger
Category: Pub, Cafe
Average price: Modest
Area: Centrum, Jordaan
Address: Nieuwe Leliestraat 34 1015 ST
Amsterdam The Netherlands
Phone: +31 20 6247426

#15
De Dampkring
Category: Coffeeshops
Average price: Modest
Area: Centrum
Address: Handboogstraat 29-1 1012 XM
Amsterdam The Netherlands
Phone: +31 20 4236040

#16
Little Collins
Category: Breakfast & Brunch,
Diners, Bar
Average price: Modest
Area: Zuid, De Pijp
Address: 1e Sweelinckstraat 19 F
1073 CL Amsterdam The Netherlands
Phone: +31 20 6732293

#17
Hard Rock Cafe Amsterdam
Category: Pub, American
Average price: Modest
Area: Centrum
Address: Max Euweplein 57-61 1017
MA Amsterdam The Netherlands
Phone: +31 20 5237625

#18
Coffeeshop Abraxas
Category: Coffeeshops
Average price: Modest
Area: Centrum
Address: Spuistraat 51 1012 ST
Amsterdam The Netherlands
Phone: +31 20 6255763

#19
Harlem Soul Food
Category: Soul Food, Bar
Average price: Modest
Area: Centrum, Haarlemmerbuurt
Address: Haarlemmerstraat 77 1013 EL
Amsterdam The Netherlands
Phone: +31 20 3301498

#20
De Tweede Kamer
Category: Nightlife
Average price: Modest
Area: Centrum
Address: Heisteeg 6 1012 WC
Amsterdam The Netherlands
Phone: +31 20 4222236

#21
Amsterdam Roest
Category: Restaurant, Bar,
Venues & Event Spaces
Average price: Inexpensive
Area: Centrum
Address: Czaar Peterstraat 213
1018 PL Amsterdam The Netherlands
Phone: +31 20 3080283

#22
Trouw Amsterdam
Category: Dance Club, Venues & Event
Spaces, Mediterranean
Average price: Modest
Area: Oost, Oosterparkbuurt
Address: Wibautstraat 131 1091 GL
Amsterdam The Netherlands
Phone: +31 20 4637788

#23
The Flying Pig Downtown
Category: Pub, Hostels
Average price: Modest
Area: Centrum
Address: Nieuwendijk 100 1012 MR
Amsterdam The Netherlands
Phone: +31 20 4206822

#24
Mata Hari
Category: Bar, Mediterranean
Average price: Modest
Area: Centrum, De Wallen
Address: Oudezijds Achterburgwal 22
1012 DM Amsterdam The Netherlands
Phone: +31 20 2050919

#25
Bar Americain
Category: Bar
Average price: Expensive
Area: Centrum
Address: Leidsekade 97 1017 PN
Amsterdam The Netherlands
Phone: +31 20 5563000

#26
SkyLounge
Category: Lounge
Average price: Expensive
Area: Centrum
Address: Oosterdoksstraat 4 1011 DK
Amsterdam The Netherlands
Phone: +31 20 5300800

#27
Brandstof
Category: Pub, Restaurant
Average price: Modest
Area: Centrum, Jordaan
Address: Marnixstraat 341 1016 TD
Amsterdam The Netherlands
Phone: +31 20 4220813

#28
In 't Aepjen
Category: Pub
Average price: Inexpensive
Area: Centrum, De Wallen
Address: Zeedijk 1 1012 AN Amsterdam
The Netherlands
Phone: +31 20 6268401

#29
Blue
Category: Sandwiches, Bar, Cafe
Average price: Modest
Area: Centrum
Address: Singel 457 1012 WP
Amsterdam The Netherlands
Phone: +31 20 4273901

#30
Genootschap der Geneugten
Category: Pub .
Average price: Modest
Area: Centrum
Address: Kerkstraat 54-HS 1017 GM
Amsterdam The Netherlands
Phone: +31 20 6250934

#31
Leidseplein
Category: Landmark
& Historical Buildings
Average price: Modest
Area: Centrum
Address: Leidseplein 1-35 1017 PR
Amsterdam The Netherlands
Phone: +31 20 6842090

#33
Struik
Category: Pub, Sandwiches
Average price: Inexpensive
Area: Centrum, Jordaan
Address: Rozengracht 160 1016 NJ
Amsterdam The Netherlands
Phone: +31 20 6254863

#32
Bitterzoet
Category: Music Venues
Average price: Modest
Area: Centrum
Address: Spuistraat 2-HS 1012 TS
Amsterdam The Netherlands
Phone: +31 20 4212318

#34
Kriterion
Category: Cinema, Pub, Music Venues
Average price: Inexpensive
Area: Plantagebuurt, Centrum
Address: Roetersstraat 170 1018 WE
Amsterdam The Netherlands
Phone: +31 20 6231708

#35
Eetcafe van Beeren
Category: GastroPub, Pub, Brasseries
Average price: Expensive
Area: Centrum
Address: Koningsstraat 54 1011 EW
Amsterdam The Netherlands
Phone: +31 20 6222329

#36
Restaurant Vapiano
Category: Italian, Bar, Pizza
Average price: Modest
Area: Centrum
Address: Oosterdokskade 145 1011 DL
Amsterdam The Netherlands
Phone: +31 20 4202025

#37
Bo Cinq
Category: Bar, French, Desserts
Average price: Expensive
Area: Centrum
Address: Prinsengracht 494 1017 KH
Amsterdam The Netherlands
Phone: +31 20 6220682

#38
Notting Hill Hotel
Category: Hotels, Nightlife, Restaurant
Average price: Exclusive
Area: Centrum
Address: Westeinde 26 1017 ZP
Amsterdam The Netherlands
Phone: +31 20 5231030

#39
Studio 80
Category: Dance Club
Average price: Expensive
Area: Centrum
Address: Rembrandtplein 17 1017 CT
Amsterdam The Netherlands
Phone: +31 20 5218333

#40
Bierfabriek
Category: Barbeque, Pub
Average price: Modest
Area: Centrum
Address: Rokin 75 1012 KL Amsterdam
The Netherlands
Phone: +31 20 5289910

#41
Café Gambrinus
Category: GastroPub, Pub, Dive Bar
Average price: Modest
Area: Zuid, De Pijp
Address: Ferdinand Bolstraat 180 1072
LV Amsterdam The Netherlands
Phone: +31 20 6717389

#42
De Koe
Category: Bar, Cafe
Average price: Modest
Area: Centrum, Jordaan
Address: Marnixstraat 381 1016 XR
Amsterdam The Netherlands
Phone: +31 20 6254482

#43
Mulligans
Category: Bar
Average price: Inexpensive
Area: Centrum
Address: Amstel 100 1017 AC
Amsterdam The Netherlands
Phone: +31 20 6221330

#44
Dvars
Category: Cocktail Bar
Average price: Expensive
Area: Centrum
Address: Reguliersdwarsstraat 44
1017 BM Amsterdam The Netherlands
Phone: +31 20 3209108

#45
Café Wheels
Category: Dive Bar, GastroPub
Average price: Modest
Area: Centrum, Negen Straatjes
Address: Wolvenstraat 4-III 1016 EP
Amsterdam The Netherlands
Phone: +31 20 6228673

#46
Vyne
Category: Wine Bar
Average price: Expensive
Area: Centrum, Negen Straatjes
Address: Prinsengracht 411 1016 HM
Amsterdam The Netherlands
Phone: +31 20 3446408

#47
Festina Lente
Category: Dive Bar
Average price: Modest
Area: Centrum, Jordaan
Address: Looiersgracht 40b 1016 VS
Amsterdam The Netherlands
Phone: +31 20 6381412

#48
Screaming Beans
Category: Pub, Wine Bar, Restaurant
Average price: Expensive
Area: West, Oud West, Helmersbuurt
Address: Eerste Constantijn
Huygensstraat 35 1054 BR Amsterdam
The Netherlands
Phone: +31 20 6160770

#49
Studio/K
Category: Dance Club,
Cinema, GastroPub
Average price: Modest
Area: Oost, Indische Buurt
Address: Timorplein 62 1094 CC
Amsterdam The Netherlands
Phone: +31 20 6920422

#50
Supperclub
Category: Dance Club
Average price: Expensive
Area: Centrum
Address: Jonge Roelensteeg 21 1012
PL Amsterdam The Netherlands
Phone: +31 20 3446400

#51
Zouk
Category: GastroPub, Pub
Average price: Modest
Area: West, Oud West, Helmersbuurt
Address: 1e C Huygensstr 45 1054 BS
Amsterdam The Netherlands
Phone: +31 20 6891133

#52
Café Gollem
Category: Pub
Average price: Modest
Area: Centrum
Address: Raamsteeg 4 1012 VZ
Amsterdam The Netherlands
Phone: +31 623 234851

#53
Bimhuis
Category: Music Venues
Average price: Modest
Area: Centrum
Address: Piet Heinkade 3 1019 BR
Amsterdam The Netherlands
Phone: +31 20 7882188

#54
Brug 34
Category: Coffee & Tea, Pub
Average price: Inexpensive
Area: Centrum
Address: Utrechtsestraat 19 1017 VH
Amsterdam The Netherlands
Phone: +31 20 2236793

#55
Pompstation Bar&Grill
Category: Restaurant, Music Venues
Average price: Expensive
Area: Oost, Zeeburg
Address: Zeeburgerdijk 52 1094 AE
Amsterdam The Netherlands
Phone: +31 20 6922888

#56
Café Parck
Category: Pub
Average price: Modest
Area: West, Oud West
Address: Overtoom 428 1054 JV
Amsterdam The Netherlands
Phone: +31 20 4125335

#57
Café Luxembourg
Category: Pub
Average price: Modest
Area: Centrum
Address: Spui 24 1012 XA Amsterdam
The Netherlands
Phone: +31 20 6206264

#58
Café P96
Category: Pub
Average price: Modest
Area: Centrum, Jordaan
Address: Prinsengracht 96 1015 DZ
Amsterdam The Netherlands
Phone: +31 20 6221864

#59
Hugo's Bar & Kitchen
Category: Restaurant, Cocktail Bar
Average price: Modest
Area: West, Frederik Hendrikbuurt
Address: Hugo de Grootplein 10 1052
KW Amsterdam The Netherlands
Phone: +31 20 7516633

#60
Café Bloemers
Category: Bar, GastroPub, Cafe
Average price: Modest
Area: Zuid, De Pijp
Address: Hemonystraat 70 1074 BT
Amsterdam The Netherlands
Phone: +31 20 4004024

#61
Novotel Amsterdam
Category: Hotels, Pub, Restaurant
Average price: Modest
Area: Zuid, Buitenveldert
Address: Europaboulevard 10 1083 AD
Amsterdam The Netherlands
Phone: +31 20 5411123

#62
Casablanca Muziek
Category: Pub, Music Venues, Karaoke
Average price: Expensive
Area: Centrum, De Wallen
Address: Zeedijk 26E 1012 AZ
Amsterdam The Netherlands
Phone: +31 612 200519

#63
Café de Dokter
Category: Pub, Jazz & Blues
Average price: Inexpensive
Area: Centrum
Address: Rozenboomsteeg 4 1012 PR
Amsterdam The Netherlands
Phone: +31 20 6264427

#64
Gollem's Proeflokaal
Category: Pub, GastroPub
Average price: Modest
Area: West, Oud West, Helmersbuurt
Address: Overtoom 160-162 1054 HP
Amsterdam The Netherlands
Phone: +31 20 6129444

#65
Café Katoen
Category: Pub
Average price: Inexpensive
Area: Centrum, De Wallen
Address: Oude Turfmarkt 153
1012 GC Amsterdam The Netherlands
Phone: +31 20 6262635

#66
Café de Dam
Category: Pub
Average price: Inexpensive
Area: Centrum, De Wallen
Address: Damstraat 4 1012 JM
Amsterdam The Netherlands
Phone: +31 20 6245331

#67
Café Thuys
Category: Pub, Food, Restaurant
Average price: Modest
Area: West, Oud West, Kinkerbuurt
Address: De Clercqstraat 129 1053 AK
Amsterdam The Netherlands
Phone: +31 20 6120898

#68
Café LUX
Category: Pub
Average price: Modest
Area: Centrum
Address: Marnixstraat 403 1017 PJ
Amsterdam The Netherlands
Phone: +31 20 4221412

#69
College Hotel
Category: Lounge, Hotels, Restaurant
Average price: Expensive
Area: Zuid, Museumkwartier
Address: Roelof Hartstraat 1 1071 VE
Amsterdam The Netherlands
Phone: +31 20 5711511

#70
Tolhuistuin
Category: Music Venues,
Performing Arts
Average price: Modest
Area: Noord
Address: Tolhuisweg 2 1031 CL
Amsterdam The Netherlands
Phone: +31 20 7630650

#71
Café De Engelbewaarder
Category: Pub, GastroPub
Average price: Modest
Area: Centrum
Address: Kloveniersburgwal 59-HS
1011 JZ Amsterdam The Netherlands
Phone: +31 20 6253772

#72
**Holland International
Canal Cruises**
Category: Nightlife, Restaurant,
Arts & Entertainment
Average price: Modest
Area: Centrum
Address: Prins Hendrikkade 33a 1012
TM Amsterdam The Netherlands
Phone: +31 20 6253035

#73
Café Kuijper
Category: Dive Bar
Average price: Modest
Area: Oost, Dapperbuurt
Address: Linnaeusstraat 79 1093 EK
Amsterdam The Netherlands
Phone: +31 20 6651926

#74
Café Restaurant Kapitein Zeppos
Category: Diners, Pub
Average price: Modest
Area: Centrum, De Wallen
Address: Gebed Zonder End 5 1012 HS
Amsterdam The Netherlands
Phone: +31 20 6242057

#75
CC MuziekCafé
Category: Jazz & Blues,
Music Venues, Cafe
Average price: Inexpensive
Area: Zuid, De Pijp
Address: Rustenburgerstraat 384 1072
HG Amsterdam The Netherlands
Phone: +31 624 236956

#76
Het Sexmuseum Amsterdam
Category: Museums, Adult
Entertainment
Average price: Inexpensive
Area: Centrum
Address: Damrak 18 1012 LH
Amsterdam The Netherlands
Phone: +31 20 6228376

#77
Getto
Category: Gay Bar, GastroPub, Pub
Average price: Modest
Area: Centrum, De Wallen
Address: Warmoesstraat 51-B 1012 HW
Amsterdam The Netherlands
Phone: +31 20 4215151

#78
Mazzo
Category: Beer, Wine & Spirits, Bar,
Restaurant
Average price: Modest
Area: Centrum, Jordaan
Address: Rozengracht 114 1016 NH
Amsterdam The Netherlands
Phone: +31 20 3446402

#79
Café de Gaeper
Category: Pub, GastroPub
Average price: Modest
Area: Centrum
Address: Staalstraat 4-IV 1011 JL
Amsterdam The Netherlands
Phone: +31 20 6233895

#80
Café Bouwman
Category: Dive Bar
Average price: Modest
Area: Centrum
Address: Utrechtsestraat 102 1017 VS
Amsterdam The Netherlands
Phone: +31 20 6265444

#81
Cafe de Kroeg
Category: Pub
Average price: Inexpensive
Area: Zuid, De Pijp
Address: Ferdinand Bolstraat 12 1072
LJ Amsterdam The Netherlands
Phone: +31 20 6711456

#82
Café Bloemers
Category: Bar, GastroPub, Cafe
Average price: Modest
Area: Zuid, De Pijp
Address: Hemonystraat 70 1074 BT
Amsterdam The Netherlands
Phone: +31 20 4004024

#83
Henry's Bar
Category: Cocktail Bar
Average price: Modest
Area: Oost, Oosterparkbuurt
Address: Oosterpark 11 1092 AE
Amsterdam The Netherlands
Phone: +31 20 3701685

#84
Cafe Brandon
Category: Pub
Average price: Modest
Area: Centrum
Address: Keizersgracht 157 1015 CL
Amsterdam The Netherlands
Phone: +31 681 942404

#85
Greenhouse Lounge
Category: Lounge
Average price: Exclusive
Area: Centrum, Haarlemmerbuurt
Address: Haarlemmerstraat 64 1013 ET
Amsterdam The Netherlands
Phone: +31 20 6277329

#86
Café de Doelen
Category: Pub, GastroPub
Average price: Modest
Area: Centrum
Address: Kloveniersburgwal 125 1011
KC Amsterdam The Netherlands
Phone: +31 20 6249023

#87
De Ebeling
Category: Bar, GastroPub
Average price: Modest
Area: West, Helmersbuurt
Address: Overtoom 50-54 1054 HK
Amsterdam The Netherlands
Phone: +31 20 6891218

#88
Mash
Category: Pub
Average price: Modest
Area: Zuid, De Pijp
Address: Gerard Douplein 9-h
1073 XE Amsterdam The Netherlands
Phone: +31 648 469747

#89
Cafe Helmers
Category: Pub
Average price: Inexpensive
Area: West, Oud West, Helmersbuurt
Address: 1e C Huygensstr 59-VI 1054
BT Amsterdam The Netherlands
Phone: +31 20 6122761

#90
Nomads
Category: Middle Eastern, Hookah Bar
Average price: Expensive
Area: Centrum, Jordaan
Address: Rozengracht 133 I 1016 LV
Amsterdam The Netherlands
Phone: +31 20 3446405

#91
Gashouder
Category: Music Venues
Average price: Modest
Area: Westerpark, West
Address: Haarlemmerweg 8-10 1014 BE
Amsterdam The Netherlands
Phone: +31 20 5974458

#92
Golden Brown Bar
Category: GastroPub, Bar, Thai
Average price: Modest
Area: West, Oud West, Helmersbuurt
Address: Jan Pieter Heijestraat 146
1054 WT Amsterdam The Netherlands
Phone: +31 20 6124076

#93
St.
Category: Irish, GastroPub, Pub
Average price: Expensive
Area: Centrum
Address: Rembrandtplein 8-10 1017 CV
Amsterdam The Netherlands
Phone: +31 20 4226886

#94
Caffe Milo
Category: Pub, Italian, GastroPub
Average price: Modest
Area: Oost, Dapperbuurt
Address: Linnaeusstraat 71-H 1093 EJ
Amsterdam The Netherlands
Phone: +31 20 4638027

#95
Kitchen & Bar Van Rijn
Category: Bar, Steakhouses
Average price: Modest
Area: Centrum
Address: Rembrandtplein 17 1017 CT
Amsterdam The Netherlands
Phone: +31 20 4500555

#96
Café The Doors
Category: Pub
Average price: Modest
Area: Centrum, Haarlemmerbuurt
Address: Singel 14 1013 GA Amsterdam
The Netherlands
Phone: +31 20 6263900

#97
Senses Restaurant
Category: French, Wine Bar
Average price: Modest
Area: Centrum
Address: Vijzelstraat 45 1017 HE
Amsterdam The Netherlands
Phone: +31 20 5306266

#98
Coco's Outback
Category: Dance Club, Australian
Average price: Modest
Area: Centrum
Address: Thorbeckeplein 8 1017 CS
Amsterdam The Netherlands
Phone: +31 20 6272423

#99
Café Cox
Category: Bar
Average price: Modest
Area: Centrum
Address: Marnixstraat 429 1017 PK
Amsterdam The Netherlands
Phone: +31 20 7959995

#100
Westerliefde
Category: Venues & Event Spaces,
Dance Club
Average price: Modest
Area: West
Address: Könneplein 4-6 1014 DD
Amsterdam The Netherlands
Phone: +31 20 6848496

#101
The Grasshopper
Category: Hookah Bar
Average price: Expensive
Area: Centrum, De Wallen
Address: Nieuwezijds Voorburgwal 59
1012 RD Amsterdam The Netherlands
Phone: +31 20 4287224

#102
Brouwerij Troost
Category: Pub, Breweries
Average price: Modest
Area: Zuid, De Pijp
Address: Cornelis Troostplein 23 1072
JJ Amsterdam The Netherlands
Phone: +31 20 7371028

#103
Cafe Fonteyn
Category: Bar, GastroPub
Average price: Modest
Area: Centrum
Address: Nieuwmarkt 13-BG 1011 JR
Amsterdam The Netherlands
Phone: +31 20 4227050

#104
Cafe Ruk en Pluk
Category: Dive Bar
Average price: Modest
Area: Oost, Oosterparkbuurt
Address: Linnaeusstraat 48-III
1092 CM Amsterdam The Netherlands
Phone: +31 20 6653248

#105
Freddy's Bar
Category:
Average price: Bar
Area: Centrum, De Wallen
Address: Hotel De l'Europe 1012 CP
Amsterdam The Netherlands
Phone: +31 20 5311707

#106
Café 't Hooischip
Category: Dive Bar, GastroPub
Average price: Modest
Area: Centrum
Address: Amstel 31 1011 PT
Amsterdam The Netherlands
Phone: +31 20 6238733

#107
Café Lange Leo
Category: Karaoke, Pub
Average price: Modest
Area: Centrum
Address: Spuistraat 326 1012 VX
Amsterdam The Netherlands
Phone: +31 20 7700162

#108
Coffeeshop Rusland
Category: Nightlife
Average price: Inexpensive
Area: Centrum, De Wallen
Address: Rusland 16-I 1012 CL
Amsterdam The Netherlands
Phone: +31 20 6279468

#109
Mazzeltof
Category:
Average price: Bar
Area: Zuid, De Pijp
Address: Ferdinand Bolstraat 40-HS
1072 LL Amsterdam The Netherlands
Phone: +31 20 6712061

#110
Café Pakhuis Wilhelmina
Category: Pub
Average price: Modest
Area: Oost
Address: Veemkade 576 1019 BL
Amsterdam The Netherlands
Phone: +31 20 4193368

#111
Jimmy Woo
Category: Dance Club
Average price: Expensive
Area: Centrum
Address: Korte Leidsedwarsstraat 18
1017 RC Amsterdam The Netherlands
Phone: +31 20 6263150

#112
Gasthuys
Category: Pub
Average price: Modest
Area: Centrum, De Wallen
Address: Grimburgwal 7-HS 1012 GA
Amsterdam The Netherlands
Phone: +31 20 6248230

#113
Café Krom
Category: Bar
Average price: Modest
Area: Centrum
Address: Utrechtsestraat 76 1017 VR
Amsterdam The Netherlands
Phone: +31 20 6245343

#114
Café Thijssen
Category: Pub, Sandwiches
Average price: Modest
Area: Centrum, Jordaan
Address: Brouwersgracht 107-II 1015
GD Amsterdam The Netherlands
Phone: +31 20 6238994

#115
SugarFactory
Category: Dance Club,
Performing Arts, Music Venues
Average price: Modest
Area: Centrum
Address: Lijnbaansgracht 238 1017 ph
Amsterdam The Netherlands
Phone: +31 20 6265006

#116
Cafe Koosje
Category: Pub
Average price: Modest
Area: Plantagebuurt, Centrum
Address: Plantage Middenlaan 37 1018
DB Amsterdam The Netherlands
Phone: +31 20 3200817

#117
Escape
Category: Dance Club
Average price: Modest
Area: Centrum
Address: Rembrandtplein 11 1017 CT
Amsterdam The Netherlands
Phone: +31 20 6204820

#118
The Bulldog Palace
Category: Bar
Average price: Modest
Area: Centrum
Address: Leidseplein 15 1017 PS
Amsterdam The Netherlands
Phone: +31 20 6271908

#119
The Bulldog Mack
Category: Pub
Average price: Expensive
Area: Centrum, De Wallen
Address: Oudezijds Voorburgwal 132
1012 GH Amsterdam The Netherlands
Phone: +31 20 6270295

#120
Cafe Cuba
Category: Bar
Average price: Modest
Area: Centrum
Address: Nieuwmarkt 3 1011 JP
Amsterdam The Netherlands
Phone: +31 20 6274919

#121
Hesp
Category: Nightlife, GastroPub
Average price: Modest
Area: Oost, Oosterparkbuurt
Address: Weesperzijde 130-131 1091
ER Amsterdam The Netherlands
Phone: +31 20 6651202

#122
D' Overkant
Category: Pub, GastroPub, Cafe
Average price: Modest
Area: Zuid, Rivierenbuurt
Address: Scheldestraat 101-105 1078
GJ Amsterdam The Netherlands
Phone: +31 20 6797366

#123
Cafe De Pels
Category: Bar
Average price: Modest
Area: Centrum, Negen Straatjes
Address: Huidenstraat 25-3 1016 ER
Amsterdam The Netherlands
Phone: +31 20 6229037

#124
Café Weber
Category: Bar
Average price: Inexpensive
Area: Centrum
Address: Marnixstraat 397 1017 PJ
Amsterdam The Netherlands
Phone: +31 20 6229910

#125
Simpel
Category: Diners, Bar
Average price: Expensive
Area: Zuid, De Pijp
Address: Ferdinand Bolstraat 11 1072
LA Amsterdam The Netherlands
Phone: +31 20 6720672

#126
WestergasTerras
Category: Pub, Cafe
Average price: Modest
Area: West
Address: Klönneplein 4-6 1014 DD
Amsterdam The Netherlands
Phone: +31 20 6848496

#127
Cafe André Lacroix
Category: Dive Bar, Beer, Wine & Spirits
Average price: Inexpensive
Area: West, Oud West
Address: Overtoom 219 1054 HV
Amsterdam The Netherlands
Phone: +31 20 6181072

#128
Casa Rosso
Category: Adult Entertainment
Average price: Expensive
Area: Centrum, De Wallen
Address: Oudezijds Achterburgwal 106-
108 1012 DS Amsterdam The
Netherlands
Phone: +31 20 6278954

#129
KU Kitchen & Bar
Category: Cocktail Bar, Asian Fusion
Average price: Modest
Area: Centrum
Address: Utrechtsestraat 114 1017 VT
Amsterdam The Netherlands
Phone: +31 20 4229424

#130
Club Up
Category: Dance Club
Average price: Modest
Area: Centrum
Address: Korte Leidsedwarsstraat 26
1017 RC Amsterdam The Netherlands
Phone: +31 20 6236985

#131
Kashmir Lounge Coffeeshop
Category: Coffeeshops
Average price: Inexpensive
Area: West, Oud West
Address: Jan Pieter Heijestraat 85-87
1053 GM Amsterdam The Netherlands
Phone: +31 20 6832268

#132
Villa Nieuwmarkt
Category: Pub, GastroPub
Average price: Modest
Area: Centrum
Address: Nieuwmarkt 25 1011 JS
Amsterdam The Netherlands
Phone: +31 20 6246410

#133
Green House
Category: Coffeeshops
Average price: Inexpensive
Area: Centrum, De Wallen
Address: Oudezijds Voorburgwal 191
1012 EW Amsterdam The Netherlands
Phone: +31 20 6271739

#134
Café Schilders
Category: Cafe, Nightlife
Average price: Modest
Area: Zuid, De Pijp
Address: Eerste van der Helststraat 45
1073 AC Amsterdam The Netherlands
Phone: +31 20 6704388

#135
Café Bar Eddy
Category: Pub
Average price: Inexpensive
Area: Zuid, De Pijp
Address: Gerard Doustraat 58 1072 VV
Amsterdam The Netherlands
Phone: +31 20 6734385

#136
Finch Cafe
Category: Pub, GastroPub
Average price: Modest
Area: Centrum, Jordaan
Address: Noordermarkt 5-HS 1015 MV
Amsterdam The Netherlands
Phone: +31 20 6262461

#137
GreenHouse
Category: Nightlife
Average price: Modest
Area: Zuid, De Pijp
Address: Tolstraat 91 1074 VG
Amsterdam The Netherlands
Phone: +31 20 6737430

#138
Toomler
Category: Performing Arts,
Comedy Club, Pub
Average price: Modest
Area: Zuid, Apollobuurt
Address: Breitnerstraat 2 1077 BL
Amsterdam The Netherlands
Phone: +31 20 6707400

#139
De Kroon
Category: Pub, Dance Club
Average price: Modest
Area: Centrum
Address: Rembrandtplein 17-I 1017 CT
Amsterdam The Netherlands
Phone: +31 20 6252011

#140
Zus & Zus
Category: European,
Cocktail Bar
Average price: Modest
Area: Zuid, West
Address: Overtoom 548 1054 LM
Amsterdam The Netherlands
Phone: +31 20 6165825

#141
Feestcafe Woody's
Category: Dance Club
Average price: Modest
Area: Centrum
Address: Thorbeckeplein 20 1017 CS
Amsterdam The Netherlands
Phone: +31 20 6227427

#142
Café de Buurvrouw
Category: Pub, Botanical Gardens
Average price: Modest
Area: Centrum, De Wallen
Address: Sint Pieterspoortsteeg 29-1
1012 HM Amsterdam The Netherlands
Phone: +31 20 6259654

#143
Coffeeshop Abraxas
Category: Coffeeshops
Area: Centrum
Address: Jonge Roelensteeg 12-BG
1012 PL Amsterdam The Netherlands
Phone: +31 20 6245852

#144
Playa Nasty
Category: Dance Club, Cafe
Average price: Modest
Area: Centrum
Address: Thorbeckeplein 6-IV 1017 CS
Amsterdam The Netherlands
Phone: +31 20 6272710

#145
Cafe de Zeemeeuw
Category: Sports Bar, Pub
Average price: Modest
Area: Centrum, De Wallen
Address: Zeedijk 102 1012 BB
Amsterdam The Netherlands
Phone: +31 20 6202097

#146
Bar Saloon
Category: Pub, GastroPub
Average price: Modest
Area: Centrum
Address: Lijnbaansgracht 270-E 1017
RL Amsterdam The Netherlands
Phone: +31 20 6230466

#147
La Bastille
Category: Bar
Average price: Expensive
Area: Centrum
Address: Lijnbaansgracht 245-HS 1017
RK Amsterdam The Netherlands
Phone: +31 20 7768301

#148
Cafe The Minds
Category: Pub
Average price: Modest
Area: Centrum
Address: Spuistraat 245-IV 1012 VP
Amsterdam The Netherlands
Phone: +31 20 6236784

#149
De Myrabelle
Category: Dive Bar, Cafe, GastroPub
Average price: Modest
Area: Centrum
Address: Vijzelgracht 1 1017 HM
Amsterdam The Netherlands
Phone: +31 20 6244109

#150
Société Wunderbar
Category: Pub, Asian Fusion
Average price: Modest
Area: Centrum
Address: Enge kapelsteeg 3 1012 NT
Amsterdam The Netherlands
Phone: +31 20 3703448

#151
Smokey
Category: Dance Club, GastroPub
Average price: Modest
Area: Centrum
Address: Rembrandtplein 18-20 1017
CV Amsterdam The Netherlands
Phone: +31 20 6237244

#152
Suzy Wong
Category: Lounge
Average price: Expensive
Area: Centrum
Address: Korte Leidsedwarsstraat 45
1017 PW Amsterdam The Netherlands
Phone: +31 20 6266769

#153
Het Bosch
Category: Lounge, Seafood, French
Average price: Expensive
Area: Zuid, Buitenveldert
Address: Jollenpad 10 1081 KC
Amsterdam The Netherlands
Phone: +31 20 6445800

#154
Café Van Daele
Category: Pub, Cafe
Average price: Expensive
Area: Centrum
Address: Paleisstraat 101 1012 ZL
Amsterdam The Netherlands
Phone: +31 20 6201415

#155
House of Bols
Category: Museums, Venues & Event
Spaces, Cocktail Bar
Average price: Modest
Area: Zuid, Museumkwartier
Address: Paulus Potterstraat 14 1071
CZ Amsterdam The Netherlands
Phone: +31 20 5708575

#156
Eik en Linde
Category: Pub, Venues & Event Spaces,
Tapas
Average price: Modest
Area: Plantagebuurt, Centrum
Address: Plantage Middenlaan 22 1018
DE Amsterdam The Netherlands
Phone: +31 20 6225716

#157
Café Sound Garden
Category: Pub
Average price: Modest
Area: Centrum, Jordaan
Address: Marnixstraat 164-166 1016 TG
Amsterdam The Netherlands
Phone: +31 20 6202853

#158
Café De Twee Zwaantjes
Category: Dive Bar, Pub
Average price: Modest
Area: Centrum, Jordaan
Address: Prinsengracht 114 1015 EA
Amsterdam The Netherlands
Phone: +31 641 464397

#159
Queen's Head
Category: Bar
Average price: Modest
Area: Centrum, De Wallen
Address: Zeedijk 20 1012 AZ
Amsterdam The Netherlands
Phone: +31 20 4202475

#160
Wijnbar DiVino
Category: Wine Bar
Average price: Modest
Area: Centrum, Jordaan
Address: Boomstraat 41a 1015 LB
Amsterdam The Netherlands
Phone: +31 20 8452207

#161
Pilsener Club DE
Category: Pub
Average price: Modest
Area: Centrum
Address: Begijnensteeg 4 1012 PN
Amsterdam The Netherlands
Phone: +31 20 6231777

#162
Café Fonk
Category: Pub, GastroPub
Average price: Modest
Area: Zuid, De Pijp
Address: Dusartstraat 51 1072 HN
Amsterdam The Netherlands
Phone: +31 20 6732487

#163
De Ruyschkamer
Category: Coffee & Tea, Pub,
Juice Bar& Smoothies
Average price: Modest
Area: Oost, Oosterparkbuurt
Address: Ruyschstraat 34 1091 CC
Amsterdam The Netherlands
Phone: +31 20 6703622

#164
Orbit Restaurant & Lounge
Category: Asian Fusion,
Japanese, Lounge
Area: Zuid, Rivierenbuurt
Address: Scheldestraat 95 1078 GJ
Amsterdam The Netherlands
Phone: +31 20 6722922

#165
Players Food & Drinks
Category: Pub, Restaurant
Average price: Modest
Area: Centrum
Address: Kleine Gartmanplantsoen 25
1017 RP Amsterdam The Netherlands
Phone: +31 20 8888886

#166
Twenty Third
Category: Bar
Average price: Exclusive
Area: Zuid, De Pijp
Address: Ferdinand Bolstraat 333 1072
LH Amsterdam The Netherlands
Phone: +31 20 6787111

#167
Coffeeshop Johnny
Category: Nightlife
Average price: Inexpensive
Area: Centrum, Jordaan
Address: Elandsgracht 3-HS 1016 TM
Amsterdam The Netherlands
Phone: +31 20 6383984

#168
Herengracht
Category: Bar, American
Average price: Expensive
Area: Centrum
Address: Herengracht 435 1017 BR
Amsterdam The Netherlands
Phone: +31 20 6162482

#169
Restaurant Barrique
Category: Wine Bar, Wineries, French
Average price: Modest
Area: Zuid, De Pijp
Address: 1072 VW 1072 VW
Amsterdam The Netherlands
Phone: +31 20 2218162

#170
A Bar
Category: Pub
Average price: Expensive
Area: Plantagebuurt, Centrum
Address: Professor tulpplein 1
1018 GX Amsterdam The Netherlands
Phone: +31 20 6226060

#171
Muziekgebouw Aan 't IJ
Category: Music Venues
Average price: Modest
Area: Centrum
Address: Piet Heinkade 1 1019 BR
Amsterdam The Netherlands
Phone: +31 20 7882010

#172
Coffeeshop 36
Category:
Average price: Coffeeshops
Area: Centrum, De Wallen
Address: Warmoesstraat 36-HS 1012
JE Amsterdam The Netherlands
Phone: +31 20 6242493

#173
Hole in the Wall
Category: Pub
Average price: Modest
Area: Centrum
Address: Leidseplein 8 1017 PT
Amsterdam The Netherlands
Phone: +31 20 6381408

#174
Café De Druif
Category: Bar
Average price: Modest
Area: Centrum
Address: Rapenburgerplein 83 1011 VJ
Amsterdam The Netherlands
Phone: +31 20 6244530

#175
Café De Pijp
Category: Pub, GastroPub
Average price: Modest
Area: Zuid, De Pijp
Address: Ferdinand Bolstraat 17-19BG
1072 LA Amsterdam The Netherlands
Phone: +31 20 6790110

#176
Café Binnen Buiten
Category: GastroPub, Bar
Average price: Modest
Area: Zuid, De Pijp
Address: Ruysdaelkade 115 1072 AN
Amsterdam The Netherlands
Phone: +31 20 6701640

#177
Dickys Grand Café
Category: Brasseries, Pub, GastroPub
Average price: Modest
Area: Zuid, WTC, Buitenveldert
Address: Gustavmahlerplein 110 1082
MA Amsterdam The Netherlands
Phone: +31 20 3444206

#178
Stanislavski
Category: Pub, Diners, Breakfast &
Brunch
Average price: Modest
Area: Centrum
Address: Leidseplein 26 1017 PT
Amsterdam The Netherlands
Phone: +31 20 7959995

#179
Majestic
Category: Pub, Breakfast & Brunch,
Cafe
Average price: Expensive
Area: Centrum, De Wallen
Address: Dam 3-7 1001 EX
Amsterdam The Netherlands
Phone: +31 20 8888883

#180
Bar Moustache
Category: Bar, Italian
Average price: Modest
Area: Centrum
Address: Utrechtsestraat 141
1017 VM Amsterdam The Netherlands
Phone: +31 20 4281074

#181
Walvis
Category: Bar, Cafe
Average price: Modest
Area: West
Address: Spaarndammerstraat 516
1013 SZ Amsterdam The Netherlands
Phone: +31 20 7739374

#182
The Old Bell
Category: Dive Bar
Average price: Modest
Area: Centrum
Address: Rembrandtplein 46 1017 CV
Amsterdam The Netherlands
Phone: +31 20 6204135

#183
Little Buddha
Category: Japanese,
Venues & Event Spaces, Lounge
Average price: Expensive
Area: Centrum
Address: Kleine Gartmanplantsoen 17
1017 RP Amsterdam The Netherlands
Phone: +31 20 5307121

#184
Lime
Category: Pub, Cocktail Bar
Average price: Modest
Area: Centrum, De Wallen
Address: Zeedijk 104 1012 BB
Amsterdam The Netherlands
Phone: +31 20 6393020

#185
Café Bedier
Category: Dive Bar
Average price: Modest
Area: Zuid, Willemspark
Address: Sophialaan 36 1075 BS
Amsterdam The Netherlands
Phone: +31 20 6624415

#186
Cafe Zürich
Category: Restaurant, Pub
Average price: Modest
Area: West, Hoofdweg en omgeving
Address: Mercatorplein 2b 1057 CB
Amsterdam The Netherlands
Phone: +31 20 7165933

#187
Rain
Category: Dance Club, Lounge
Average price: Modest
Area: Centrum
Address: Rembrandtplein 44 1017 CV
Amsterdam The Netherlands
Phone: +31 20 6267078

#188
Cafe Langereis
Category: Coffee & Tea, Bar
Average price: Inexpensive
Area: Centrum
Address: Amstel 202 1017 AH
Amsterdam The Netherlands
Phone: +31 20 7850641

#189
Sociëteit De Kring
Category: Bar
Average price: Modest
Area: Centrum
Address: Kleine-Gartmanplantsoen 7-9
1017 RP Amsterdam The Netherlands
Phone: +31 20 6236985

#190
Café Eijlders
Category: Pub
Average price: Modest
Area: Centrum
Address: Korte Leidsedwarsstraat
47-HS 1017 PW Amsterdam
The Netherlands
Phone: +31 20 6242704

#191
Biblos
Category: Bar
Average price: Modest
Area: Centrum
Address: Lijnbaansgracht 243 1017 PH
Amsterdam The Netherlands
Phone: +31 20 4272848

#192
Cafe Euro Pub
Category: Pub
Average price: Modest
Area: Centrum, De Wallen
Address: Dam 5-7 1012 JS Amsterdam
The Netherlands
Phone: +31 20 4200563

#193
Odeon
Category: Dance Club,
Venues & Event Spaces, Restaurant
Average price: Modest
Area: Centrum
Address: Singel 460 1017 AW
Amsterdam The Netherlands
Phone: +31 20 5218555

#194
Coffeeshop Rokerij
Category: Lounge
Average price: Expensive
Area: Centrum
Address: Amstel 8 1017 AA
Amsterdam The Netherlands
Phone: +31 20 6200484

#195
Cannibale Royale
Category: Bar, Burgers, Cafe
Average price: Modest
Area: Centrum
Address: Handboogstraat 17-19 1012
XM Amsterdam The Netherlands
Phone: +31 617 716455

#196
Cafe de Punt
Category: Pub, Cafe
Average price: Modest
Area: Zuid, De Pijp
Address: Tweede Jacob van
Campenstraat 150 1073 XZ
Amsterdam The Netherlands
Phone: +31 20 6734251

#197
Mulliner's Wijnlokaal
Category: Wine Bar
Average price: Modest
Area: Centrum
Address: Lijnbaansgracht 267-HS 1017
RL Amsterdam The Netherlands
Phone: +31 20 6279782

#198
Surprise Bar
Category: Pub, Dance Club
Average price: Modest
Area: Centrum
Address: Leidsekruisstraat 41-43 1017
RG Amsterdam The Netherlands
Phone: +31 20 6236328

#199
Club NL
Category: Dance Club
Average price: Expensive
Area: Centrum
Address: Nieuwezijds Voorburgwal 169
1012 RK Amsterdam The Netherlands
Phone: +31 20 6236157

#200
Club Dauphine
Category: Music Venues, Dance Club
Average price: Expensive
Area: Oost, Watergraafsmeer
Address: Prins Bernhardplein 175 1097
BL Amsterdam The Netherlands
Phone: +31 20 4621646

#201
Theater Bellevue
Category: Performing Arts,
Music Venues
Average price: Modest
Area: West
Address: Leidsekade 90-AHS 1017 PN
Amsterdam The Netherlands
Phone: +31 20 5305300

#202
Satellite Sportscafe
Category: Pub, Sports Bar, Dance Club
Average price: Modest
Area: Centrum
Address: Leidseplein 11 1017 PS
Amsterdam The Netherlands
Phone: +31 20 4272529

#203
Cafe Gollem 2
Category: Pub, Dive Bar
Average price: Modest
Area: Zuid, De Pijp
Address: Daniel Stalpertstraat 74 1072
XK Amsterdam The Netherlands
Phone: +31 20 6129444

#204
Restaurant View
Category: Diners, Bar, Vegetarian
Average price: Modest
Area: Centrum
Address: Oosterdokskade 133 1011 DL
Amsterdam The Netherlands
Phone: +31 20 3708059

#205
Café L' Affiche
Category: Pub
Average price: Modest
Area: West
Address: Jacob van Lennepstraat 39/HS
1053 HB Amsterdam The Netherlands
Phone: +31 20 6121959

#206
Poollokaal De Gracht
Category: Pool Halls
Average price: Modest
Area: Plantagebuurt, Centrum
Address: Nieuwe Achtergracht 110 1018
WT Amsterdam The Netherlands
Phone: +31 20 6202008

#207
Jeffrey's Café
Category: Pub, Dance Club
Average price: Modest
Area: Zuid, De Pijp
Address: Eerste Sweelinckstraat 11
1073 CK Amsterdam The Netherlands
Phone: +31 20 4711332

#208
Coffeeshop Blue Bird
Category: Pub
Average price: Modest
Area: Centrum
Address: Sint Antoniesbreestraat 71
1011 HB Amsterdam The Netherlands
Phone: +31 20 6225232

#209
Café Aen't Water
Category: Bar
Average price: Modest
Area: Centrum, De Wallen
Address: Oudezijds Voorburgwal 2a
1012 GC Amsterdam The Netherlands
Phone: +31 652 006618

#210
Stones Café
Category:
Average price: Coffeeshops
Area: Centrum, De Wallen
Address: Warmoesstraat 91 1012 HZ
Amsterdam The Netherlands
Phone: +31 20 6241406

#211
Hunters Bar
Category: Pub
Average price: Modest
Area: Centrum, De Wallen
Address: Warmoesstraat 35 1012 HV
Amsterdam The Netherlands
Phone: +31 20 4278955

#212
De Barderij
Category: Dive Bar
Average price: Modest
Area: Centrum, De Wallen
Address: Zeedijk 14 1012 AX
Amsterdam The Netherlands
Phone: +31 20 4205132

#213
CREA Café
Category: Pub
Average price: Inexpensive
Area: Plantagebuurt, Centrum
Address: Nieuwe Achtergracht 170 1018
WV Amsterdam The Netherlands
Phone: +31 20 5251400

#214
Edel
Category: Wine Bar, Cafe
Average price: Modest
Area: West
Address: Postjesweg 1 1057 DT
Amsterdam The Netherlands
Phone: +31 20 7995000

#215
Poco Loco
Category: Pub, GastroPub
Average price: Modest
Area: Centrum, De Wallen
Address: Nieuwmarkt 24 1012 CR
Amsterdam The Netherlands
Phone: +31 20 6242937

#216
Dante Kitchen & Bar
Category: Pub, Italian
Average price: Modest
Area: Centrum
Address: Spuistraat 320 1012 VX
Amsterdam The Netherlands
Phone: +31 20 6246266

#217
Cafe de Poort
Category: Bar
Average price: Modest
Area: Centrum, Haarlemmerbuurt
Address: Haarlemmerdijk 4 1013 JD
Amsterdam The Netherlands
Phone: +31 20 6247283

#218
Eerste Klas Grand Café
Category: Bar, Restaurant
Average price: Expensive
Area: Centrum
Address: Stationsplein 15 1012 AB
Amsterdam The Netherlands
Phone: +31 20 6250131

#219
XtraCold Amsterdam
Category: Lounge
Average price: Modest
Area: Centrum
Address: Amstel 194-196 1017 AG
Amsterdam The Netherlands
Phone: +31 20 3205700

#220
De Bekeerde Suster
Category: Pub
Average price: Modest
Area: Centrum, De Wallen
Address: Kloveniersburgwal 6 1012 CT
Amsterdam The Netherlands
Phone: +31 20 4230112

#221
Café Heuvel
Category: Pub
Average price: Modest
Area: Centrum
Address: Prinsengracht 568 1017 KR
Amsterdam The Netherlands
Phone: +31 20 6226354

#222
Club 8
Category: Bar, Pool Halls
Average price: Modest
Area: West, De Baarsjes
Address: Admiraal de Ruijterweg 56-B
1056 GL Amsterdam The Netherlands
Phone: +31 20 6851703

#223
Café Lowietje
Category: Pub
Average price: Modest
Area: Centrum, Jordaan
Address: 3e Goudsbloemdwarsstraat 2
1015 KA Amsterdam The Netherlands
Phone: +31 20 4278198

#224
De Roode Leeuw
Category: Pub, Hotels, Restaurant
Average price: Modest
Area: Centrum
Address: Damrak 93-94 1012 LP
Amsterdam The Netherlands
Phone: +31 20 5550666

#225
Cafe Klasen
Category: Bar
Average price: Modest
Area: Zuid, Rivierenbuurt
Address: Maasstraat 55 1078 HD
Amsterdam The Netherlands
Phone: +31 20 6723744

#226
Cafe Schinkelhaven
Category: GastroPub, Pub
Average price: Modest
Area: Zuid
Address: Amstelveenseweg 126 1075
XL Amsterdam The Netherlands
Phone: +31 20 6719509

#227
Café Stevens
Category: Pub, GastroPub
Average price: Modest
Area: Centrum
Address: Geldersekade 123 1011 EN
Amsterdam The Netherlands
Phone: +31 20 6206970

#228
The Power Zone
Category: Dance Club
Average price: Modest
Area: Oost
Address: Daniel Goedkoopstraat 1-3
1096 BD Amsterdam The Netherlands
Phone: +31 20 6818866

#229
Sing Sing
Category: Asian Fusion, Pub
Average price: Modest
Area: Zuid, Willemspark
Address: Cornelis Krusemanstraat 15
1075 NB Amsterdam The Netherlands
Phone: +31 20 4704475

#230
Chupitos
Category: Bar
Average price: Modest
Area: Centrum
Address: Zieseniskade 25 1017 RT
Amsterdam The Netherlands
Phone: +31 641 221163

#231
Sarphaat
Category: Coffee & Tea,
GastroPub, Pub
Average price: Modest
Area: Zuid, De Pijp
Address: Ceintuurbaan 157-A 1072 GB
Amsterdam The Netherlands
Phone: +31 20 6751565

#232
The Oyster Club
Category: European,
Lounge, Cocktail Bar
Average price: Exclusive
Area: Zuid, Stadionbuurt
Address: Olympisch Station 35 1076 DE
Amsterdam The Netherlands
Phone: +31 20 5708400

#233
De Heeren Van Aemstel
Category: Pub
Average price: Modest
Area: Centrum
Address: Thorbeckeplein 5 1017 CS
Amsterdam The Netherlands
Phone: +31 20 6202173

#234
BananenBar
Category: Adult Entertainment
Average price: Expensive
Area: Centrum, De Wallen
Address: Oudezijds Achterburgwal 37
1012 DA Amsterdam The Netherlands
Phone: +31 20 6224670

#235
Staring at Jacob
Category: American, Breakfast &
Brunch, Pub
Average price: Inexpensive
Area: West, Oud West
Address: Jacob van Lennepkade 215
1054 ZP Amsterdam The Netherlands
Phone: +31 624 427473

#236
Café Spargo
Category: Dive Bar
Average price: Modest
Area: Oost, Dapperbuurt
Address: Linnaeusstraat 37-39 1093 EG
Amsterdam The Netherlands
Phone: +31 20 6941140

#237
ARC
Category: Bar
Average price: Expensive
Area: Centrum
Address: Reguliersdwarsstraat 44 1017
BM Amsterdam The Netherlands
Phone: +31 20 6897070

#238
Ludwig II
Category: Gay Bar, Coffee & Tea
Average price: Modest
Area: Centrum
Address: Reguliersdwarsstraat 37 1017
BK Amsterdam The Netherlands
Phone: +31 20 6161181

#239
Dutch Flowers
Category: Nightlife
Average price: Modest
Area: Centrum
Address: Singel 387 1012 WN
Amsterdam The Netherlands
Phone: +31 20 6247624

#240
Savoy Bar
Category: Bar
Average price: Modest
Area: Centrum
Address: Korte Reguliersdwarsstraat 1
1017 BH Amsterdam The Netherlands
Phone: +31 20 6272507

#241
Café de Zwart
Category: Pub
Average price: Modest
Area: Centrum
Address: Spuistraat 334 1012 VX
Amsterdam The Netherlands
Phone: +31 20 6246511

#242
Puerto Pata Negra
Category: Spanish, Lounge
Average price: Modest
Area: Oost, Zeeburg
Address: Oostelijke handelskade 999
1019 BW Amsterdam The Netherlands
Phone: +31 20 4191793

#243
Temple Bar
Category: Pub
Average price: Modest
Area: Centrum, De Wallen
Address: Kloveniersburgwal 2 1012 CT
Amsterdam The Netherlands
Phone: +31 20 4274400

#244
Maloe Melo
Category: Bar
Average price: Inexpensive
Area: Centrum, Jordaan
Address: Lijnbaansgracht 163-III 1016
VX Amsterdam The Netherlands
Phone: +31 20 4204592

#245
Players
Category: Sports Bar
Average price: Modest
Area: Centrum, De Wallen
Address: Warmoesstraat 170 1012 JK
Amsterdam The Netherlands
Phone: +31 20 6204481

#246
Café Rooie Nelis
Category: Pub
Average price: Modest
Area: Centrum, Jordaan
Address: Laurierstraat 101-II 1016 PK
Amsterdam The Netherlands
Phone: +31 20 6244167

#247
Winston Belushi's Bar
Category: Pub
Average price: Modest
Area: Centrum, De Wallen
Address: Warmoesstraat 129 1012 NL
Amsterdam The Netherlands
Phone: +31 20 6231380

#248
Cafe Dijk 120
Category: Pub
Average price: Modest
Area: Centrum, De Wallen
Address: Zeedijk 120 1012 BB
Amsterdam The Netherlands
Phone: +31 20 6247107

#249
**Café 't Genootschap
der Geneugten**
Category: Pub
Average price: Modest
Area: Centrum
Address: Kerkstraat 54-hs 1017 GM
Amsterdam The Netherlands
Phone: +31 20 6250934

#250
In de Buurt
Category: GastroPub, Bar
Average price: Expensive
Area: Centrum
Address: Lijnbaansgracht 246 1017 RK
Amsterdam The Netherlands
Phone: +31 20 6164787

#251
Restaurant La Margarita
Category: Bar, Caribbean
Average price: Modest
Area: Centrum
Address: Reguliersdwarsstraat 47 1017
BK Amsterdam The Netherlands
Phone: +31 20 6230707

#252
CousCousClub
Category: Moroccan, Cocktail Bar
Average price: Modest
Area: Zuid, De Pijp
Address: Ceintuurbaan 346 1072 GP
Amsterdam The Netherlands
Phone: +31 20 6733539

#253
Café Havelaar
Category: Bar
Average price: Modest
Area: Centrum
Address: Voetboogstraat 22-24 1012 XL
Amsterdam The Netherlands
Phone: +31 20 6385953

#254
La Tertulia
Category:
Average price: Coffeeshops
Area: Centrum, Jordaan
Address: Prinsengracht 312 1016 HX
Amsterdam The Netherlands
Phone: +31 20 6238503

#255
Café Mulder
Category: Bar
Average price: Modest
Area: Centrum
Address: Weteringschans 163 1017 XD
Amsterdam The Netherlands
Phone: +31 20 6237874

#256
De Pont
Category: Pub, Venues & Event Spaces
Average price: Modest
Area: Noord
Address: Buiksloterweg 3-5 1031 CC
Amsterdam The Netherlands
Phone: +31 20 6363388

#257
IQ Creative
Category: Wine Bar, Lounge, Brasseries
Average price: Modest
Area: Centrum
Address: Jonge Roelensteeg 21 1012
PL Amsterdam The Netherlands
Phone: +31 20 3446400

#258
Pinguin
Category: Nightlife
Average price: Modest
Area: Centrum, Negen Straatjes
Address: Berenstraat 5-B 1016 GG
Amsterdam The Netherlands
Phone: +31 20 7720821

#259
Kadinsky Coffeeshop
Category: Nightlife
Average price: Modest
Area: Centrum
Address: Zoutsteeg 14 1012 LX
Amsterdam The Netherlands
Phone: +31 20 6204715

#260
Cafe Sarphaat
Category: Pub, Brasseries
Average price: Modest
Area: Zuid, De Pijp
Address: Ceintuurbaan 157-A 1072 GB
Amsterdam The Netherlands
Phone: +31 20 6751565

#261
The End
Category: Karaoke
Average price: Modest
Area: Centrum, De Wallen
Address: Nieuwebrugsteeg 32 1012 AH
Amsterdam The Netherlands
Phone: +31 649 048839

#262
Koetjes en Kalfjes
Category: Restaurant, Pub
Average price: Expensive
Area: Zuid, WTC
Address: Gustav Mahlerplein 14 1082
MA Amsterdam The Netherlands
Phone: +31 20 6440811

#263
Cafe Batavia 1920
Category: British, Bar, Coffee & Tea
Area: Centrum, De Wallen
Address: Prins Hendrikkade 85 1012 AE
Amsterdam The Netherlands
Phone: +31 20 6234086

#264
Café de Gouden Florijn
Category: Dive Bar
Average price: Inexpensive
Area: Centrum, Jordaan
Address: Rozengracht 28-WINK 1016
NC Amsterdam The Netherlands
Phone: +31 20 6273817

#265
Old Sailor
Category: Pub
Average price: Expensive
Area: Centrum, De Wallen
Address: Oudezijds Achterburgwal 39-A
1012 DA Amsterdam The Netherlands
Phone: +31 20 6247739

#266
Holland Village Amsterdam
Category: Music Venues, European
Average price: Modest
Area: Centrum
Address: Entrepotdok 7-8 1018 AD
Amsterdam The Netherlands
Phone: +31 20 6241876

#267
Werck
Category: Bar, Tapas
Average price: Exclusive
Area: Centrum
Address: Prinsengracht 277 1016 GW
Amsterdam The Netherlands
Phone: +31 20 6274079

#268
Café 16cc
Category: Music Venues, Pub, Cinema
Average price: Inexpensive
Area: Centrum
Address: Kadijksplein 16 1018 AC
Amsterdam The Netherlands
Phone: +31 20 6270236

#269
Café Hegeraad
Category: Pub, Dive Bar
Average price: Modest
Area: Centrum, Jordaan
Address: Noordermarkt 34 1015 NA
Amsterdam The Netherlands
Phone: +31 20 6245565

#270
Tennisclub Kattenlaan
Category: Mediterranean, Pub, Tennis
Average price: Modest
Area: Zuid
Address: Kattenlaan 13 1054 KA
Amsterdam The Netherlands
Phone: +31 641 370983

#271
Roode Bioscoop
Category: Music Venues, Performing
Arts, Venues & Event Spaces
Average price: Inexpensive
Area: Centrum, Haarlemmerbuurt
Address: Haarlemmerplein 7 1013 HP
Amsterdam The Netherlands
Phone: +31 20 6257500

#272
Amstel XXX Hoek
Category: Restaurant, Pub
Average price: Modest
Area: Centrum
Address: Zwanenburgwal 15
1011 VW Amsterdam The Netherlands
Phone: +31 20 6209039

#273
Plan B
Category: Sports Bar, Pool Halls
Average price: Expensive
Area: West, Oud West
Address: Overtoom 209 1054 HT
Amsterdam The Netherlands
Phone: +31 20 8456221

#274
De II Prinsen
Category: Pub
Average price: Modest
Area: Centrum
Address: Prinsenstraat 27 1015 DB
Amsterdam The Netherlands
Phone: +31 20 6249722

#275
Café Dorst
Category: Pub
Average price: Modest
Area: Oost, Centrum, Dapperbuurt
Address: Zeeburgerdijk 3 1093 SJ
Amsterdam The Netherlands
Phone: +31 20 6685797

#276
The Three Sisters
Category: Pub, Food
Average price: Expensive
Area: Centrum
Address: Rembrandtplein 19 1017 CT
Amsterdam The Netherlands
Phone: +31 20 6263346

#277
OCCII
Category: Music Venues
Average price: Inexpensive
Area: Zuid
Address: Amstelveenseweg 134
1075 XL Amsterdam The Netherlands
Phone: +31 20 6717778

#278
Ter Brugge
Category: Pub, GastroPub
Average price: Modest
Area: Zuid, West
Address: Overtoom 578 1054 LN
Amsterdam The Netherlands
Phone: +31 20 6129983

#279
Taboo
Category: Gay Bar
Average price: Modest
Area: Centrum
Address: Reguliersdwarsstraat 45
1017 BK Amsterdam The Netherlands
Phone: +31 20 3344411

#280
Blinq
Category: Dance Club, Cafe
Average price: Modest
Area: Centrum
Address: Kleine-Gartmanplantsoen
5-BG 1017 RP Amsterdam The
Netherlands
Phone: +31 20 3304000

#281
Sopranos Pianobar
Category: Bar, Jazz & Blues
Area: Centrum
Address: Paardenstraat 11-15
1017 CX Amsterdam The Netherlands
Phone: +31 20 4288211

#282
de Koningshut
Category: Pub
Average price: Modest
Area: Centrum
Address: Spuistraat 269 1012 VR
Amsterdam The Netherlands
Phone: +31 20 6264276

#283
Café Schuim
Category: Pub, Sandwiches
Average price: Modest
Area: Centrum
Address: Spuistraat 189 1012 VN
Amsterdam The Netherlands
Phone: +31 20 6389357

#284
Rembrandt Corner
Category: Bar, GastroPub
Average price: Modest
Area: Centrum
Address: Jodenbreestraat 2 1011 NK
Amsterdam The Netherlands
Phone: +31 20 6274463

#285
Beurs Van Berlage Café
Category: Venues & Event Spaces,
Breakfast & Brunch, Pub
Average price: Modest
Area: Centrum, De Wallen
Address: Beursplein 2 1012 ZJ
Amsterdam The Netherlands
Phone: +31 20 5304146

#286
Café Corso
Category: Bar
Average price: Modest
Area: Centrum, De Wallen
Address: Oudezijds Achterburgwal 26
1012 DM Amsterdam The Netherlands
Phone: +31 20 6244120

#287
Saigon
Category: Vietnamese, Lounge, Cafe
Average price: Modest
Area: Centrum
Address: Leidsestraat 95 1017 NZ
Amsterdam The Netherlands
Phone: +31 20 7370848

#288
Butcher's Tears
Category: Bar, Breweries
Average price: Inexpensive
Area: Zuid
Address: Karperweg 45 1075 LB
Amsterdam The Netherlands
Phone: +31 653 909777

#289
Strand West
Category: GastroPub, Pub
Average price: Modest
Area: West
Address: Stavangerweg 900
1013 AX Amsterdam The Netherlands
Phone: +31 20 6826310

#290
Mulder
Category: Bar
Area: Centrum
Address: 1e Weteringdwarsstraat 2-4
1017 TN Amsterdam The Netherlands
Phone: +31 20 6647247

#291
Le Patron Anonyme
Category: Pub
Average price: Modest
Area: Centrum
Address: Vijzelgracht 63 1017 HP
Amsterdam The Netherlands
Phone: +31 641 311623

#292
Café Marcella
Category: Pub
Average price: Inexpensive
Area: Centrum
Address: Amstelveld 21 1017 JD
Amsterdam The Netherlands
Phone: +31 20 6231900

#293
Kamer 401
Category: Pub
Average price: Modest
Area: Centrum
Address: Marnixstraat 401 1017 PJ
Amsterdam The Netherlands
Phone: +31 20 6200614

#294
The Rookies
Category: Nightlife, Hotels
Average price: Modest
Area: Centrum
Address: Korte Leidsedwarsstraat
145-BG 1017 PZ Amsterdam
The Netherlands
Phone: +31 20 6390978

#295
Café Krull
Category: GastroPub, Pub
Average price: Modest
Area: Zuid, De Pijp
Address: Sarphatipark 2 1072 PA
Amsterdam The Netherlands
Phone: +31 20 6620214

#296
Cafe De Vriendschap
Category: Dive Bar, Pub
Average price: Modest
Area: Centrum
Address: Nieuwmarkt 1 1011 JP
Amsterdam The Netherlands
Phone: +31 20 6248112

#297
Club Roses
Category: Dance Club,
Venues & Event Spaces
Average price: Modest
Area: Centrum, Jordaan
Address: Rozengracht 133
1016 LV Amsterdam The Netherlands
Phone: +31 20 4162211

#298
Tuin 10
Category: Pub
Average price: Modest
Area: Centrum, Jordaan
Address: Tweede Tuindwarsstraat 10
1015 RZ Amsterdam The Netherlands
Phone: +31 20 3702361

#299
't Loosje
Category: Pub, GastroPub
Average price: Modest
Area: Centrum, De Wallen
Address: Nieuwmarkt 34 1011 JP
Amsterdam The Netherlands
Phone: +31 20 6274919

#300
Café Chaos
Category: GastroPub, Pub
Average price: Modest
Area: Centrum, Jordaan
Address: Looiersgracht 144 1016 VT
Amsterdam The Netherlands
Phone: +31 20 6235269

#301
Café de Eland
Category: Pub
Average price: Modest
Area: Centrum
Address: Prinsengracht 296
1016 HW Amsterdam The Netherlands
Phone: +31 20 6237654

#302
Melodyline
Category: Pub
Average price: Modest
Area: Oost
Address: Willem Fenegastraat 12
1096 BN Amsterdam The Netherlands
Phone: +31 20 6929650

#303
Amstel Fifty Four
Category: Pub, Gay Bar
Average price: Modest
Area: Centrum
Address: Amstel 54 1017 AB
Amsterdam The Netherlands
Phone: +31 629 557092

#304
Eetcafe de Jordaan
Category: Dive Bar
Average price: Modest
Area: Centrum, Jordaan
Address: Elandsgracht 45 1016 TN
Amsterdam The Netherlands
Phone: +31 20 6275863

#305
De Keu
Category: Pool Halls
Average price: Modest
Area: West, Helmersbuurt
Address: Eerste Helmersstraat 5-7
1054 CX Amsterdam The Netherlands
Phone: +31 20 2300551

#306
Terzijde
Category: Pub
Average price: Modest
Area: Centrum
Address: Kerkstraat 59 1017 GC
Amsterdam The Netherlands
Phone: +31 20 6262301

#307
Club Smokey
Category: Dance Club
Average price: Inexpensive
Area: Centrum
Address: Rembrandtplein 18-20
1017 CV Amsterdam The Netherlands
Phone: +31 20 4222194

#308
Cafe Reynders
Category: Pub
Average price: Modest
Area: Centrum
Address: Leidseplein 6 1017 PT
Amsterdam The Netherlands
Phone: +31 20 6234419

#309
Molentje Café, 't
Category: Pub, Dive Bar
Average price: Modest
Area: Centrum
Address: Singel 278 1016 AC
Amsterdam The Netherlands
Phone: +31 20 6244984

#310
Café Tapvreugd
Category: Pub, Cafe
Average price: Modest
Area: Centrum, De Wallen
Address: Oude Hoogstraat 11
1012 CD Amsterdam The Netherlands
Phone: +31 20 6233609

#311
De Fietskantine
Category: Bike, Coffeeshops
Area: West, Oud West
Address: Overtoom 141 1054 HG
Amsterdam The Netherlands
Phone: +31 616 365494

#312
Paleis Van de Weemoed
Category: Performing Arts,
Venues & Event Spaces, Music Venues
Average price: Modest
Area: Centrum, De Wallen
Address: Oudezijds Voorburgwal 15
1012 EH Amsterdam The Netherlands
Phone: +31 20 6256964

#313
Kade West
Category: Brasseries, Cafe, Dive Bar
Average price: Modest
Area: West, Oud West, Da Costabuurt
Address: Kinkerstraat 87 1053 DH
Amsterdam The Netherlands
Phone: +41 20 618 38 58

#314
Café de Nieuwe Lelie
Category: Pub, Dive Bar
Average price: Inexpensive
Area: Centrum, Jordaan
Address: Nieuwe Leliestraat 83
1015 SL Amsterdam The Netherlands
Phone: +31 20 6225493

#315
Cafe Gewaeght
Category: Pub
Average price: Modest
Area: Centrum, De Wallen
Address: Nieuwmarkt 16 1012 CR
Amsterdam The Netherlands
Phone: +31 20 6240927

#316
Café de Kletskop
Category: Pub
Average price: Inexpensive
Area: Centrum, De Wallen
Address: Zeedijk 10 1012 AX
Amsterdam The Netherlands
Phone: +31 20 6225728

#317
Red Light Bar
Category: Pub, Coffeeshops
Average price: Modest
Area: Centrum, De Wallen
Address: Oudezijds Achterburgwal 61
1012 DB Amsterdam The Netherlands
Phone: +31 20 6382951

#318
Café Scharrebier
Category: Bar
Average price: Modest
Area: Centrum
Address: Rapenburgerplein 1-II
1011 VA Amsterdam The Netherlands
Phone: +31 20 6248101

#319
Park 118
Category: Adult Entertainment
Area: Zuid, De Pijp
Address: Sarphatipark 118-I 1073 ED
Amsterdam The Netherlands
Phone: +31 20 6723022

#320
't Koggeschip De Wilde Man
Category: Pub
Average price: Inexpensive
Area: Centrum
Address: Singel 43 1012 VC
Amsterdam The Netherlands
Phone: +31 20 6230815

#321
Café de Parel
Category: Pub
Average price: Inexpensive
Area: Centrum, Jordaan
Address: Westerstraat 266 1015 MT
Amsterdam The Netherlands
Phone: +31 20 6245219

#322
Louis
Category: Cafe, Pub
Average price: Modest
Area: Centrum
Address: Singel 43 1015 AA
Amsterdam The Netherlands
Phone: +31 20 5314230

#323
Café de Bron
Category: Bar
Average price: Modest
Area: West, Oud West, Helmersbuurt
Address: Jan Pieter Heijestraat 133-135
1054 ME Amsterdam The Netherlands
Phone: +31 20 4126237

#324
Prins Café,
Category: Bar, GastroPub
Area: Centrum, Jordaan
Address: Korte Prinsengracht 124
1015 EA Amsterdam The Netherlands
Phone: +31 20 6249382

#325
Kantine Apollohal
Category: Sports Bar, Active Life
Average price: Modest
Area: Zuid, Apollobuurt
Address: Apollolaan 4 1077 BA
Amsterdam The Netherlands
Phone: +31 20 6713910

#326
Figurantenbar
Category: Pub
Average price: Modest
Area: West, Oud West
Address: Rhijnvis Feithstraat 9 1054 TT
Amsterdam The Netherlands
Phone: +31 650 411825

#327
Cafe Emmelot
Category: Pub
Average price: Modest
Area: Centrum, De Wallen
Address: Oudezijdse Voorburgwal 52
1012 GE Amsterdam The Netherlands
Phone: +31 20 6221626

#328
Café Blek
Category: GastroPub, Dive Bar
Average price: Modest
Area: Zuid, Rivierenbuurt
Address: Waalstraat 48 1078 BV
Amsterdam The Netherlands
Phone: +31 20 3707744

#329
Grandcafé Vrienden
Category: Lounge
Average price: Modest
Area: Zuid, De Pijp
Address: Marie Heinekenplein 33 1072
MH Amsterdam The Netherlands
Phone: +31 20 6704661

#330
Café Toko
Category: Pub
Average price: Modest
Area: Zuid, De Pijp
Address: Albert Cuypstraat 124-BG
1072 EA Amsterdam The Netherlands
Phone: +31 20 6709370

#331
Café de Spuyt
Category: Pub
Average price: Modest
Area: Centrum
Address: Korte Leidsedwarsstraat 86-II
1017 RD Amsterdam The Netherlands
Phone: +31 20 6248901

#332
Café 't Spui-Tje
Category: Pub
Average price: Modest
Area: Centrum
Address: Spuistraat 318-IV 1012 VX
Amsterdam The Netherlands
Phone: +31 20 6267684

#333
Café Party Crew
Category: Dance Club
Average price: Modest
Area: Centrum
Address: Rembrandtplein 31 1017 CT
Amsterdam The Netherlands
Phone: +31 20 6233740

#334
Karma Café
Category: Pub
Average price: Modest
Area: Centrum
Address: Nieuwe Nieuwstraat 20 1012
NH Amsterdam The Netherlands
Phone: +31 20 3206042

#335
East of Eden
Category: Pub
Average price: Modest
Area: Oost, Dapperbuurt
Address: Linnaeusstraat 11-A 1093 EC
Amsterdam The Netherlands
Phone: +31 20 6650743

#336
Café Welling
Category: Dive Bar
Average price: Modest
Area: Zuid, Museumkwartier
Address: J.W.Brouwerstraat 32 1071
NC Amsterdam The Netherlands
Phone: +31 20 6620205

#337
Mensjelief
Category: Nightlife, GastroPub
Average price: Modest
Area: West
Address: Nova Zemblastraat 586
1013 RP Amsterdam The Netherlands
Phone: +31 20 7371953

#338
Barney's Coffeeshop
Category: Pub
Average price: Expensive
Area: Centrum, Haarlemmerbuurt
Address: Haarlemmerstraat 102-BG
1013 EW Amsterdam The Netherlands
Phone: +31 20 6259761

#339
Lovers Powerzone
Category: Bowling, Lounge, Burgers
Average price: Modest
Area: Centrum
Address: De Ruyterkade 153
1011 AC Amsterdam The Netherlands
Phone: +31 20 7607600

#340
The Amsterdam Ice Bar
Category: Pub
Average price: Modest
Area: Centrum
Address: Amstel 194-196 BG
1017 AG Amsterdam The Netherlands
Phone: +31 20 3205700

#341
Teasers
Category: Cafe, Sports Bar
Average price: Expensive
Area: Centrum
Address: Damrak 36 1012 LK
Amsterdam The Netherlands
Phone: +31 20 4218411

#342
Café De Zon
Category: Bar
Average price: Modest
Area: Centrum, De Wallen
Address: Nieuwmarkt 2 1012 CR
Amsterdam The Netherlands
Phone: +31 20 6249064

#343
Restaurant AS
Category: Diners, Wine Bar
Average price: Exclusive
Area: Zuid, WTC
Address: Prinses Irenestraat 19 1077
WT Amsterdam The Netherlands
Phone: +31 20 6440100

#344
Café Ruis onder de Bomen
Category: Pub
Average price: Modest
Area: Zuid, De Pijp
Address: Van der Helstplein 9
1073 AR Amsterdam The Netherlands
Phone: +31 20 3640354

#345
Grand Cafe Mynt
Category: Bar, Cafe
Area: Centrum
Address: Newendijk 123-125
1012 MD Amsterdam The Netherlands
Phone: +31 20 5289544

#346
Cafe Wester
Category: Dive Bar
Average price: Modest
Area: Centrum, Jordaan
Address: Nieuwe Leliestraat 2
1015 SP Amsterdam The Netherlands
Phone: +31 20 7580846

#347
Bourbon street
Category: Jazz & Blues
Average price: Modest
Area: Centrum
Address: Leidsekruisstraat 6-8
1017 RH Amsterdam The Netherlands
Phone: +31 20 6233440

#348
Bar Huf
Category: European, Bar
Average price: Modest
Area: Centrum
Address: Reguliersdwarsstraat 43
1017 BK Amsterdam The Netherlands
Phone: +31 20 3039561

#349
Disco Dolly
Category: Bar, Dance Club
Area: Centrum
Address: Handboogstraat 11/HS
1012 XM Amsterdam The Netherlands
Phone: +31 20 6201779

#350
The Cave
Category: Bar
Average price: Modest
Area: Centrum
Address: Prinsengracht 472-IV ST
1017 KG Amsterdam The Netherlands
Phone: +31 20 6268939

#351
Dan Murphys Irish Pub
Category: Pub
Average price: Modest
Area: Centrum
Address: Leidseplein 24-1 1017 PT
Amsterdam The Netherlands
Phone: +31 20 4223285

#352
Cafe DEL Mondo
Category: Pub
Average price: Modest
Area: Centrum, De Wallen
Address: Nieuwmarkt 28 1012 CS
Amsterdam The Netherlands
Phone: +31 20 6241373

#353
La Vie En Proost
Category: Adult Entertainment
Area: Centrum, De Wallen
Address: Bethlehemsteeg 23 1076 XP
Amsterdam The Netherlands
Phone: +31 20 6261635

#354
Dapper
Category: Brasseries, Dive Bar
Average price: Modest
Area: West, Oud West
Address: Jacob van Lennepkade 58-60
1053 ML Amsterdam The Netherlands
Phone: +31 20 6180757

#355
Frontline Café
Category: Bar
Average price: Modest
Area: Centrum, De Wallen
Address: Geldersekade 95 1011 EM
Amsterdam The Netherlands
Phone: +31 20 4210527

#356
Chris Scholten Café
Category: Pub
Average price: Inexpensive
Area: Zuid, De Pijp
Address: Van Woustraat 104 1073 LR
Amsterdam The Netherlands
Phone: +31 20 6797524

#357
Cafe Roos
Category: Pub, Pool Halls
Average price: Modest
Area: Zuid, De Pijp
Address: Ferdinand Bolstraat 158 1072
LT Amsterdam The Netherlands
Phone: +31 20 6723249

#358
Café Tapmarin
Category: Pub, GastroPub
Average price: Modest
Area: Zuid, De Pijp
Address: Van Woustraat 130-1 1073 LT
Amsterdam The Netherlands
Phone: +31 20 6727525

#359
Jefferson
Category: Bar, Brasseries
Average price: Expensive
Area: Zuid, Hoofddorppleinbuurt
Address: Vliegtuigstraat 16-18 1059 CL
Amsterdam The Netherlands
Phone: +31 20 6173804

#360
Hotel Café Corner House
Category: Pub, Hotels
Average price: Expensive
Area: Centrum
Address: Nieuwezijds Voorburgwal
119-121 1012 RH Amsterdam
The Netherlands
Phone: +31 20 6241326

#361
Café Noorderster
Category: Pub, Dive Bar
Average price: Modest
Area: West
Address: Houtmankade 9 1013 MP
Amsterdam The Netherlands
Phone: +31 20 6242904

#362
Café de Oude Wester
Category: Pub, Diners
Average price: Modest
Area: Centrum, Jordaan
Address: Rozengracht 2 1016 NB
Amsterdam The Netherlands
Phone: +31 20 6257502

#363
Bar Oldenhof
Category: Wine Bar,
Jazz & Blues, Cocktail Bar
Average price: Expensive
Area: Centrum, Jordaan
Address: Elandsgracht 84 1016 TZ
Amsterdam The Netherlands
Phone: +31 20 7513273

#364
The Bulldog N 90
Category: Bar
Average price: Expensive
Area: Centrum, De Wallen
Address: Oudezijds Voorburgwal 90-II
1012 GG Amsterdam The Netherlands
Phone: +31 20 6259864

#365
Café 't Stoplicht
Category: Pub, Dive Bar
Average price: Inexpensive
Area: West, De Baarsjes
Address: Witte de Withstraat 153 1057
XT Amsterdam The Netherlands
Phone: +31 20 4898888

#366
Café de Jaren
Category: Bar
Average price: Modest
Area: Centrum, De Wallen
Address: Nieuwe Doelenstraat 20-22
1012 CP Amsterdam The Netherlands
Phone: +31 20 6255771

#367
North Sea Jazz Club
Category: Jazz & Blues,
Restaurant, Dance Club
Average price: Expensive
Area: West
Address: Pazzanistraat 1 1014 DB
Amsterdam The Netherlands
Phone: +31 20 7220980

#368
't Narretje
Category: Dive Bar
Average price: Inexpensive
Area: Zuid, Rivierenbuurt
Address: Rijnstraat 254 1079 HW
Amsterdam The Netherlands
Phone: +31 20 6610887

#369
Fitch & Shui
Category: Lounge
Average price: Modest
Area: Zuid, WTC
Address: Strawinskylaan 77 1077 XW
Amsterdam The Netherlands
Phone: +31 20 3331527

#370
Cafe Kingfisher
Category: Pub, GastroPub
Average price: Modest
Area: Zuid, De Pijp
Address: Ferdinand Bolstraat 24-II
1072 LK Amsterdam The Netherlands
Phone: +31 20 6712395

#371
Bar Paul
Category: Bar
Area: Centrum
Address: Reguliersdwarsstraat 41
1017 BK Amsterdam The Netherlands
Phone: +31 653 845347

#372
El Punto Latino
Category: Bar, Music Venues
Area: Centrum
Address: Lange Leidsedwarsstraat 35
1017 NG Amsterdam The Netherlands
Phone: +31 20 4202235

#373
Dopey's Elixer
Category: Dive Bar, GastroPub
Average price: Modest
Area: Zuid, De Pijp
Address: Lutmastraat 49 1072 JP
Amsterdam The Netherlands
Phone: +31 20 6716946

#374
Lido Club
Category: Dance Club
Average price: Modest
Area: West
Address: Holland Casino Amsterdam
1017 MB Amsterdam The Netherlands
Phone: +31 20 5211111

#375
Club Roque
Category: Dance Club, Gay Bar
Average price: Modest
Area: Centrum
Address: Amstel 178 1017 AE
Amsterdam The Netherlands
Phone: +31 20 4210900

#376
Ruig
Category: Bar, Cafe
Area: Centrum
Address: Nieuwezijds Voorburgwal 260
1012 RS Amsterdam The Netherlands
Phone: +31 20 2330569

#377
Chapter 21
Category: Bar, Dance Club
Area: Centrum
Address: Jonge Roelensteeg 21 1012
PL Amsterdam The Netherlands
Phone: +31 627 412532

#378
Café Zwart
Category: Bar
Area: Centrum, De Wallen
Address: Dam 15 1012 JS Amsterdam
The Netherlands
Phone: +31 20 6240950

#379
Tripel
Category: Bar, Cafe
Area: Centrum, Jordaan
Address: Lijnbaansgracht 161 1016 VX
Amsterdam The Netherlands
Phone: +31 20 3706421

#380
Jet Lounge
Category: Bar
Area: Centrum
Address: Westermarkt 25 1016 DJ
Amsterdam The Netherlands
Phone: +31 20 6247744

#381
Pleinzicht
Category: Dive Bar
Average price: Modest
Area: Centrum, De Wallen
Address: Oudezijds Voorburgwal 75-3
1012 EL Amsterdam The Netherlands
Phone: +31 20 6247444

#382
Bar 117
Category: Coffee & Tea, Pub
Average price: Modest
Area: Centrum, Jordaan
Address: In Boom Chicago 1016 LV
Amsterdam The Netherlands
Phone: +31 20 2170400

#383
NLTracks
Category: Music Venues
Average price: Modest
Area: Centrum
Address: Singel 146 1015 AG
Amsterdam The Netherlands
Phone: +31 20 7787266

#384
Irish Pub Slainte
Category: Pub
Average price: Inexpensive
Area: Centrum, De Wallen
Address: Oudekerksplein 34 1012 HZ
Amsterdam The Netherlands
Phone: +31 20 6255974

#385
The Eagle Bar
Category: Bar
Average price: Inexpensive
Area: Centrum, De Wallen
Address: Warmoestraat 90 1012 HZ
Amsterdam The Netherlands
Phone: +31 627 8634

#386
CUE Bar
Category: Bar
Area: Centrum
Address: Utrechtsestraat 16-Winkel
1017 VN Amsterdam The Netherlands
Phone: +31 653 261716

#387
New Dorrius
Category: Bar, European, Sandwiches
Area: Centrum
Address: Nieuwendijk 60 1012 MP
Amsterdam The Netherlands
Phone: +31 20 5211750

#388
Pianola Museum
Category: Music Venues
Average price: Expensive
Area: Centrum, Jordaan
Address: Westerstraat 106-1 1015 MN
Amsterdam The Netherlands
Phone: +31 20 6279624

#389
Noah's Arq
Category: GastroPub, Pub
Average price: Expensive
Area: Centrum
Address: Prins Hendrikkade 194 1011
TD Amsterdam The Netherlands
Phone: +31 20 7371809

#390
Podium Mozaïek
Category: Music Venues,
Venues & Event Spaces
Average price: Modest
Area: West, Bos en Lommer
Address: Bos en Lommerweg 191 1055
DT Amsterdam The Netherlands
Phone: +31 20 5800381

#391
Argos
Category: Gay Bar
Average price: Modest
Area: Centrum, De Wallen
Address: Warmoesstraat 95 1012 HZ
Amsterdam The Netherlands
Phone: +31 20 6243807

#392
Rembrandt Bar
Category: Pub
Average price: Modest
Area: Centrum
Address: Rembrandtplein 3 1017 CT
Amsterdam The Netherlands
Phone: +31 20 6230688

#393
Rijnbar
Category: Pub, Dive Bar
Average price: Modest
Area: Zuid, Rivierenbuurt
Address: Rijnstraat 1 1078 PT
Amsterdam The Netherlands
Phone: +31 20 6705851

#394
Het Feest Van Joop
Category: Dance Club
Average price: Expensive
Area: Centrum
Address: Lange Leidsedwarsstraat
39-3 1017 NG Amsterdam
The Netherlands
Phone: +31 20 6271780

#395
Luminaa
Category: Lounge, Restaurant
Average price: Modest
Area: Centrum
Address: Leidseplein 22-HS 1017 PT
Amsterdam The Netherlands
Phone: +31 20 4215684

#396
Club Lite
Category: Dance Club,
Venues & Event Spaces, Music Venues
Average price: Modest
Area: West, Bos en Lommer
Address: Van Galenstraat 24 1051 KM
Amsterdam The Netherlands
Phone: +31 625 456518

#397
The Bulldog Energy
Category: Nightlife
Average price: Inexpensive
Area: Centrum, De Wallen
Address: Oudezijds Voorburgwal 218
1012 GJ Amsterdam The Netherlands
Phone: +31 20 6382593

#398
Café de Pul
Category: Bar
Average price: Modest
Area: Centrum, De Wallen
Address: Oudezijds Achterburgwal
116-I BG 1012 DT Amsterdam
The Netherlands
Phone: +31 20 6266343

#399
Rue De Sèvres
Category:
Average price: Bar,
Breakfast & Brunch, Cafe
Area: West, Bos en Lommer
Address: Jan van Galenstraat 92h 1056
CD Amsterdam The Netherlands
Phone: +31 20 4122594

#400
Victoria Hotel Bar
Category: Champagne Bar
Average price: Expensive
Area: Centrum
Address: Damrak 1-5 1012 LG
Amsterdam The Netherlands
Phone: +31 20 6234255

#401
Café de Karpershoek
Category: Pub
Average price: Inexpensive
Area: Centrum
Address: Martelaarsgracht 2 1012 TP
Amsterdam The Netherlands
Phone: +31 20 6247886

#402
De Engel Van Amsterdam
Category: Gay Bar, Dive Bar
Average price: Modest
Area: Centrum, De Wallen
Address: Zeedijk 21 1012 AP
Amsterdam The Netherlands
Phone: +31 20 4276381

#403
Moes
Category: Restaurant, Pub
Average price: Expensive
Area: Centrum
Address: Prins Hendrikkade 142 1011
AT Amsterdam The Netherlands
Phone: +31 20 6235477

#404
Café Amstelstroom
Category: Bar
Average price: Modest
Area: Oost, Oosterparkbuurt
Address: Weesperzijde 40 1091 EE
Amsterdam The Netherlands
Phone: +31 20 6654662

#405
Café de Zeepost
Category: Pub
Average price: Inexpensive
Area: Centrum, De Wallen
Address: Prins Hendrikkade 88 1012 AE
Amsterdam The Netherlands
Phone: +31 20 6220450

#406
Café Onder de Ooievaar
Category: Pub
Average price: Modest
Area: Centrum
Address: Utrechtsestraat 119 1017 VL
Amsterdam The Netherlands
Phone: +31 20 6246836

#407
Weekend
Category: Lounge, Cafe
Average price: Modest
Area: Zuid
Address: Europaboulevard 7 1079 PC
Amsterdam The Netherlands
Phone: +31 20 6618400

#408
Club Paradise
Category:
Average price: Adult Entertainment
Area: Noord
Address: Schaafstraat 26 1021 KE
Amsterdam The Netherlands
Phone: +31 20 6373416

#409
Thuis Aan De Amstel
Category: Pub, Cafe
Average price: Modest
Area: Oost
Address: Korte Ouderkerkerdijk 40
1096 AC Amsterdam The Netherlands
Phone: +31 20 3547520

#410
Café BOS
Category: Pub, Dive Bar
Average price: Modest
Area: Zuid
Address: Amstelveenseweg 226
1075 XT Amsterdam The Netherlands
Phone: +31 20 6621448

#411
Café de Zuid
Category: Bar
Average price: Modest
Area: Oost, Java Eiland
Address: Azartplein 2-A 1019 PD
Amsterdam The Netherlands
Phone: +31 20 4191787

#412
Mellow Yellow
Category: Nightlife
Average price: Modest
Area: Centrum
Address: Vijzelstraat 103 1017 HN
Amsterdam The Netherlands
Phone: +31 20 8465828

#413
Kaap de Goede Hoop
Category: GastroPub, Pub
Average price: Modest
Area: Zuid, West
Address: Overtoom 534 1054 LL
Amsterdam The Netherlands
Phone: +31 20 6854043

#414
Bar Lempicka
Category: Brasseries, Cocktail Bar
Average price: Modest
Area: Plantagebuurt, Centrum
Address: Sarphatistraat 23 1018 EV
Amsterdam The Netherlands
Phone: +31 20 6220209

#415
Nacht Café Deniz
Category: Bar
Average price: Inexpensive
Area: Zuid, De Pijp
Address: Albert Cuypstraat 226
1073 BN Amsterdam The Netherlands
Phone: +31 641 973182

#416
The Flying Dutchman
Category: Bar
Area: Centrum
Address: Martelaarsgracht 13
1012 TN Amsterdam The Netherlands
Phone: +31 20 6221076

#417
Hotel V
Category: Lounge, Hotels
Average price: Modest
Area: Centrum
Address: Weteringschans 136
1017 XV Amsterdam The Netherlands
Phone: +31 20 6623233

#418
Café Otten
Category: Pub
Average price: Modest
Area: Centrum
Address: Reguliersbreestraat 44
1017 CN Amsterdam The Netherlands
Phone: +31 20 6247313

#419
Schaakcafé Het Hok
Category: Bar
Area: Centrum
Address: Lange Leidsedwarsstraat
134 1017 NN Amsterdam
The Netherlands
Phone: +31 20 6243133

#420
The News
Category: Bar
Area: Centrum
Address: Korte Leidsedwarsstraat
77 1017 PW Amsterdam
The Netherlands
Phone: +31 20 6261838

#421
Museum Cafe Mokum
Category: Pub, Coffee & Tea
Average price: Modest
Area: Centrum
Address: Kalverstraat 92 1012 PH
Amsterdam The Netherlands
Phone: +31 20 6236736

#422
Thorbeckeplein
Category: Local Flavor, Bar
Average price: Expensive
Area: Centrum
Address: Thorbeckeplein 1017 CS
Amsterdam The Netherlands
Phone: +31 20 4212284

#423
Café De Pool
Category: Bar
Average price: Modest
Area: Centrum, De Wallen
Address: Oude Hoogstraat 8-BG 1012
CE Amsterdam The Netherlands
Phone: +31 20 6248710

#424
Café Zwart Op de Dam
Category: Bar
Average price: Expensive
Area: Centrum, De Wallen
Address: Dam 15 1012 JS
Amsterdam The Netherlands
Phone: +31 20 8888881

#425
Koekenbier
Category: Pub, Dive Bar
Average price: Modest
Area: Zuid, De Pijp
Address: Daniel Stalpertstraat 56-BG
1072 XJ Amsterdam The Netherlands
Phone: +31 20 6702753

#426
Café de Laurierboom
Category: Pub
Average price: Inexpensive
Area: Centrum, Jordaan
Address: Laurierstraat 76 1016 PN
Amsterdam The Netherlands
Phone: +31 20 6233015

#427
Mozzarella Bar
Category: Bar, Italian
Area: West, Oud West, Helmersbuurt
Address: Eerste Constantijn
Huygensstraat 41 1054 BR Amsterdam
The Netherlands
Phone: +31 20 7893320

#428
Café Mansro
Category: Bar
Area: Zuid, De Pijp
Address: Eerste Sweelinckstraat 13
1073 CL Amsterdam The Netherlands
Phone: +31 20 6644554

#429
Café Old Wembley
Category: Sports Bar
Average price: Inexpensive
Area: Centrum, De Wallen
Address: Monnikenstraat 12 1012 BP
Amsterdam The Netherlands
Phone: +31 20 4271667

#430
Speak Easy
Category: Coffeeshops
Average price: Inexpensive
Area: Centrum, De Wallen
Address: Oudebrugsteeg 4 1012 JP
Amsterdam The Netherlands
Phone: +31 20 6247621

#431
Café Van Beeren
Category: Pub
Average price: Modest
Area: Centrum
Address: Nieuwendijk 129 1012 MD
Amsterdam The Netherlands
Phone: +31 20 6226656

#432
Sexodrom
Category: Adult Entertainment
Area: Centrum
Address: Nieuwendijk 74 1012 MP
Amsterdam The Netherlands
Phone: +31 20 6279668

#433
Café-Koffiehuis de Zwijger
Category: Bar, Coffee & Tea
Area: West, De Baarsjes
Address: Willem de Zwijgerlaan 157
1056 JL Amsterdam The Netherlands
Phone: +31 655 307340

#434
Hoopman Irish Pub
Category: Pub, Irish
Average price: Inexpensive
Area: Centrum
Address: Leidseplein 4 1017 PT
Amsterdam The Netherlands
Phone: +31 20 6381408

#435
Eagle Amsterdam
Category: Gay Bar
Average price: Modest
Area: Centrum, De Wallen
Address: Warmoesstraat 90
1012 JH Amsterdam The Netherlands
Phone: +31 627 043550

#436
Hunters
Category: Coffeeshops
Average price: Modest
Area: Centrum, De Wallen
Address: Warmoesstraat 24
1012 JD Amsterdam The Netherlands
Phone: +31 20 3203854

#437
Zuidpool
Category: Lounge, Dance Club
Average price: Expensive
Area: Zuid
Address: Europaplein 22 1078 GZ
Amsterdam The Netherlands
Phone: +31 20 6392589

#438
Tales & Spirits
Category: Cocktail Bar, European
Average price: Expensive
Area: Centrum
Address: Lijnbaanssteeg 5-7
1012 TE Amsterdam The Netherlands
Phone: +31 655 356467

#439
Panama
Category: Dance Club
Average price: Modest
Area: Oost
Address: Oostelijke Handelskade
4 1019 BM Amsterdam
The Netherlands
Phone: +31 20 3118680

#440
Café Vivelavie
Category: Pub
Average price: Exclusive
Area: Centrum
Address: Amstelstraat 7 1017 DA
Amsterdam The Netherlands
Phone: +31 20 6240114

#441
Easy Times
Category: Coffeeshops
Average price: Modest
Area: Centrum
Address: Prinsengracht 476 1017 KG
Amsterdam The Netherlands
Phone: +31 20 6265709

#442
Café Kobalt
Category: GastroPub, Pub
Average price: Modest
Area: Centrum, Haarlemmerbuurt
Address: Singel 2-A 1013 GA
Amsterdam The Netherlands
Phone: +31 20 3202059

#443
Bar Berlijn
Category:
Average price: Bar, Cafe
Area: West, Da Costabuurt
Address: Potgieterstraat 35 1053 XR
Amsterdam The Netherlands
Phone: +31 20 6124662

#444
Café de Hartjes
Category: Bar
Average price: Modest
Area: Centrum, De Wallen
Address: Nieuwebrugsteeg 25
1012 AG Amsterdam The Netherlands
Phone: +31 20 3202420

#445
Escort Amsterdam
Category: Adult Entertainment
Area: Centrum, Jordaan
Address: Tuinstraat 69 1015 NZ
Amsterdam The Netherlands
Phone: +31 20 7163702

#446
Coffeeshop Nice Place
Category: Bar
Area: Zuid, De Pijp
Address: Van Ostadestraat 290
1073 TW Amsterdam The Netherlands
Phone: +31 644 671575

#447
De Kleine Karseboom
Category: Bar
Area: Centrum
Address: 1012 MB 1012 MB
Amsterdam The Netherlands
Phone: +31 627 521017

#448
5And33
Category: Bar, Mediterranean
Area: Centrum
Address: Martelaarsgracht 5
1012 TM Amsterdam The Netherlands
Phone: +31 20 8205333

#449
Club Golden Key
Category: Adult Entertainment
Area: West, Oud West, Helmersbuurt
Address: Overtoom 294 1054 JC
Amsterdam The Netherlands
Phone: +31 20 6124078

#450
Palladium
Category: Bar, Brasseries, Food
Average price: Expensive
Area: Centrum
Address: Kleine-Gartmanplantsoen 7
1017 RP Amsterdam The Netherlands
Phone: +31 655 778621

#451
Snappers
Category: Cocktail Bar, Mediterranean
Area: Centrum
Address: Reguliersdwarsstraat 21
1017 BJ Amsterdam The Netherlands
Phone: +31 20 8458144

#452
Česko-Slovenský
Category: Bar, Cafe
Area: Centrum
Address: Amstel 14 1017 AA
Amsterdam The Netherlands
Phone: +31 640 762392

#453
café Mon Ami
Category: Bar
Area: Centrum
Address: Amstelstraat 34 1017 DA
Amsterdam The Netherlands
Phone: +31 20 6262243

#454
Girls Company
Category: Adult Entertainment
Average price: Modest
Area: Centrum, De Wallen
Address: Bethaniendwarsstraat 12 1012
CB Amsterdam The Netherlands
Phone: +31 20 4226100

#455
Café De Dam, Louis Bar
Category: Bar, Cafe
Area: Centrum
Address: Singel 43 1012 JM
Amsterdam The Netherlands
Phone: +31 20 6245331

#456
Cafe Rosman
Category: Pub
Average price: Modest
Area: West, Bos en Lommer
Address: Willem De Zwijgerlaan 333
1055 RB Amsterdam The Netherlands
Phone: +31 20 3415696

#457
Cafe Verhulst
Category: Brasseries, Pub
Area: Zuid, Museumkwartier
Address: Johannes Verhulststraat 105
1071 MX Amsterdam The Netherlands
Phone: +31 20 7723872

#458
Ibiza Lounge
Category: Lounge
Average price: Inexpensive
Area: Centrum
Address: Lange Leidsedwarsstraat
41 1017 NG Amsterdam
The Netherlands
Phone: +31 648 616684

#459
Supreme Escort Amsterdam
Category: Adult Entertainment
Area: Centrum, De Wallen
Address: Bethaniëndwarsstraat 10 - 12
1012 CB Amsterdam The Netherlands
Phone: +31 611 369170

#460
Escorts Elegance
Category: Adult Entertainment
Area: Centrum, De Wallen
Address: Bethaniendwarsstraat 10 -12
1012 CB Amsterdam The Netherlands
Phone: +31 652 516520

#461
Escort Sexclusive
Category: Adult Entertainment
Area: Centrum
Address: Korte Keizersstraat 20 1011
GH Amsterdam The Netherlands
Phone: +31 620 770005

#462
Cafe Tetra
Category: Bar
Area: Centrum
Address: Nieuwezijds Voorburgwal 89
1012 SH Amsterdam The Netherlands
Phone: +31 641 582778

#463
De Burgh
Category: Bar, Cafe, Pool Halls
Area: Centrum, De Wallen
Address: Oudezijds Achterburgwal 52
1012 DP Amsterdam The Netherlands
Phone: +31 20 6257465

#464
Mehkong River
Category: Bar
Area: Centrum, De Wallen
Address: Oudezijds Voorburgwal 20
1012 GD Amsterdam The Netherlands
Phone: +31 20 6226992

#465
Coffeeshop Blue Sea
Category: Bar
Area: Zuid, De Pijp
Address: Van Woustraat 87 1074 AE
Amsterdam The Netherlands
Phone: +31 20 6761991

#466
Cocktails and Dreamz
Category: Lounge
Average price: Inexpensive
Area: Plantagebuurt, Centrum
Address: Plantage Muidergracht 87
1010 TN Amsterdam The Netherlands
Phone: +31 20 4200421

#467
Adult Escort Agency
Category: Adult Entertainment
Area: Centrum
Address: Laagte Kadijk 1-A 1018 BA
Amsterdam The Netherlands
Phone: +31 20 6266426

#468
Escort Service
Escort-4U Amsterdam
Category: Adult Entertainment
Area: West, Bos en Lommer
Address: Mercatorstraat 119-1
1056 RC Amsterdam The Netherlands
Phone: +31 20 7722481

#469
Happy People Coffeeshop
Category: Hookah Bar
Average price: Inexpensive
Area: Oost, Dapperbuurt
Address: Dapperstraat 2 1093 BT
Amsterdam The Netherlands
Phone: +31 20 6931869

#470
Hotel Arena
Category: Cafe, Bar
Area: Oost, Oosterparkbuurt
Address: 's-Gravesandestraat 51
1092 AA Amsterdam The Netherlands
Phone: +31 20 8502400

#471
Luus
Category: Cafe, Bar
Area: Zuid, WTC
Address: Beethovenstraat 180-182
1077 JX Amsterdam The Netherlands
Phone: +31 20 6727762

#472
Amstel Exclusive Erotic Meeting Point
Category: Adult Entertainment
Area: Zuid, Rivierenbuurt
Address: Amstelkade 34 1078 AE
Amsterdam The Netherlands
Phone: +31 20 6751183

#473
Café De Krommerdt
Category: Bar
Area: West, De Baarsjes
Address: Witte de Withstraat 188
1057 ZL Amsterdam The Netherlands
Phone: +31 20 6182425

#474
De Staatsman
Category: Bar
Area: West, Staatsliedenbuurt
Address: Van Limburg Stirumstraat 115
1051 BA Amsterdam The Netherlands
Phone: +31 20 6866633

#475
Bar Upstairs
Category: Bar
Area: Oost, Watergraafsmeer
Address: Eerste Ringdijkstraat 4 1097
BC Amsterdam The Netherlands
Phone: +31 20 6651171

#476
SoVine
Category: Wine Bar
Average price: Modest
Area: Zuid
Address: Amstelveenseweg 152
1075 XM Amsterdam The Netherlands
Phone: +31 652 618606

#477
Café Nol
Category: Dive Bar
Average price: Modest
Area: Centrum, Jordaan
Address: Westerstraat 109 1015 LX
Amsterdam The Netherlands
Phone: +31 20 6245380

#478
Drie Fleschjes Proeflokaal
Category: Bar
Average price: Modest
Area: Centrum
Address: Gravenstraat 18 1012 NM
Amsterdam The Netherlands
Phone: +31 20 6248443

#479
The Last Waterhole
Category: Pub
Average price: Modest
Area: Centrum
Address: Korte Leidsedwarsstraat 49
1017 PW Amsterdam The Netherlands
Phone: +31 20 6208904

#480
Brix Food 'n' Drinx
Category: Asian Fusion, Lounge
Average price: Modest
Area: Centrum, Negen Straatjes
Address: Wolvenstraat 16 1016 EP
Amsterdam The Netherlands
Phone: +31 20 6390351

#481
Easy Times
Category: Coffeeshops
Average price: Modest
Area: Centrum
Address: Prinsengracht 476 1017 KG
Amsterdam The Netherlands
Phone: +31 20 6265709

#482
Café 't Smalle
Category: Pub
Average price: Modest
Area: Centrum, Jordaan
Address: Egelantiersgracht 12 1015 RL
Amsterdam The Netherlands
Phone: +31 20 6239617

#483
Café Kadijk
Category: Diners, GastroPub
Average price: Modest
Area: Centrum
Address: Kadijksplein 5 1018 AB
Amsterdam The Netherlands
Phone: +31 617 744411

#484
Prik
Category: Gay Bar
Average price: Modest
Area: Centrum
Address: Spuistraat 109 1012 SV
Amsterdam The Netherlands
Phone: +31 20 3200002

#485
Boom Chicago
Category: Comedy Club, Cocktail Bar
Average price: Modest
Area: Centrum, Jordaan
Address: Rozengracht 117 1016 LV
Amsterdam The Netherlands
Phone: +31 20 2170400

#486
O'Donnell's Irish Pub
Category: Bar, Irish
Average price: Modest
Area: Zuid, De Pijp
Address: Ferdinand Bolstraat 5-II
1072 LA Amsterdam The Netherlands
Phone: +31 20 4700357

#487
Bolle Jan
Category:
Average price: Bar
Area: Centrum
Address: Korte Reguliersdwarsstraat
3 1017 BH Amsterdam
The Netherlands
Phone: +31 20 6259376

#488
Donny's Fine Food & Cocktails
Category: Cocktail Bar, Asian Fusion
Area: Centrum
Address: Lange Leidsedwarsstraat
33 1017 NG Amsterdam
The Netherlands
Phone: +31 20 4285858

#489
Mansro
Category: Bar
Area: Zuid, De Pijp
Address: Govert Flinckstraat 286-Al
1073 CG Amsterdam The Netherlands
Phone: +31 20 7757783

#490
De Barderij
Category: Bar
Area: Centrum, De Wallen
Address: Haarlemmerdijk 94 2hg 1013
JG Amsterdam The Netherlands
Phone: +31 622 404733

#491
Nachtcafé De Zottekop
Category: Bar
Area: Zuid, De Pijp
Address: Ceintuurbaan 186 1072 GC
Amsterdam The Netherlands
Phone: +31 20 6703031

#492
Desire Escort Amsterdam
Category: Adult Entertainment
Area: Centrum, De Wallen
Address: 1012 CC Amsterdam The
Netherlands
Phone: +31 615 591094

#493
Café Same Place
Category: Bar
Area: West, Frederik Hendrikbuurt
Address: Nassaukade 120 1052 EC
Amsterdam The Netherlands
Phone: +31 20 4751981

#494
Wijnbar Boelen & Boelen
Category: French, Wine Bar
Average price: Modest
Area: Zuid, De Pijp
Address: 1e van der Helststraat 50
1072 NV Amsterdam The Netherlands
Phone: +31 20 6712242

#495
Tendermoments
Escort Amsterdam
Category: Adult Entertainment
Area: Centrum
Address: 1012 AA Amsterdam
The Netherlands
Phone: +31 657 184751

#496
Michael S Boys Escorts
Category: Adult Entertainment
Area: Zuid, Willemspark
Address: Vondelkerkstraat 15-HS
1054 KX Amsterdam The Netherlands
Phone: +31 651 569322

#497
Café Verhoeff
Category: Pub
Average price: Modest
Area: Centrum, De Wallen
Address: Zeedijk 12 1012 AX
Amsterdam The Netherlands
Phone: +31 20 6222297

#498
Café Papeneiland
Category: Pub
Average price: Expensive
Area: Centrum, Jordaan
Address: Prinsengracht 2 1015 DV
Amsterdam The Netherlands
Phone: +31 20 6241989

#499
New York
Category: Bar
Area: Oost, Dapperbuurt
Address: Linnaeusstraat 83-III 1093 EK
Amsterdam The Netherlands
Phone: +31 20 4684741

#500
De Knoest
Category: Coffee & Tea, Dive Bar
Area: Oost, Dapperbuurt
Address: Dapperplein 23 1093 GP
Amsterdam The Netherlands
Phone: +31 20 6941882

TOP 200 CANNABIS COFFEE SHOPS

Recommended by Locals & Trevelers
(From #1 to #200)

#1
Barney's Coffeeshop
Category: Cannabis Coffee House
Address: Haarlemmerstraat 102,
1013 EW Amsterdam
Phone: +31 20 6259761

#2
Dampkring Haarlemmerstraat
Category: Cannabis Coffee House
Address: Haarlemmerstraat 44,
1013 ES Amsterdam
Phone: +31 20 4279716

#3
Kuil, de (420 Cafe)
Category: Cannabis Coffee House
Address: Oudebrugsteeg 27,
1012 JN Amsterdam
Phone: +31 20 6234848

#4
Homegrown Fantasy
Category: Cannabis Coffee House
Address: Nieuwezijds Voorburgwal 87a,
1012 RE Amsterdam
Phone: +31 20 6124009

#5
Blue Bird
Category: Cannabis Coffee House
Address: St. Antoniesbreestr. 71,
1011 HB Amsterdam
Phone: +31 20 6225232

#6
De Dampkring
Category: Cannabis Coffee House
Address: Handboogstraat 29,
1012 XM Amsterdam
Phone: +31 20 6380705

#7
Abraxas
Category: Cannabis Coffee House
Address: Jonge Roelensteeg 12-14,
1012 PL Amsterdam
Phone: +31 20 6245852

#8
Grey Area
Category: Cannabis Coffee House
Address: Oude Leliestraat 2,
1015 AW Amsterdam
Phone: +31 20 4204301

#9
Amnesia
Category: Cannabis Coffee House
Address: Herengracht 133,
1015 BG Amsterdam
Phone: +31 20 4277874

#10
The Dolphin's
Category: Cannabis Coffee House
Address: Kerkstraat 39,
1017 GB Amsterdam
Phone: +31 20 7743336

#11
The Old Church
Category: Cannabis Coffee House
Address: Oudekerksplein 54,
1012 HA Amsterdam
Phone: +31 20 4201264

#12
Babylon
Category: Cannabis Coffee House
Address: Beursstraat 27,
1012 JV Amsterdam
Phone: +31 20 4270609

#13
Voyagers
Category: Cannabis Coffee House
Address: Geldersekade 2,
1012 BH Amsterdam
Phone: +31 20 6246871

#14
Blues Brothers
Category: Cannabis Coffee House
Address: Nieuwendijk 89,
1012 MC Amsterdam
Phone: +31 20 6273845

#15
Grasshopper
Category: Cannabis Coffee House
Address: Oudebrugsteeg 16,
1012 JP Amsterdam
Phone: +31 20 6261259

#16
Green House Red Light
Category: Cannabis Coffee House
Address: Oudezijds Voorburgwal 191,
1012 EW Amsterdam
Phone: +31 20 6271739

#17
Resin
Category: Cannabis Coffee House
Address: Hekelveld 7,
1012SN Amsterdam
Phone: +31 20 4229838

#18
Prix d'Ami
Category: Cannabis Coffee House
Address: Haringpakkerssteeg 3,
1012 LR Amsterdam
Phone: +31 20 6271019

#19
Basjoe, Koffiehuis
Category: Cannabis Coffee House
Address: Kloveniersburgwal 62,
1012 CX Amsterdam
Phone: +31 20 6273858

#20
The Bushdoctor
Category: Cannabis Coffee House
Address: Thorbeckeplein 28,
1017 Amsterdam
Phone: +31 20 3307475

#21
Free I
Category: Cannabis Coffee House
Address: Reguliersdwarsstraat 70,
1017 BN Amsterdam
Phone: +31 20 6227727

#22
Paradox
Category: Cannabis Coffee House
Address: 1e Bloemdwarsstraat 2,
1016 KS Amsterdam
Phone: +31 20 6235639

#23
Funny People
Category: Cannabis Coffee House
Address: Nieuwebrugsteeg 24,
1012 AH Amsterdam
Phone: +31 20 6238663

#24
Stone's Cafe
Category: Cannabis Coffee House
Address: Warmoesstraat 91,
1012 HZ Amsterdam
Phone: +31 20 6241406

#25
Grasshopper 2
Category: Cannabis Coffee House
Address: Nieuwezijds Voorburgwal 59,
1012 RD Amsterdam
Phone: +31 20 6246753

#26
Rusland
Category: Cannabis Coffee House
Address: Rusland 16,
1012 CL Amsterdam
Phone: +31 20 6279468

#27
Abraxas Too
Category: Cannabis Coffee House
Address: Spuistraat 51,
1012 ST Amsterdam
Phone: +31 20 6226241

#28
Popeye
Category: Cannabis Coffee House
Address: Haarlemmerstraat 63,
1013 EK Amsterdam
Phone: +31 20 3206589

#29
Hunters
Category: Cannabis Coffee House
Address: Warmoesstraat 24,
1012JD Amsterdam
Phone: +31 20 3201197

#30
Rokerij II
Category: Cannabis Coffee House
Address: Singel 8,
1013 GA Amsterdam
Phone: +31 20 4226643

#31
Baba
Category: Cannabis Coffee House
Address: Warmoesstraat 64,
1012 JH Amsterdam
Phone: +31 20 6241409

#33
Doors, the
Category: Cannabis Coffee House
Address: Singel 14,
1013 GA Amsterdam
Phone: +31 20 6263900

#32
Coffeeshop 137
Category: Cannabis Coffee House
Address: Brouwersgracht 137,
1015 GE Amsterdam
Phone: +31 20 6270764

#34
Ben
Category: Cannabis Coffee House
Address: Kolksteeg 10,
1012 PT Amsterdam
Phone: +31 20 6237006

#35
Green House United
Category: Cannabis Coffee House
Address: Haarlemmerstraat 64hs,
1013 ET Amsterdam
Phone: +31 20 4272998

#36
De Kroon
Category: Cannabis Coffee House
Address: Oudebrugsteeg 26,
1012 JP Amsterdam
Phone: +31 20 3307805

#37
Hill Street Blues
Category: Cannabis Coffee House
Address: Warmoesstraat 52a,
1012 JG Amsterdam
Phone: +31 20 6223164

#38
Extase
Category: Cannabis Coffee House
Address: Oude Hoogstraat 2,
1012 CD Amsterdam
Phone: +31 20 6233058

#39
Sheeba
Category: Cannabis Coffee House
Address: Warmoestraat 73,
1012HX Amsterdam
Phone: +31 20 6240357

#40
Coffeeshop 36
Category: Cannabis Coffee House
Address: Warmoesstraat 36,
1012 JE Amsterdam
Phone: +31 20 6242493

#41
Rasta Baby
Category: Cannabis Coffee House
Address: Prins Hendrikkade 6-7,
1012 TK Amsterdam
Phone: +31 20 6247403

#42
Dutch Flowers
Category: Cannabis Coffee House
Address: Singel 387,
1012 WN Amsterdam
Phone: +31 20 6247624

#43
La Grotte
Category: Cannabis Coffee House
Address: Haarlemmerstraat 34,
1013 ES Amsterdam
Phone: +31 20 6253400

#44
Pick Up The Pieces
Category: Cannabis Coffee House
Address: Oude Hoogstraat 5,
1012 CD Amsterdam
Phone: +31 20 6260534

#45
Mellow Yellow
Category: Cannabis Coffee House
Address: Vijzelgracht 33,
1017 HN Amsterdam
Phone: +31 20 6380436

#46
Happy Feelings
Category: Cannabis Coffee House
Address: Kerkstraat 51,
1017 GC Amsterdam
Phone: +31 20 6391154

#47
Club Media
Category: Cannabis Coffee House
Address: Gerard Doustraat 83-85,
1072 VN Amsterdam
Phone: +31 20 6645889

#48
The Green Place
Category: Cannabis Coffee House
Address: Kloveniersburgwal 4,
1012 CT Amsterdam
Phone: +31 62 2096816

#49
Boerejongens
Category: Cannabis Coffee House
Address: Baarsjesweg 239,
1058 AA Amsterdam
Phone: +31 20 6182128

#50
The Bulldog No. 90
Category: Cannabis Coffee House
Address: Oudezijds Voorburgwal 90,
1012 GG Amsterdam
Phone: +31 20 6259864

#51
City Hall
Category: Cannabis Coffee House
Address: Oudezijds Voorburgwal 189,
1012 EW Amsterdam
Phone: +31 20 6263985

#52
Betty Too
Category: Cannabis Coffee House
Address: Reguliersdwarsstraat 29,
1017 BJ Amsterdam
Phone: +31 20 6270333

#53
The Bulldog Rockshop
Category: Cannabis Coffee House
Address: Singel 12,
1013 GA Amsterdam
Phone: +31 20 6278900

#54
The Bulldog Energy
Category: Cannabis Coffee House
Address: Oudezijds Voorburgwal 218,
1012 GJ Amsterdam
Phone: +31 20 6382593

#55
Soft Temple
Category: Cannabis Coffee House
Address: Gravenstraat 5,
1012 NL Amsterdam
Phone: +31 20 6229140

#56
Carmona
Category: Cannabis Coffee House
Address: 2e Jan van der Heijdenstraat
43, 1074 BA Amsterdam
Phone: +31 20 4004026

#57
The Bulldog Lounge
Category: Cannabis Coffee House
Address: Spuistraat 7,
1012 SP Amsterdam
Phone: +31 20 4200282

#58
Anyday
Category: Cannabis Coffee House
Address: Spuistraat 19,
1012SP Amsterdam
Phone: +31 20 4208698

#59
Tweede Kamer
Category: Cannabis Coffee House
Address: Heisteeg 6,
1012 WC Amsterdam
Phone: +31 20 4222236

#60
High Time
Category: Cannabis Coffee House
Address: Wijde Kerksteeg 3,
1012 GW Amsterdam
Phone: +31 20 6202315

#61
Cum Laude
Category: Cannabis Coffee House
Address: Langebrugsteeg 7a,
1012 GB Amsterdam
Phone: +31 20 6204715

#62
Rokerij III
Category: Cannabis Coffee House
Address: Elandsgracht 53,
1016 TN Amsterdam
Phone: +31 20 6230938

#63
Lion Of Judah
Category: Cannabis Coffee House
Address: Oudezijds Voorburgwal 47,
1012EJ Amsterdam
Phone: +31 20 6242723

#64
Greenhouse Effect
Category: Cannabis Coffee House
Address: Warmoesstraat 53-55,
1012 HW Amsterdam
Phone: +31 20 6244974

#65
Kadinsky
Category: Cannabis Coffee House
Address: Rosmarijnsteeg 9,
1012 RP Amsterdam
Phone: +31 20 6247023

#66
Utopia
Category: Cannabis Coffee House
Address: Nieuwezijds Voorburgwal 132,
1012 SH Amsterdam
Phone: +31 20 6261295

#67
Bagheera
Category: Cannabis Coffee House
Address: Kloveniersburgwal 60,
1012 CX Amsterdam
Phone: +31 20 6270384

#68
Route 99
Category: Cannabis Coffee House
Address: Haringpakkerssteeg 8,
1012 LR Amsterdam
Phone: +31 20 6279134

#69
Free Adam
Category: Cannabis Coffee House
Address: Oude Hoogstraat 13,
1012 CD Amsterdam
Phone: +31 20 6279910

#70
Stix 1
Category: Cannabis Coffee House
Address: Utrechtsestraat 21,
1017 VH Amsterdam
Phone: +31 20 6383325

#71
Yo-Yo
Category: Cannabis Coffee House
Address: 2e Jan van der Heijdenstraat
79,
1072 TZ Amsterdam
Phone: +31 20 6647173

#72
Stone's Corner
Category: Cannabis Coffee House
Address: Warmoesstraat 59,
1012 HW Amsterdam
Phone: +31 20 6245588

#73
Rokerij IV
Category: Cannabis Coffee House
Address: Amstel 8,
1017 AA Amsterdam
Phone: +31 20 6200484

#74
The Noon
Category: Cannabis Coffee House
Address: Zieseniskade 22,
1017 RT Amsterdam
Phone: +31 20 6250720

#75
Atlantis
Category: Cannabis Coffee House
Address: Daniël Stalpertstraat 78,
1072 XK Amsterdam
Phone: +31 20 6732353

#76
De Graal
Category: Cannabis Coffee House
Address: Albert Cuypstraat 25,
1072 CK Amsterdam
Phone: +31 20 4711791

#77
Arabica Lounge
Category: Cannabis Coffee House
Address: Amstelstraat 45,
1017 DA Amsterdam
Phone: +31 20 3203596

#78
When Nature Calls
Category: Cannabis Coffee House
Address: Keizersgracht 508,
1017 EJ Amsterdam
Phone: +31 20 3300700

#79
Little
Category: Cannabis Coffee House
Address: Vijzelgracht 47,
1017 HP Amsterdam
Phone: +31 20 4201386

#80
Get Down To It
Category: Cannabis Coffee House
Address: Korte Leidsedwarsstraat
77-79, 1017 PW Amsterdam
Phone: +31 20 4202012

#81
The Bulldog Palace
Category: Cannabis Coffee House
Address: Leidseplein 17,
1017 PS Amsterdam
Phone: +31 20 4223444

#82
Happiness
Category: Cannabis Coffee House
Address: Orteliusstraat 193,
1056NP Amsterdam
Phone: +31 20 4893929

#83
Hunters (II)
Category: Cannabis Coffee House
Address: Warmoestraat 37,
1012HV Amsterdam
Phone: +31 20 6120107

#84
Kashmir
Category: Cannabis Coffee House
Address: Jan Pieter Heijestraat 82,
1053 GS Amsterdam
Phone: +31 20 6180683

#85
Sensemillia
Category: Cannabis Coffee House
Address: Meer en Vaart 177/B,
1068 LA Amsterdam
Phone: +31 20 6198846

#86
Old Amsterdam
Category: Cannabis Coffee House
Address: Amstelstraat 35,
1017 DA Amsterdam
Phone: +31 20 6220422

#87
Route 66
Category: Cannabis Coffee House
Address: Warmoesstraat 77,
1012 HX Amsterdam
Phone: +31 20 6220695

#88
Monaco
Category: Cannabis Coffee House
Address: Spuistraat 118,
1012 VA Amsterdam
Phone: +31 20 6229644

#89
Pi Kunst en Koffie
Category: Cannabis Coffee House
Address: 2e Laurierdwarsstraat 64,
1016 RC Amsterdam
Phone: +31 20 6225960

#90
Reefer House
Category: Cannabis Coffee House
Address: Sint Antoniesbreestraat 77,
1011 HB Amsterdam
Phone: +31 20 6233615

#91
Siberië
Category: Cannabis Coffee House
Address: Brouwersgracht 11,
1015 GA Amsterdam
Phone: +31 20 6235909

#92
Easy Times
Category: Cannabis Coffee House
Address: Prinsengracht 476,
1017 KG Amsterdam
Phone: +31 20 6241572

#93
Stix-2
Category: Cannabis Coffee House
Address: Korte Koningsstraat 2,
1011 GA Amsterdam
Phone: +31 20 6240645

#94
Andalucia
Category: Cannabis Coffee House
Address: Halvemaansteeg 1,
1017 CR Amsterdam
Phone: +31 20 6253668

#95
Top
Category: Cannabis Coffee House
Address: Prinsengracht 480,
1017 KG Amsterdam
Phone: +31 20 6384108

#96
The Rookies
Category: Cannabis Coffee House
Address: Korte Leidsedwarsstraat
145-147, 1017 PZ Amsterdam
Phone: +31 20 6390978

#97
Top Weazle
Category: Cannabis Coffee House
Address: Vechtstraat 63,
1079 JA Amsterdam
Phone: +31 20 6611514

#98
Gierenest 't
Category: Cannabis Coffee House
Address: Amstelveenseweg 61,
1075 VV Amsterdam
Phone: +31 20 6620985

#99
De Prijs
Category: Cannabis Coffee House
Address: Surinamestraat 7,
1058 GJ Amsterdam
Phone: +31 20 6690620

#100
Future
Category: Cannabis Coffee House
Address: Prins Hendrikkade 102,
1011 AH Amsterdam
Phone: +31 20 6811319

#101
The Stud
Category: Cannabis Coffee House
Address: Niasstraat 31,
1095 TV Amsterdam
Phone: +31 20 6940983

#102
Bullwackie
Category: Cannabis Coffee House
Address: Woestduinstraat 76,
1058 TJ Amsterdam
Phone: +31 20 6179295

#103
Het Ballonnetje
Category: Cannabis Coffee House
Address: Roetersstraat 12,
1018 WD Amsterdam
Phone: +31 20 6228027

#104
Pablo Picasso
Category: Cannabis Coffee House
Address: Haarlemmerstraat 6,
1013 ER Amsterdam
Phone: +31 20 6388079

#105
Chapiteau
Category: Cannabis Coffee House
Address: Van Boetzelaerstraat 31,
1051 CT Amsterdam
Phone: +31 20 6822548

#106
La Tertulia
Category: Cannabis Coffee House
Address: Prinsengracht 312,
1016 HX Amsterdam
Phone: +31 20 6238503

#107
The Doors Palace
Category: Cannabis Coffee House
Address: Spuistraat 46,
1012 TV Amsterdam
Phone: +31 20 6250996

#108
Ooiervaartje 't
Category: Cannabis Coffee House
Address: Ooievaarsweg 10,
1021 GZ Amsterdam
Phone: +31 20 6372215

#109
Best Friends
Category: Cannabis Coffee House
Address: Niasstraat 1,
1095 AS Amsterdam
Phone: +31 20 3623654

#110
De Barentsz
Category: Cannabis Coffee House
Address: Barentszstraat 130,
1013 NS Amsterdam
Phone: +31 20 4202530

#111
The Pool Dog
Category: Cannabis Coffee House
Address: Hekelveld 7,
1012SN Amsterdam
Phone: +31 20 4229838

#112
Touche
Category: Cannabis Coffee House
Address: Kwakersstraat 8,
1053 WC Amsterdam
Phone: +31 20 6167908

#113
Green House Namaste
Category: Cannabis Coffee House
Address: Waterlooplein 345,
1011 PG Amsterdam
Phone: +31 20 6225499

#114
Old Style
Category: Cannabis Coffee House
Address: Martelaarsgracht 24,
1012TR Amsterdam
Phone: +31 20 6270021

#115
Bros
Category: Cannabis Coffee House
Address: Waterlandplein 24,
1024 LV Amsterdam
Phone: +31 20 6370018

#116
Baywatch
Category: Cannabis Coffee House
Address: Marnixstraat 333,
1016 TC Amsterdam
Phone: +31 20 6384014

#117
Bronx
Category: Cannabis Coffee House
Address: Marnixstraat 92,
1015 VZ Amsterdam
Phone: +31 20 7798939

#118
The Saint
Category: Cannabis Coffee House
Address: Regulierssteeg 2,
1017 CP Amsterdam
Phone: +31 20 3300074

#119
Cum Laude
Category: Cannabis Coffee House
Address: Langebrugsteeg 7a,
1012 GB Amsterdam
Phone: +31 20 3305936

#120
Ruthless
Category: Cannabis Coffee House
Address: Hoofdweg 174,
1057 DC Amsterdam
Phone: +31 20 4123057

#121
Het Gelderse
Category: Cannabis Coffee House
Address: Geldersekade 54,
1012 BK Amsterdam
Phone: +31 20 4207211

#122
Otherside, the
Category: Cannabis Coffee House
Address: Reguliersdwarsstraat 6,
1017 BM Amsterdam
Phone: +31 20 4211014

#123
Remember
Category: Cannabis Coffee House
Address: Oudezijds Achterburgwal 81,
1012 DC Amsterdam
Phone: +31 20 4227176

#124
Het Oerwoud
Category: Cannabis Coffee House
Address: Warmoesstraat 70,
1012 JH Amsterdam
Phone: +31 20 4288477

#125
Yamama
Category: Cannabis Coffee House
Address: 1e Oosterparkstraat 47,
1091 GV Amsterdam
Phone: +31 20 4639518

#126
Space Mountain
Category: Cannabis Coffee House
Address: Dusartstraat 22,
1072 HS Amsterdam
Phone: +31 20 4712331

#127
De Supermarkt
Category: Cannabis Coffee House
Address: Frederik Hendrikstraat 69,
1052 HL Amsterdam
Phone: +31 20 4862497

#128
Flashback
Category: Cannabis Coffee House
Address: Hudsonstraat 138/HS,
1057 SR Amsterdam
Phone: +31 20 4896115

#129
The Loft
Category: Cannabis Coffee House
Address: Jan van Galenstraat 285,
1056CA Amsterdam
Phone: +31 20 6126953

#130
Gouden Boon
Category: Cannabis Coffee House
Address: Da Costastraat 51,
1053 ZD Amsterdam
Phone: +31 20 6163347

#131
Terminator
Category: Cannabis Coffee House
Address: Admiraal de Ruijterweg 104,
1056GP Amsterdam
Phone: +31 20 6169558

#132
Tweedy
Category: Cannabis Coffee House
Address: Vondelstraat 104,
1054 GR Amsterdam
Phone: +31 20 6180334

#133
Coffeeshop 96
Category: Cannabis Coffee House
Address: Jan Pieter Heijestraat 96,
1053GT Amsterdam
Phone: +31 20 6186084

#134
Rock-It
Category: Cannabis Coffee House
Address: Nieuwmarkt 12,
1012 CR Amsterdam
Phone: +31 20 6200617

#135
Freeworld Coffeeshop
Category: Cannabis Coffee House
Address: Nieuwendijk 30,
1012 MK Amsterdam
Phone: +31 20 6200902

#136
Kadinsky
Category: Cannabis Coffee House
Address: Zoutsteeg 14,
1012 LX Amsterdam
Phone: +31 20 6204715

#137
Hollywood
Category: Cannabis Coffee House
Address: Nieuwendijk 1,
1012 LZ Amsterdam
Phone: +31 20 6208070

#138
Flower Power
Category: Cannabis Coffee House
Address: Rozengracht 139,
1016 LV Amsterdam
Phone: +31 20 6226198

#139
Keteltje 't
Category: Cannabis Coffee House
Address: Marnixstraat 74,
1015 VX Amsterdam
Phone: +31 20 6226998

#140
Rokerij I
Category: Cannabis Coffee House
Address: Lange Leidsedwarsstraat 41,
1017 NG Amsterdam
Phone: +31 20 6229442

#141
Down Town
Category: Cannabis Coffee House
Address: Reguliersdwarsstraat 31,
1017 BJ Amsterdam
Phone: +31 20 6229958

#142
Sensi Museum Coffeeshop
Category: Cannabis Coffee House
Address: Oude Doelenstraat 20,
1012ED Amsterdam
Phone: +31 20 6235267

#143
Meuwese Espresso
Category: Cannabis Coffee House
Address: Rokin 119-121,
1012 KP Amsterdam
Phone: +31 20 6241243

#144
Oude Kerk
Category: Cannabis Coffee House
Address: Oudezijds Voorburgwal 47,
1012EJ Amsterdam
Phone: +31 20 6242723

#145
Sevilla
Category: Cannabis Coffee House
Address: Utrechtsestraat 14,
1017 VN Amsterdam
Phone: +31 20 6244820

#146
Highway
Category: Cannabis Coffee House
Address: Lange Niezel 25,
1012 GS Amsterdam
Phone: +31 20 6250775

#147
Spirit
Category: Cannabis Coffee House
Address: Westerstraat 121,
1015 LZ Amsterdam
Phone: +31 20 6254650

#148
Number One
Category: Cannabis Coffee House
Address: Oude Hoogstraat 4,
1012 CE Amsterdam
Phone: +31 20 6262904

#149
Freeland
Category: Cannabis Coffee House
Address: Lange Niezel 27,
1012 GS Amsterdam
Phone: +31 20 6273279

#150
Atlas
Category: Cannabis Coffee House
Address: Parlevinker 8,
1034 PZ Amsterdam
Phone: +31 20 6315100

#151
Dread Rock
Category: Cannabis Coffee House
Address: Oudezijds Voorburgwal 67,
1012 EK Amsterdam
Phone: +31 20 6383534

#152
Johnny
Category: Cannabis Coffee House
Address: Elandsgracht 3,
1016 TM Amsterdam
Phone: +31 20 6383984

#153
Relax
Category: Cannabis Coffee House
Address: Binnen Oranjestraat 9,
1013 HZ Amsterdam
Phone: +31 20 6391058

#154
Global Chillage
Category: Cannabis Coffee House
Address: Kerkstraat 51,
1017GC Amsterdam
Phone: +31 20 6391154

#155
Het Trefpunt
Category: Cannabis Coffee House
Address: Zeeburgerdijk 33,
1093 SL Amsterdam
Phone: +31 20 6639327

#156
Nachtegaal
Category: Cannabis Coffee House
Address: Krugerplein 22,
1091 KZ Amsterdam
Phone: +31 20 6635599

#157
Jabba
Category: Cannabis Coffee House
Address: Achillesstraat 104,
1076 RH Amsterdam
Phone: +31 20 6648279

#158
Pacific
Category: Cannabis Coffee House
Address: Balthasar Floriszstraat 10,
1071 VC Amsterdam
Phone: +31 20 6710318

#159
Goed Goed
Category: Cannabis Coffee House
Address: Churchilllaan 86,
1078 EL Amsterdam
Phone: +31 20 6718633

#160
De Keeper
Category: Cannabis Coffee House
Address: Van Woustraat 193,
1074 AN Amsterdam
Phone: +31 20 6732972

#161
Green House South
Category: Cannabis Coffee House
Address: Tolstraat 91,
1074 VG Amsterdam
Phone: +31 20 6737430

#162
Blue Sea
Category: Cannabis Coffee House
Address: Van Woustraat 87,
1074 AE Amsterdam
Phone: +31 20 6761991

#163
Hugo de Groot
Category: Cannabis Coffee House
Address: Frederik Hendrikstraat 123hs,
1052 HP Amsterdam
Phone: +31 20 6817979

#164
The Dream
Category: Cannabis Coffee House
Address: Witte de Withstraat 30-A,
1057 XZ Amsterdam
Phone: +31 20 6853847

#165
Cheech & Chong's
Category: Cannabis Coffee House
Address: Marco Polostraat 225,
1056 DL Amsterdam
Phone: +31 20 6854810

#166
Cheech & Chongs II
Category: Cannabis Coffee House
Address: De Clercqstraat 30,
1052 NE Amsterdam
Phone: +31 20 6854810

#167
Coffeeshop 156
Category: Cannabis Coffee House
Address: Hudsonstraat 156,
1057 Amsterdam
Phone: +31 20 6855308

#168
Tuintje, 't
Category: Cannabis Coffee House
Address: Overtoom 451,
1054 KH Amsterdam
Phone: +31 20 6854513

#169
Sensemillia II
Category: Cannabis Coffee House
Address: Gillis van Ledenberchstraat
135-HS,
1052 VE Amsterdam
Phone: +31 20 6865144

#170
Lucifera
Category: Cannabis Coffee House
Address: Frederik Hendrikstraat 22,
1052 HV Amsterdam
Phone: +31 20 6868408

#171
Risky Business
Category: Cannabis Coffee House
Address: Bos en Lommerweg 163,
1055 DS Amsterdam
Phone: +31 20 6880715

#172
The Point
Category: Cannabis Coffee House
Address: 3e Oosterparkstraat 73,
1091 JV Amsterdam
Phone: +31 20 6935555

#173
The Power
Category: Cannabis Coffee House
Address: Wibautstraat 115,
1091 GL Amsterdam
Phone: +31 20 6940360

#174
Magic
Category: Cannabis Coffee House
Address: Herengracht 287,
1016 BL Amsterdam
Phone: +31 20 7715093

#175
Het Wonder
Category: Cannabis Coffee House
Address: Huidenstraat 13a,
1016 ER Amsterdam
Phone: +31 20 7772799

#176
Kingston
Category: Cannabis Coffee House
Address: Beursstraat 27,
1012 JV Amsterdam
Phone: +31 20 4270609

#177
Blue Lagoon
Category: Cannabis Coffee House
Address: Overtoom 342,
1054 JE Amsterdam
Phone: +31 20 6126232

#178
Bunkertje 't
Category: Cannabis Coffee House
Address: Rietwijkerstraat 34,
1059 Amsterdam
Phone: +31 20 6171424

#179
Wild Style
Category: Cannabis Coffee House
Address: Oudezijds Voorburgwal 250,
1012 GK Amsterdam
Phone: +31 20 6229655

#180
Biba
Category: Cannabis Coffee House
Address: Hazenstraat 15,
1016 SM Amsterdam
Phone: +31 20 6261134

#181
Balou
Category: Cannabis Coffee House
Address: Halvemaansteeg 5,
1017 CR Amsterdam
Phone: +31 20 6275653

#182
Betty's
Category: Cannabis Coffee House
Address: Rijnstraat 75,
1079 GX Amsterdam
Phone: +31 20 6445896

#183
De Bommel
Category: Cannabis Coffee House
Address: Balboastraat 19,
1057 VT Amsterdam
Phone: +31 20 6854509

#184
Catch 33
Category: Cannabis Coffee House
Address: Nassaukade 33,
1052 CK Amsterdam
Phone: +31 20 4862444

#185
The Coin
Category: Cannabis Coffee House
Address: Warmoesstraat 37,
1012 HV Amsterdam
Phone: +31 20 6120107

#186
Costa Rica
Category: Cannabis Coffee House
Address: Da Costastraat 76,
1053 ZR Amsterdam
Phone: +31 20 6165889

#187
Heavenly
Category: Cannabis Coffee House
Address: Knollendamstraat 5,
1013 TL Amsterdam
Phone: +31 20 4869735

#188
Melilla
Category: Cannabis Coffee House
Address: Agatha Dekenstraat 40,
1053 AR Amsterdam
Phone: +31 20 6122278

#189
Baris
Category: Cannabis Coffee House
Address: Agatha Dekenstraat 31,
1053 AM Amsterdam
Phone: +31 20 6129920

#190
Future, Café
Category: Cannabis Coffee House
Address: Osdorperban 152,
1069 ZR Amsterdam
Phone: +31 20 6195488

#191
Front Page
Category: Cannabis Coffee House
Address: Zoutsteeg 14,
1012 LX Amsterdam
Phone: +31 20 6204715

#192
De Waeghals
Category: Cannabis Coffee House
Address: Korte Koningsstraat 2,
1011 GA Amsterdam
Phone: +31 20 6240645

#193
K. Marong
Category: Cannabis Coffee House
Address: Tweede Laurierdwarsstraat 44,
1016 RB Amsterdam
Phone: +31 20 6241907

#194
Rockland
Category: Cannabis Coffee House
Address: Raadhuisstraat 8,
1016 DE Amsterdam
Phone: +31 20 6248890

#195
Koffiekeldertje 't
Category: Cannabis Coffee House
Address: Frederiksplein 4,
1017 XM Amsterdam
Phone: +31 20 6263424

#196
Trinity
Category: Cannabis Coffee House
Address: Sarphatistraat 87,
1018 EZ Amsterdam
Phone: +31 20 6266283

#197
Paradise
Category: Cannabis Coffee House
Address: Damstraat 8-10,
1012 JM Amsterdam
Phone: +31 20 6269939

#198
Het Filiaal
Category: Cannabis Coffee House
Address: Papaverweg 2,
1032 KH Amsterdam
Phone: +31 20 6376172

#199
Twilight Zone
Category: Cannabis Coffee House
Address: Lange Niezel 7,
1012 GS Amsterdam
Phone: +31 20 6381528

#200
NogalWiedes
Category: Cannabis Coffee House
Address: Czaar Peterstraat 122,
1018 PV Amsterdam
Phone: +31 20 6391783